MICROSOFT VISUAL BASIC®
GAME PROGRAMMING
FOR TEENS

JONATHAN S. HARBOUR

THOMSON
———*———™
COURSE TECHNOLOGY
Professional ■ Trade ■ Reference

ISBN: 1-59200-587-X

Library of Congress Catalog Card Number: 2004114414

Printed in the United States of America

04 05 06 07 08 BH 10 9 8 7 6 5 4 3 2 1

THOMSON

™

COURSE TECHNOLOGY

Professional ■ Trade ■ Reference

Thomson Course PTR, a division of Course Technology
25 Thomson Place
Boston, MA 02210
http://www.courseptr.com

SVP, Thomson Course Technology PTR:
Andy Shafran

Publisher:
Stacy L. Hiquet

Senior Marketing Manager:
Sarah O'Donnell

Marketing Manager:
Heather Hurley

Manager of Editorial Services:
Heather Talbot

Acquisitions Editor:
Mitzi Koontz

Senior Editor:
Mark Garvey

Associate Marketing Manager:
Kristin Eisenzopf

Marketing Coordinator:
Jordan Casey

Project Editor:
Scott Harris/Argosy Publishing

Technical Reviewer:
Maneesh Sethi

Teen Reviewer:
Andrew Nguyen

PTR Editorial Services Coordinator:
Elizabeth Furbish

Copy Editor:
Tonya Cupp

Interior Layout Tech:
Kate Binder

Cover Designer:
Mike Tanamachi

CD-ROM Producer:
Brandon Penticuff

Indexer:
Maureen Shepherd

Proofreader:
Jan Cocker

For my Grandmother,
Myrt Cremeen

ACKNOWLEDGMENTS

This book would not have been possible were it not for the hard-working editors, artists, proofreaders, marketers, indexers, layout specialists, and managers at Premier Press (Course PTR). Thank you to everyone at Premier Press and Argosy Publishing for doing such great work: Mitzi Koontz, Scott Harris, Jenny Davidson, Brandon Penticuff, Emi Smith, Stacy Hiquet, Andy Shafran, Sarah O'Donnell, Heather Hurley, Mark Garvey, Heather Talbot, Kristin Eisenzopf, Jordan Casey, Elizabeth Furbish, Mike Tanamachi, Tonya Cupp, Kate Binder, Maureen Shepherd, and Jan Crocker. Thank you to Maneesh Sethi for his technical review of the manuscript. I believe you will find this a solid book due to all of their efforts.

Thanks to my wonderful wife, Jennifer, and our rambunctious little ones, Jeremiah and Kayleigh, and our third one on the way. You guys make every aspect of our lives together a joy, and it is a privilege to share mine with you.

I am extremely grateful to Reiner Prokein for the use of his extraordinary artwork at Reiner's Tilesets (http://www.reinerstileset.de). I can honestly say I would not have even attempted to create the RPG in this book without Reiner's incredible talent at hand. Artwork is everything! Thank you for providing your high-quality tiles and sprites to the world.

I also owe my thanks and appreciation to Robin B. for his excellent level editor, Mappy (http://www.tilemap.co.uk). In addition, thank you to Daniel Sczepansky at Cosmigo for Pro Motion (http://www.cosmigo.com), the powerful sprite animation software featured in this book.

About the Author

JONATHAN S. HARBOUR has been an avid gamer and programmer for 17 years, having started with early systems like the Commodore PET, Apple II, and Tandy 1000. He holds a bachelor of science degree in computer information systems and enjoys writing code in several languages, including C, C++, and VB. He has experience with several platforms, including Windows, Linux, Pocket PC, and Game Boy Advance. Jonathan has written nine books on the subjects of game programming, application development, console programming, cross-platform programming, and console modding. He maintains a Web site dedicated to game programming at http://www.jharbour.com.

Contents at a Glance

CONTENTS

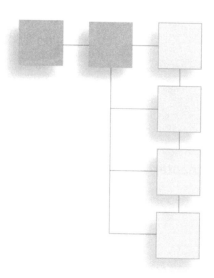

PART II: CREATING AN INTERACTIVE GAME WORLD   63

PART V: FINISHING TOUCHES   327

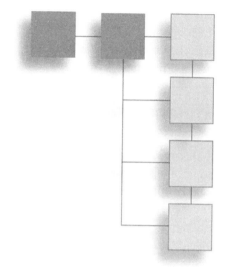

INTRODUCTION

Greetings! This book teaches you how to create your own role-playing game (RPG) using Visual Basic and DirectX. I teach you, step-by-step, how to construct each part of the game using DirectX components such as Direct3D. If you think RPGs are fun to play, wait until you start working on your very own! Constructing an RPG is far more interesting than playing one, because you are in complete control over the RPG world, and you can let your imagination loose to create adventures for others to enjoy.

Visual Basic and DirectX

Before you can get to the point where you can design an adventure and build an RPG with Visual Basic, you need to learn the language and get up to speed on DirectX. My goal with this book is to teach you just what you need to know in order to make this happen, without going into detail. You learn what you need to know to construct an RPG and nothing more. You might choose to use a product such as RPG Maker, rather than writing your own RPG with Visual Basic. That is certainly a good alternative, but wouldn't it be more interesting to have complete control over how the game works? Certainly you can create many complete RPGs of your own design with RPG Maker in the time it takes to build just one RPG from scratch and doing all of your own programming. But after writing your own code, you have learned a promising skill—game programming! In addition, you have complete creative control over how the game operates.

Pacing and Experience

This book reads like a hobby book, with no pressure and limited goals, because the primary purpose is to help you have fun learning about game programming. Typing long source-code listings out of a book is not fun, so I don't ask you to do that in every single chapter. Instead, you learn to write short programs to demonstrate the major topics in each chapter, and over time you get the hang of it. There is no memorization required here, as I'm a firm believer that repetition—practice—is the best way to learn, not theory and memorization.

Prerequisites

The goal of this book is to teach you how to create a complete RPG from scratch. You need to know Visual Basic in advance, because I do not spend any time explaining how to program in Visual Basic. Programming an RPG is a serious challenge before even considering the impact of going over DirectX at the same time. In addition, the small size of this book prevents me from doing anything other than focusing on that primary goal. If you are not at least somewhat familiar with the Visual Basic language, then I strongly recommend that you pick up a primer on the language before you dive head-first into this book. (One good example is Michael Vine's *Visual Basic Programming for the Absolute Beginner*.) Otherwise, you are more than likely to get lost within the first few chapters.

Which Version of Visual Basic?

This book focuses exclusively on Visual Basic 6.0. There is no support whatsoever for Visual Basic .NET, which is a wholly different product from 6.0. You may use any version of Visual Basic 6.0, including the Learning Edition, to run the programs presented in this book. In addition, you may use Visual Basic 5.0 if you do not have 6.0, because the compiler behind both of these versions is nearly the same. I have tested the code on 5.0 and 6.0 and found it to work.

Which Version of DirectX?

This book uses DirectX 8.0, because that is the last version of DirectX supported by Visual Basic 6.0. To say that it is a limitation is an extreme exaggeration, because DirectX 8 is a powerful, full-featured game library with very advanced 3D support—the likes of which is not even used in this book. In this book, I teach you how to build a complete 2D-based RPG. There is no need for any advanced features (such as those you find in DirectX 9). The sample programs use Direct3D surfaces and textures entirely.

Contacting the Author

I maintain a Web site at http://www.jharbour.com, which has information about this book that you may find useful. This site also features an active online forum where you can pose questions and keep up to date with the latest discussions about Visual Basic 6.0 with other programmers and VB fans. If you have any problems working through this book, feel free to stop by the site or just email me directly at support@jharbour.com.

Conventions Used in This Book

The following styles are used in this book to highlight important portions of text. You will find Note, Tip, and Caution boxes here and there throughout the book.

note

This is what a note looks like. Notes are additional information related to the text.

tip

This is what a tip looks like. Tips give you pointers in the current tutorial.

caution

This is what a caution looks like. Cautions provide you with guidance and what to do or not do in a given situation.

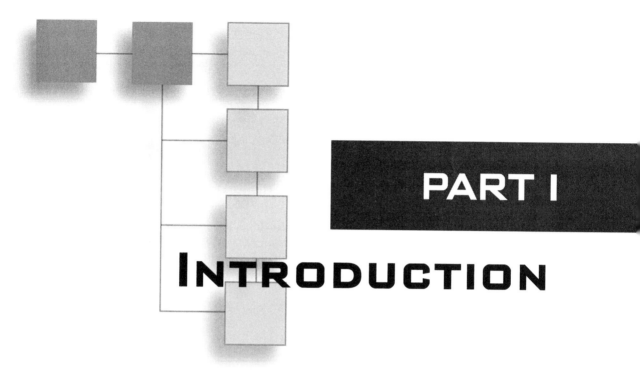

PART I

INTRODUCTION

W elcome to the first part of the book. This part includes two chapters that help get the ball rolling with regard to writing games with Visual Basic using the DirectX library. You learn how to create a Visual Basic game project that uses the DirectX type library and learn a little bit about the game project that you work on throughout the book. The second chapter provides a solid introduction to DirectX, explaining each of the components, as well as showing you how to write your first DirectX program.

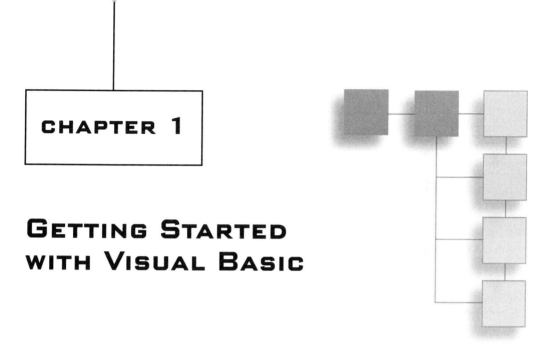

CHAPTER 1

GETTING STARTED WITH VISUAL BASIC

Welcome to the first chapter of *Visual Basic Game Programming for Teens*. This chapter gives you a little overview of what to expect in the book. You also get an introduction to Visual Basic by seeing how to create a reference to the DirectX type library and making sure that DirectX is installed properly. The chapter then goes on to present an overview of the sample game that you develop in this book as a learning tool and example of what you can do with Visual Basic.

Here is a breakdown of the major topics in this chapter:

- Game programming
- Getting started with DirectX
- Overview of the Game Project

Game Programming

Visual Basic is a good tool to use for writing games because the language is easy to learn and supports DirectX, the industry-standard game development library for Windows. This book treats Visual Basic like a professional game development language, powered by DirectX 8.1, completely ignoring the form-based application development features that make Visual Basic so popular in the business world.

To get into the core subject as quickly as possible, I have decided to forego a tutorial on the Visual Basic language itself and assume that you either already know Visual Basic or can learn it quickly enough to keep up with this book. After all, you want to learn how to write games, not write business programs, right? Well, in order to do that in these few pages, I jump right into the code, explaining everything as you read along, rather than explaining how to program with Visual Basic first. Seriously, hundreds of books teach the basics of Visual Basic 6.0 (which is what I use in this book), so I would rather just stick to game programming. If you feel that you are completely lost within the next few chapters, my advice is to pick up a Visual Basic primer to get up to speed and then return to this book. Nothing in here is confusing, but a lot of information is presented in a fast pace, so you don't want to get left behind.

note

Although I recommend a Visual Basic primer if you are completely new to the language, you should still be able to follow along and get the gist of what is going on, even if you don't understand every detail. To write a complete game in Visual Basic, however, some assumptions must be made, and that includes at least a working understanding of Visual Basic. If you have absolutely no experience with Visual Basic, I recommend you first read *Visual Basic for the Absolute Beginner* by Michael Vine.

Get Your Feet Wet First, Ask Questions Later

I have chosen to just jump into game programming without explaining everything about Visual Basic, well, mainly due to the size of this book, but secondly, because every page spent covering the basics is one that could have been used to accomplish the main goal of teaching you how to write a killer game with Visual Basic!

"What type of game might that be?" you might be wondering. For every great game idea that someone has, a thousand more ideas are waiting to be thought up by a creative person. One thing I want you to do while reading this book is learn to think outside the box. I realize that is a cliché that you have heard many times, but it is an important concept because it helps you visualize the point very clearly. Most people, and most programmers for that matter, are unable to think beyond the experience of their collected memories. A very rare person is able to think about something absolutely, completely foreign, the likes of which has never been thought of before. The phrase "thinking outside the box" can mean many things, depending on the context, but when I'm talking about writing a game, I mean you should think of ideas that are *above and beyond* what has already been done.

tip

Before you can let your creativity flow, you first need a foundation in the basics of programming, so you aren't always bogged down not knowing how to make your imagination come to life on the screen.

Do you really think John Carmack, John Romero, and Adrian Carmack were basing Doom on their memories of Pac-Man back in 1993? It's entirely possible that Doom is older than you are (or at least older than you were before you could play games). Many of the current generation don't understand what all the hoopla over Doom is about—it's because games were so different back then. In 1993, I was playing Sid Meier's Civilization on my PC, Super Mario World on my Super NES (which you might recognize as Super Mario Advance 2 on your GBA), and Dragon Crystal on my Game Gear. The fact is, most people did *not* play games back then, unlike today where almost everyone *does* play games! A game like Doom was unbelievable at the time, which is why people are still sharing fond memories about it today; that is why Doom 3 was created; that is why David Kushner wrote the book *Masters of Doom*. This game (Doom), unlike any other before it, was so dramatically different from all the other games at the time that a whole new genre was created: the first-person shooter (FPS). FPS games dominate the world of games today unlike any other genre.

Let Your Creativity Fly

The important thing to realize, though, is that thinking outside the box and coming up with something unprecedented is just the first step toward creating a new product. You must have the technical know-how to pull it off. In the field of video games, that means you must be a skilled programmer. If you are just getting started, then this book is perfect because Visual Basic allows you to practice some of your game ideas without getting too bogged down with a difficult programming language (like C or C++). These languages have a tendency to suck away all of your time and leave your mind numb and unable to think creatively. Writing solid code has a tendency to do that to a person, which is why it is a huge help when you start with a not-too-difficult language like Visual Basic. After you have figured out the basics, then you can move on to a more difficult subject like Dark-BASIC or Blitz Basic. You may not ever need to learn C or C++ to become a great game programmer.

---

tip

You don't need to be an expert C or C++ programmer to write a killer game! All it takes is good artwork, a good story, and well-written code.

Creativity, Talent, and Hard Work

I have seen some super high-quality games written with DarkBASIC and Blitz Basic. After you have finished with this book, I encourage you to read *Beginner's Guide to DarkBASIC Game Programming* (by Jonathan S. Harbour and Joshua R. Smith) as well as *Game Programming for Teens* (by Maneesh Sethi), which, despite the title, is actually a book about learning Blitz Basic. Once you have mastered all of these BASIC books and have created your own games, maybe then you will be interested in learning a more difficult language like C.

I wrote a book about writing games with C, called *Game Programming All In One, 2nd Edition*, which uses the Allegro game library and is a great step because you get a lot of experience with C coding while doing advanced graphics programming using Allegro. Normally, you have to use DirectX when you want to write games with C or C++, because almost every game programming book out there is about DirectX. However, Allegro uses DirectX behind the scenes, so you can get your feet wet with C and Allegro without taking that huge plunge into the depths of hard-core programming topics (which become overwhelming very quickly).

I have to say that technical programming language skill is about equal in importance with your creativity. I've known some very talented programmers who don't have an ounce of creativity in their bones, and so they are not able to do anything unique and interesting without someone *else* giving them the ideas first. It's okay to be a person like that, where you are really, really good at programming but not very creative; you can always borrow ideas from other games and things like movies, and leave the ideas to a game designer or another person who needs your technical skills. It doesn't matter if you have the technical or creative bent, because you really need to learn anything and everything you can in order to be an elite game developer.

The Sky Is the Limit

Did you know that you can write your own games for the Game Boy Advance? I'm talking about the GBA, GBA SP, *and* the GBA DS models. Imagine seeing your own games running on the GBA. Would that be the coolest thing ever, or what? That's something you definitely *can* do once you have learned enough and mastered a few programming languages, as I have suggested in the previous few paragraphs. All console programming, such as that for the GBA, is done in C or C++ (usually one or the other; it's up to the programmer at that point).

tip

For more information on GBA programming, you can download my free e-book *Programming the Game Boy Advance* from my Web site at http://www.jharbour.com. This e-book is intermediate to advanced, assuming that you already know how to program in C. I know several people who read this e-book, followed my suggestions, and then got hired as GBA programmers for major game companies!

Did you know that you can also write your own games for the Xbox? A project is currently in the works at SourceForge.net to produce an open-source Xbox development kit that allows anyone to compile the source code for a program (or a game) that runs on the Xbox. Pretty cool, huh?

You don't need to limit your creative juices to just what you *think* is possible. In fact, don't limit yourself at all, and don't assume that you *can't* do anything, even if you have tried and failed. If you can imagine something, no matter how out of this world it might seem, then it's possible to build it. That is what human imagination is all about. What Jules Verne imagined back in the late 1890s—ideas that were so crazy that everyone laughed at them—suddenly became a reality fewer than 70 years later. Imagine that—people riding around in horse carriages, on dirt or cobblestone roads, and some crazy writer suggests that people will walk on the moon. What a lunatic! Right? If you lived in 1890, you probably would have thought he was crazy, because it's easy for us to make fun of people after the fact (something called *hindsight*). Jules Verne described the rocket ship that would blast off the Earth with an explosion of mighty power that would lift the huge rocket off the ground and propel the men into space so they could land on the moon. Doesn't that sound familiar? If you have ever watched a video of the Apollo 11 mission, it is uncanny how Jules Verne described the launch 70 years before that time. Even today, the space shuttles are launched from the ground into orbit using the same basic technology, although the rockets are a lot more powerful and more efficient today than they were three decades ago.

Learn the Trade

The most technically skilled programmers are often those who copy the most creatively talented people in the world. From that perspective, people are still copying the work of John Carmack (of id Software), who continues cranking out unbelievable game engines, while the vast majority of game developers are trying to keep up or succumb to Carmack's genius and end up paying to use his latest game engine. Carmack is one of the few who possesses both unmatched technical skill and incredible creative talent. While he was born with the talent, he learned the technical skill purely from hard work, putting in an unbelievable number of hours at his keyboard, experimenting, tweaking, and trying new things, day after day, month after month, year after year—and he is still going at it.

If your whole purpose is just to have some fun while learning how to write your own game, and you have no real desire to become a master of it, that is perfectly okay! I am one of those people. I just love writing games for my enjoyment and that of others, and I don't really care if my latest game is bad. If you are approaching game development from the standpoint of a hobby, the whole point is to have fun. If you want to get serious, attend a game-development college, and then get a job as a professional game developer, you probably take the subject a little more seriously. There is a benefit to just treating this subject as a hobby: no deadlines or pressure and the freedom to do whatever you want. Have you always wanted to create your very own role-playing game (or another type of game), and decided to learn how to do it on your own? That's great! In fact, that is largely the direction this book takes. If your goal is to do this for a living, then I wish you the very best; this book may be your first stepping stone on the path toward that dream.

When I suggest you think outside the box, therefore, I'm advising that you try not to succumb to the "been there, done that" mentality of creating yet-another-mod (using a game engine like Battlefield 1942), or another Tetris clone, or another version of Breakout. These terrific learning experiences are very common, because these latter two types of games are easy to make and demonstrate important concepts in 2D game programming. A game engine mod, on the other hand, is an entirely different issue; most *mods* require little or no programming. They are merely conversions with new 3D models and game levels to match a new theme (as is the case with Desert Combat (a Battlefield 1942 mod) and Counter-Strike (a Half-Life mod). Try to come up with some completely original game ideas and develop them; no matter how simple a game concept is, if it's a brand new idea, then it will probably be interesting! Of course, the fun factor is entirely up to you, the game's designer and programmer.

Getting Started with DirectX

I would like to get a head start in this first chapter by showing you how to create a new project in Visual Basic and add a reference to DirectX to it. This allows you to start writing DirectX code in Visual Basic. Going over the topic now is good because Chapter 2 jumps into the first of many chapters on DirectX, and you eventually learn how to use bitmaps, how to create sprites, how to read keyboard and mouse input, how to play sound effects and music, and so on. It all begins here!

Start with a new Visual Basic project. Start Visual Basic; you should automatically see the New Project dialog appear over a blank Visual Basic project. See Figure 1.1.

Always choose Standard EXE as the project type when working on a game in Visual Basic. When you choose this project type, Visual Basic creates a new project and adds a default form to the project for you, as shown in Figure 1.2.

This is the usual starting point for a program in Visual Basic, which is exactly what you need at this point: a blank canvas with which to work. Visual Basic normally uses forms with controls to build an application, such as a business database that tracks customers. That you are using Visual Basic to write games is kind of odd, as it was never designed as a game development tool. On the other hand, Visual C++ was designed for game development and does have features useful in a game project. With its simple language, GUI editor, and built-in compiler, Visual Basic is easy to learn and use, which is why it has become such a popular choice.

If you press F5 or choose Run, Start from the menu, the program quickly compiles and runs, with a useless blank window called Form1 popping up. The Visual Basic form makes it easy to initialize a DirectX program, because the form has all the properties of a standard window (something that you have to create the hard way in a language like C).

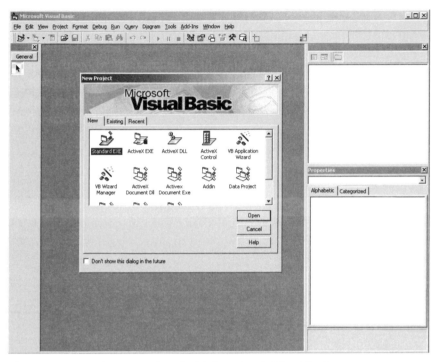

Figure 1.1 Creating a new Standard EXE project in Visual Basic.

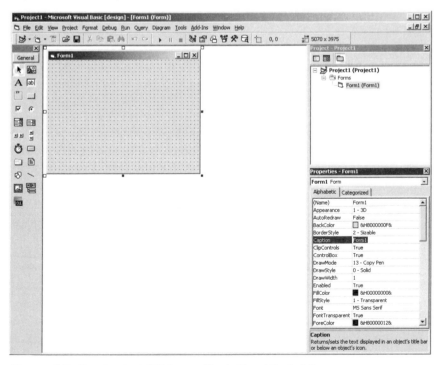

Figure 1.2 The standard GUI form editor in Visual Basic 6.0.

The following section shows you how to add DirectX support to a Visual Basic program. If you haven't already installed the DirectX Software Development Kit (SDK) on your PC, then you should install that before going any further. The CD-ROM provides a version of DirectX that specifically supports Visual Basic, providing just the DirectX 8 for Visual Basic Type Library. You can get away with just this and need not install the complete DirectX SDK, which includes all the files needed for writing DirectX programs in C or C++.

You should also install Service Pack 6 (SP6) for Visual Basic (or the full Visual Studio), which is what the programs in this book support. Some differences between a stock install of Visual Basic and the changes in SP6 require you to update your version of Visual Studio or Visual Basic with SP6. This service pack also includes all of the changes from SP1 through SP5 and fixes a lot of old bugs in Visual Basic. You can download the latest updates and service packs for Microsoft software from http://msdn.microsoft.com/downloads/.

Adding a Reference to the DirectX Type Library

To add DirectX support to your Visual Basic program, follow these steps:

1. Open the Project menu and select References. This brings up the References dialog, which is a list of type libraries and ActiveX objects available in your system.

2. Scroll down the list to the Ds. You should find two items on the list referring to DirectX:

   ■ DirectX 7 for Visual Basic Type Library
   ■ DirectX 8 for Visual Basic Type Library

3. Choose the second item, DirectX 8, as shown in Figure 1.3.

Testing the DirectX Reference

Now that DirectX has been added to the project as a reference, you should be able to view the DirectX objects using IntelliSense while writing source code. Take a peek to see if DirectX is, indeed, now available to your Visual Basic program. Returning to the form view of Visual Basic, you can click the View Code button above the Project Explorer on the right side of the window (see Figure 1.4), or by selecting Code from the View menu, as shown in Figure 1.5.

Alternately, you can double-click the form itself to bring up the source code editor, with a focus on the Form_Load event, which is perfect! If you opened the code window using a method other than double-clicking the form, then you can automatically create the Form_Load event using the two drop-down lists above the code editor, as shown in Figure 1.6. (Form_Load is run automatically by Visual Basic when the program first starts up.)

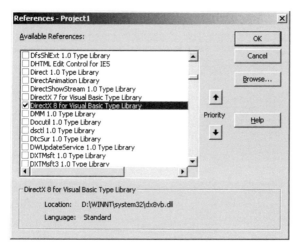

Figure 1.3 Adding a reference to the DirectX 8 type library for Visual Basic.

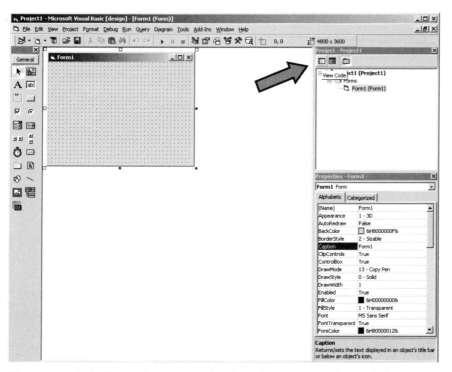

Figure 1.4 Switching to the source code editor view using the View Code icon.

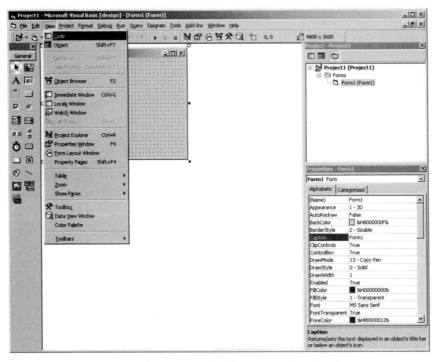

Figure 1.5 Switching to the source code editor view using the View menu.

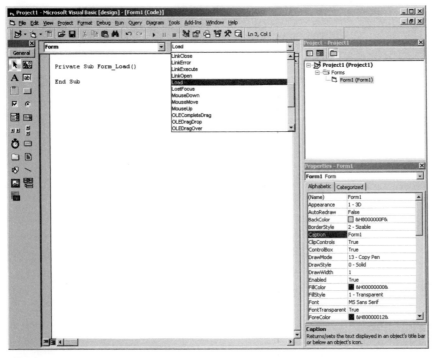

Figure 1.6 Selecting Load from the list of events for the Form.

Or you can always just type in the Form_Load event yourself! Are you a fast typist? There isn't much to type:

```
Private Sub Form_Load()
End Sub
```

Position the cursor *inside* Form_Load and type the following to see if the DirectX reference is working:

```
Dim directx As DirectX8
```

Before you even finish typing the last word, you should see IntelliSense pop up with a list of libraries available to your program. If you have the DirectX type library installed correctly, the drop-down list should show the DirectX8 library, which you see in Figure 1.7. If you see that, then congratulations: you are ready to get cracking with DirectX and can move onto the really good stuff! If you don't see it, then you need to install the DirectX 8 for Visual Basic Type Library again, along with (perhaps?) the DirectX run-time library. Do you have DirectX already installed? The type library only functions by exposing the objects in the run-time library (while the type library doesn't explicitly require the full DirectX SDK).

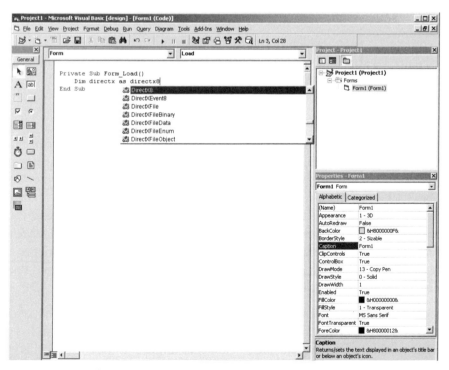

Figure 1.7 Verifying that the DirectX type library reference is working.

Ready to Write Some Code?

I would love to jump right in and demonstrate a sample Direct3D program right here and now. The reality is there's no simple way to explain how to set up Direct3D in just a few short pages without getting really involved in how to create the DirectX objects and initialize Direct3D; doing something simple like loading a bitmap and displaying it on the screen takes quite a few lines of code.

I don't want you to get bogged down in that much code so soon! Instead, I want to go over the plans for a sample game project that you work on throughout the book. I think you will really have fun writing this game from one chapter to the next, so explore that now and I'll reserve the technical details of DirectX for the upcoming chapters. Right now you're just preparing to study the things you need to build a complete game. First you come up with a goal, then you determine how to meet the goal from a technical standpoint, and then you start working toward the goal.

Overview of the Game Project

This book uses a single Game Project to teach the subject and give an overall picture of how the topics in each chapter are put to use in a real game. The alternative is to forego a sample game altogether or just use simple mini games (which are not much more than graphics demos, really) in each chapter to explain how a new subject you have learned can be put to use.

This game is entirely 2D based, which is still the standard for most *role-playing games (RPGs)* today. Figure 1.8 shows the game as it will look when you are finished with it in this book's last chapter.

Building a Role-Playing Game

I chose to create a complete RPG for this book because no other subject digs deeper into the depths of game programming than a real RPG with all of the functionality you expect from this genre. Since I come from the old school of gaming, I am still fond of classics like Ultima VII: The Black Gate. My second choice was a game based on *Star Trek*, but there are the obvious copyright problems when using a TV show as the basis for a game. If you really love some subject such as *Star Trek*, then I encourage you to go ahead and write a game about that subject and then give it away to your friends. The learning experience is enhanced when you are working on a game about a subject that you really enjoy and that has a lot of texture, with a huge background story surrounding it.

The RPG you create as an overall learning experience is called Celtic Crusader and takes place in the ancient land of mythical England. While the ancient Celtic civilization has a lot of history and myth, the background story is not very important here. The goal is to write a complete game while learning important new skills with each new chapter.

Figure 1.8 Celtic Crusader is a game you create from scratch in this book.

The Story

The premise of the story is basically this: Norwegian Vikings have been invading England and Ireland for centuries, conquering and then being driven off in rebellions. The story in Celtic Crusader does not include just fantasy creatures like you might find in some RPGs, such as vampires, skeletons (see Figure 1.9), werewolves, giant snakes, giant spiders, dragons (see Figure 1.10), and the like.

note

The images shown here for the Celtic Crusader game were created by Reiner "Tiles" Prokein, who makes them freely available to the public to be used for any purpose (including commercial games). You may browse Reiner's sprites and tiles at http://www.reinerstileset.de.

While fantasy characters are a lot of fun to kill in most RPGs, and Celtic Crusader has a lot of creatures to fight (such as the Skeleton Knight shown in Figure 1.11), this game also features some human characters that your player will encounter.

Figure 1.9 A Skeleton Archer.

Figure 1.10 A dragon.

Figure 1.11 A Skeleton Knight.

Good Guys Versus Bad Guys

I am taking this game in a slightly different direction and following a real-world scenario, like you might find in the Ultima and Legend of Zelda series. There are a lot of human characters in Celtic Crusader (as you learn in the next few chapters), and the player can choose from several character classes. In addition to some fantasy creatures, the game features an invading Viking army for the primary quest of the game. See Figures 1.12 and 1.13.

Good *non-player characters (NPCs)* also help the player (or whom the player must help) to successfully complete the game's primary quest or subquests. See Figures 1.14 and 1.15.

Adventure Game or Dungeon Hack?

Two types of classic RPGs exist in my opinion: adventure game and dungeon hack. The typical dungeon hack is made up of a town where you can equip your character (purchase weapons, armor, and so on) using the treasure you find in the dungeon, which is usually

Figure 1.12 A Viking knight.

Figure 1.13 A Viking archer.

Figure 1.14 This white mage is a good NPC.

Figure 1.15 This mighty warrior is a good NPC.

made up of many levels and driving deep into the Earth, and is often portrayed as a gold mine that became infested with evil creatures. While you are killing bad guys, your experience is going up and you are finding gold. As your experience goes up, your skills go up as well, and this is reflected by your character's level. A level-20 warrior, for instance, can dispatch level-5 skeleton archers with the back of his hand, so to speak, while a level-18 fire dragon poses a serious threat! This type of game is typically very simple in concept, lacking any serious storyline or plot—hence the term *dungeon hack*. Diablo and Dungeon Siege epitomize this type of game.

The other type of RPG, the adventure game, usually takes place on the surface rather than in a deep mine, and does involve an often deep storyline with multiple subquests to challenge the player. This game allows the player's character to gain experience, weapons, and special items such as armor, amulets, magic rings, and so on. While the main quest of an adventure RPG might be very, very difficult, the subquests allow the player's character to reach a level sufficient to beat the game's main quest. The subquests offer plenty of opportunity for a creative game designer to insert fascinating stories and interactions with NPCs like the one in Figure 1.16. Ultima VII is a good example of this type of game.

Figure 1.16 An interesting
female NPC.

I must admit, the latter is my choice type of RPG between the two, because in an adventure RPG, you can create multiple towns across the countryside and allow the player to explore a vast world. The dungeon hack is a lot of fun, I'll admit, and both types of RPG have merit.

Describing the Player's Character

The most robust RPGs usually allow the player to create a custom character to play, although in recent years this has taken a back seat to hack-and-slash games like Baldur's Gate (which is okay because it introduces another type of gamer to the great fun had with an RPG and gives the type of person who would not normally play an RPG a glimpse into a bigger world). You can usually choose from five character types:

1. Warrior Class

Figure 1.17 The Warrior
character class.

2. Knight Class

Figure 1.18 The Swordsman character class.

3. Thief Class

Figure 1.19 The Thief character class.

4. Archer/Scout Class

Figure 1.20 The Archer
character class.

5. Mage Class

Figure 1.21 The Mage
character class.

This is just a glimpse at a larger game that you have an opportunity to create in this book!
Of course, you can tweak and modify the game to suit your own imagination and you will
have the technical know-how after reading this book to do just that.

Summary

This chapter has introduced you to the main concepts that you learn in the book. Here you learned how to take the first step toward writing games with Visual Basic by including support for the DirectX type library. You then learned how to determine whether the DirectX installation is working, so you can reference the DirectX components from within Visual Basic. This chapter was short on details but tall on ideas, presenting a glimpse of the Celtic Crusader game, an RPG that you create while following along in this book from one chapter to the next, learning new game programming topics. The next chapter shows you how to write your first DirectX program, which is the first step toward starting this great-looking game.

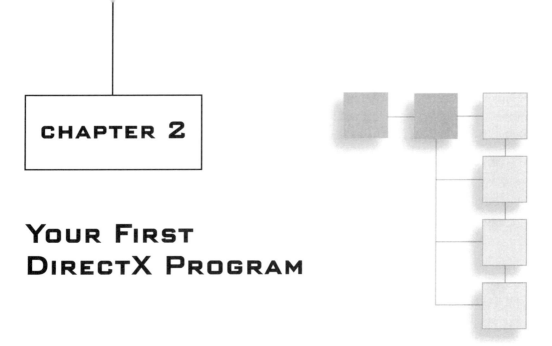

CHAPTER 2

YOUR FIRST DIRECTX PROGRAM

This chapter takes you through the process of writing a complete program that loads a bitmap file and displays the image on the screen using Direct3D. You learn all about surfaces in this chapter, as well as how to tap into DirectX. You need to learn about several DirectX components, which appear in this chapter, because they are used throughout the rest of the book. You might be surprised to learn that Direct3D is used to draw bitmaps on the screen, but the truth is, Direct3D is just as good for making 2D games (like Age of Mythology and Civilization III) as it is for 3D games (like Doom 3). Before you get started working on a role-playing game, you need to start with the basics of how to set up Direct3D for drawing 2D graphics on the screen. This chapter shows you how to do just that.

- Initializing DirectX
- Loading and displaying a bitmap file

Initializing DirectX

Although you may already know some programming, I have to assume that you are a complete beginner, which is a challenge, because I don't want to explain things you already know, but also don't want this material to be too difficult. It's like walking a tightrope, a fine line where I want to make it understandable for a beginner, but challenging at the same time. In my experience, the best way to accomplish both goals is by covering the easy stuff early on (like in this chapter), and then gradually build up to more challenging subjects later on. I recommend you read each chapter in order. Then, if you want to learn more about a certain subject, you can go back after you have finished the book. In more advanced books you find chapters that don't explain everything and that assume you understand, because you need to know a lot of things in advance (called *prerequisites*) just to draw a pixel on the screen.

Creating a New Project

Start by creating a new project in Visual Basic and adding a reference to the DirectX 8 type library, which you just learned about in the first chapter.

1. If you haven't already fired up Visual Basic, do that now.

   You should see the New Project dialog come up. If it doesn't, then open the File menu and select New Project to open it; this was covered in the last chapter.

2. Visual Basic should create a new project for you and add a new form to the project called Form1.

   Now, the most important step here, again, is to add DirectX support to your program.

3. Do this by opening the Project menu and selecting References.

4. Then search for DirectX 8 for Visual Basic Type Library from the list and click the checkbox.

5. Close the dialog.

Your program now has DirectX support, as you learned in the last chapter. If, for some reason, you do not see "DirectX 8 for Visual Basic Type Library" in the list of components, then you may need to install the DirectX SDK (which is provided on the CD-ROM under \DirectX). This may be the case if you are still using an older OS like Windows 2000. If you are using Windows XP or later, then you automatically have DirectX 8 installed, and you may just need the Visual Basic type library. I have included this on the CD-ROM as well, under \DirectX (look for dx8vbsdk.exe to install it). You do not need the complete DirectX SDK to write DirectX programs with Visual Basic.

The DirectX and Direct3D Objects

Now it's time to write some code. The easiest way to get started is to double-click somewhere on Form1. That opens the code window and adds a Form_Load subroutine to the program (which you also learned about already in the previous chapter, but I'm going over it to refresh your memory).

First, you must declare and create a variable for the primary DirectX object:

```
Dim dx As DirectX8
Set dx = New DirectX8
```

This main object controls all the other DirectX components that your program uses. For example, to create the Direct3D object, you must use the DirectX object to create it:

```
Dim d3d As Direct3D8
Set d3d = dx.Direct3DCreate()
```

See how that works? First you created the DirectX object, and then you used it to create the Direct3D object by calling the `Direct3DCreate` function, available only in the DirectX object. You can't just call this function from anywhere, because it is built into the DirectX object (which I have called `dx`). Since the `Direct3DCreate` function is located inside an object, it is properly called a *method*.

I have always found it confusing to call subroutines and functions by a different name just because they are inside a class or object or something else. To keep the discussion simple, I like to just call them *subroutines* and *functions*. Although, you should keep in mind that many people prefer to call subroutines *procedures* instead, which is more in line with other programming languages. Since Visual Basic uses Function to define a function, and Sub to define a procedure, I will just use the term *Subroutine* because I personally think that is easier to understand.

Here is an example of a function, so you get an idea about what I'm talking about:

```
Function DoThis() As Boolean
    MsgBox "I'm doing this!"
    DoThis = True
End Function
```

Now let me show you an example of a subroutine:

```
Sub DoThat()
    MsgBox "I'm doing that!"
End Sub
```

Do you see how the function has `As Boolean` as part of the first line, while the subroutine doesn't have that? Functions are different from subroutines because a function must return a value, while a subroutine just does something and doesn't return anything. In case you were wondering, Sub comes from the ancient version of the BASIC language, which had a GOSUB command that would jump to a different line in the program (yes, BASIC code used to have line numbers) and then the RETURN command told BASIC to return to part of the program right after the GOSUB line. Here is an example:

```
10 PRINT "Hi, this is a BASIC program."
20 PRINT "Line numbers are dumb."
30 PRINT "I'm going to run a subroutine..."
40 GOSUB 100
50 PRINT "I'm baaaaaaaack!"
60 END
100 PRINT "This is a subroutine."
110 RETURN
```

This sort of thing is completely irrelevant today, but it is interesting to know why Visual Basic uses the term *Sub* to define what all other programming languages just call a *procedure*. If I accidentally say *procedure* somewhere in the book, don't have a cow—it means the same thing as *subroutine*. But you don't care either way, right? You just want to make your own version of Fable and I'm wasting time here?

This does bring back some fond memories from a while back when I was mainly using DarkBASIC for all of my games. This is a really cool programming language (which comes with a complete editor and compiler and everything in one package) that you should check out. In case you are interested, I wrote a book with a good friend of mine who works as a professional game programmer (he worked on games like Hot Wheels and Real War); the book is called *Beginner's Guide to DarkBASIC Game Programming*. Okay, moving along . . . . (I didn't realize you learned so fast, so I'll pick up the pace.)

Creating the Primary Device

After you have taken care of the DirectX and Direct3D objects, you need to create a variable to take care of the Direct3D device, which represents the video card. Initializing the device takes a little more than just creating a variable for it. The device has to be configured so Direct3D knows how you plan to use it. This is where you set things like the screen resolution, color depth, windowed or full-screen mode; and if you're doing 3D, you also have to set up the 3D rendering options as well (which I won't bother doing here).

tip

A *double buffer*—also called *back buffer*—is a duplicate of the screen, stored in memory, where you send all graphics output to. By working with this scratch pad in memory, and then drawing the whole double buffer to the screen all at once, you greatly improve the quality of the game, reducing flicker and screen refresh problems.

There are a lot of options here, so I'm just going to show you the presentation parameters needed for each program instead of going over all of the options up front. First create a variable:

```
Dim d3dpp As D3DPRESENT_PARAMETERS
```

Then use d3dpp to set the presentation parameters that you want to use for Direct3D. For starters, here is how you set the parameters for a simple Direct3D program that has an automatically updated double buffer:

```
d3dpp.hDeviceWindow = Me.hWnd
d3dpp.BackBufferCount = 1
d3dpp.BackBufferWidth = 640
d3dpp.BackBufferHeight = 480
```

```
d3dpp.SwapEffect = D3DSWAPEFFECT_DISCARD
d3dpp.Windowed = 1
d3d.GetAdapterDisplayMode D3DADAPTER_DEFAULT, dispmode
d3dpp.BackBufferFormat = dispmode.Format
```

The last two lines are very important, and if not included the program won't run at all! Gack! (That's the sound I make when my programs crash.) You can set the format yourself, as there are a lot of options for the display screen settings, but using the current color depth of the Windows desktop is the safest way to ensure the program runs. I know it's ridiculous today to think about this, but it's possible, however unlikely, that some PCs in the world don't have a 32-bit video card (especially in some countries where new hardware is difficult to come by). So, you could just configure Direct3D to use the best video mode, but it's better to use the current format.

The rest of the presentation parameters are pretty obvious. Set the window handle (hDeviceWindow) to point to Form1. Then you set the back buffer count, width, and height (the back buffer is the same as a double buffer). Now you can actually create the Direct3D device:

```
Set d3ddev = d3d.CreateDevice( _
    D3DADAPTER_DEFAULT, _
    D3DDEVTYPE_HAL, _
    hWnd, _
    D3DCREATE_SOFTWARE_VERTEXPROCESSING, _
    d3dpp)
```

This sort of ugly-looking code shows the five parameters, each listed on a separate line so the function is easier to read. I don't want you to even worry about what these parameters mean or what they do at this point. For one thing, they are primarily related to doing 3D (and this book focuses on doing 2D) and another thing, it's too soon to be concerned with such details.

In Visual Basic, when you want to split a line, you use the _ (underscore) character at the end of one line, and then you can continue on the next line. I do this a lot in the book so the code won't wrap around like this:

```
Set d3ddev = d3d.CreateDevice(D3DADAPTER_DEFAULT, D3DDEVTYPE_HAL, hWnd,
D3DCREATE_SOFTWARE_VERTEXPROCESSING, d3dpp)
```

That might save some space, but it's more difficult to explain and definitely makes it harder to change the function parameters. It is always preferable to write code that is easier to read, rather than writing code that takes up less space. The compiler doesn't care what the code looks like, so you should make it as easy to read as possible. I've had problems reading my own code many times over the years; I'll write a program and then come back to it a couple years later and won't be able to understand any of it! For this reason, I make all of my code easier to read and insert a lot of comments (usually above each block of code that does something important). Okay, that is all there is to initializing Direct3D in your program, and at this point, Direct3D takes over your program (so to speak).

caution

If you set d3dpp.Windowed = 0, then Direct3D immediately switches to full-screen mode. If you don't have some sort of code in your program to catch the Escape key or something, then you are stuck—the only solution left to you is to Ctrl+Alt+Del, bring up the Task Manager, and then kill the process (which shuts down Visual Basic as well). Don't try setting d3dpp.Windowed = 0 until you have some code in your program to let it escape. I always include a way that terminates the program by either pressing the Escape key or closing the window. It is best to develop a game in windowed mode until it's finished, and then switch to full screen before you distribute it.

What can you do after DirectX has been initialized? The sky's the limit, really. This is the point where you start drawing graphics on the screen and is the starting point for your game. For this first program, I'll just have you clear the screen with a certain color and then refresh the screen. The next program (later in this chapter) shows you how to take it to the next step, loading a bitmap file and displaying it on the screen.

The InitDirectX Program

The InitDirectX program is shown in the following listing. When you run the program, it looks like Figure 2.1.

```
'----------------------------------------------------------
' Visual Basic Game Programming for Teens
' Chapter 2 - InitDirectX program
'----------------------------------------------------------

Dim dx As DirectX8
Dim d3d As Direct3D8
Dim d3dpp As D3DPRESENT_PARAMETERS
Dim dispmode As D3DDISPLAYMODE
Dim d3ddev As Direct3DDevice8

Private Sub Form_Load()

    'create the DirectX object
    Set dx = New DirectX8

    'create the Direct3D object
    Set d3d = dx.Direct3DCreate()
```

Figure 2.1 The InitDirectX program reminds me of the game Birth of the Federation.

```
'set the display device parameters for windowed mode
d3dpp.hDeviceWindow = Me.hWnd
d3dpp.BackBufferCount = 1
d3dpp.BackBufferWidth = 640
d3dpp.BackBufferHeight = 480
d3dpp.SwapEffect = D3DSWAPEFFECT_DISCARD
d3dpp.Windowed = 1
d3d.GetAdapterDisplayMode D3DADAPTER_DEFAULT, dispmode
d3dpp.BackBufferFormat = dispmode.Format

'create the Direct3D primary device
Set d3ddev = d3d.CreateDevice( _
    D3DADAPTER_DEFAULT, _
    D3DDEVTYPE_HAL, _
    hWnd, _
    D3DCREATE_SOFTWARE_VERTEXPROCESSING, _
    d3dpp)

End Sub
```

```
Private Sub Form_Paint()
    'clear the window with red color
    d3ddev.Clear 0, ByVal 0, D3DCLEAR_TARGET, RGB(255, 0, 0), 1#, 0

    'refresh the window
    d3ddev.Present ByVal 0, ByVal 0, 0, ByVal 0
End Sub

Private Sub Form_QueryUnload(Cancel As Integer, UnloadMode As Integer)
    Shutdown
End Sub

Private Sub Form_KeyDown(KeyCode As Integer, Shift As Integer)
    If KeyCode = 27 Then Shutdown
End Sub

Private Sub Shutdown()
    Set d3ddev = Nothing
    Set d3d = Nothing
    Set dx = Nothing
    End
End Sub
```

Loading and Displaying a Bitmap File

The ability to load a bitmap file is at the core of a game, and is an absolutely essential, make-or-break, mission-critical thing that just has to work or the game might as well be running on Pioneer 11 out beyond the orbit of Pluto. (Yeah, maybe it runs, but you won't see anything.)

By the way, did you know that NASA now has a project in the works called Interstellar Probe? You can read about it at http://interstellar.jpl.nasa.gov/. You know, sometimes I get the feeling that programming a game is more of a challenge than programming a NASA spacecraft. But since I have never done the latter, I can't really justify that feeling.

The New LoadBitmap Project

The InitDirectX program was a good starting point as far as showing you how to write the initialization code for Direct3D, but it didn't do anything at all. Let's take it a little further by writing some new code that loads a bitmap file and displays the image on the screen. This chapter does not fully go into the use of bitmaps, as that is reserved for a future chapter. However, I will show you how to load a bitmap and then copy it to the back buffer, which is then displayed on the screen. This program has DirectX initialization code in a special subroutine that you can reuse in future programs. The program uses some constants you can easily change to adjust how the program runs. Speaking of which, the program is shown in Figure 2.2.

I recommend starting with a new, blank project for this program, rather than modifying the last program, because a lot of the code is different. Create a new project in Visual Basic; go into Project, References and select the reference to DirectX 8 for Visual Basic Type Library to add DirectX support to the program. You can then open the code window for Form1 and get started on the program.

Variables

Let me go over it from a top-down fashion, explaining the code as if you are reading it, because that is easier to follow. First you have the program comment, constants, and variable definitions:

```
'-------------------------------------------------------
' Visual Basic Game Programming for Teens
' Chapter 2 - LoadBitmap program
'-------------------------------------------------------
```

Figure 2.2 The LoadBitmap program demonstrates how to use Direct3D surfaces.

```
Const SCREENWIDTH As Long = 640
Const SCREENHEIGHT As Long = 480
Const FULLSCREEN As Boolean = False
Const C_BLACK As Long = &H0
Const C_RED As Long = &HFF0000


'the DirectX objects
Dim dx As DirectX8
Dim d3d As Direct3D8
Dim d3dx As New D3DX8
Dim dispmode As D3DDISPLAYMODE
Dim d3dpp As D3DPRESENT_PARAMETERS
Dim d3ddev As Direct3DDevice8


'some surfaces
Dim backbuffer As Direct3DSurface8
Dim surface As Direct3DSurface8
```

As you can see, this code is quite a bit of an improvement over the last program that you worked on just a few minutes ago, so you're making good progress already! First, I have declared some constants at the top. These are values that you can easily change at the top of the program, affecting things like the resolution and windowed mode. I've also created two color constants so it's easier to change the background clearing color (and you use color in other areas later on). Next, you see two groups of variables: the DirectX objects and some surfaces are defined. The surface variables are something new that you haven't seen before.

Direct3DSurface8 is a class, just like DirectX8, Direct3D8, and D3DX8 (which is just a helper class that includes a function for loading bitmap files). Classes are an *object-oriented programming (OOP)* concept. I don't want to get into OOP in this book, because it might be a better way to write code, but adds confusion that I'm not willing to inject into the equation of your learning process at this point. If you are dissatisfied with that explanation (and have a little more experience with Visual Basic than the average reader), then I can recommend my previous book for you, titled *Visual Basic Game Programming with DirectX*. That book uses OOP extensively in every chapter and builds a complete game library out of classes that you can use to create 2D or 3D games (and many sample games are included). This is a rather large book that is not for beginners—it covers things like multiplayer programming with DirectPlay (including how to build a game server), 3D collision detection, and many other subjects. In many ways, the book you are now holding is better because it is focused on a single game and does include something the more advanced book doesn't cover: Direct3D surfaces. I recommend that book only if you finish this book and want to learn how to program in Visual Basic with OOP.

Program Startup

Let's look at the Form_Load subroutine next. (This is an event that runs automatically when the form is first displayed by Visual Basic.)

```
Private Sub Form_Load()
    'set up the main form
    Form1.Caption = "LoadBitmap"
    Form1.ScaleMode = 3
    Form1.Width = Screen.TwipsPerPixelX * (SCREENWIDTH + 12)
    Form1.Height = Screen.TwipsPerPixelY * (SCREENHEIGHT + 30)
    Form1.Show

    'initialize Direct3D
    InitDirect3D Me.hwnd, SCREENWIDTH, SCREENHEIGHT, FULLSCREEN

    'get reference to the back buffer
    Set backbuffer = d3ddev.GetBackBuffer(0, D3DBACKBUFFER_TYPE_MONO)

    'load the bitmap file
    Set surface = LoadSurface(App.Path & "\sky.bmp")

End Sub
```

Some new code in Form_Load requires some explanation. The first group of code sets some properties for Form1 that are important in a game in general. The Caption property identifies the program. ScaleMode, Width, and Height are used to set the form's size. The Screen.TwipsPerPixelX and Screen.TwipsPerPixelY properties return twip values (which differs with each video card and is related to dot pitch). The original goal was to provide a way to measure the screen in a way that is equivalent to a printed page. As a result, Visual Basic scales objects on a form using twips rather than pixels, and so you just want to change the scale mode to pixels. Along with some additional space for the border around the form, this code sets the form so it is sized correctly for your requested resolution (using SCREENWIDTH and SCREENHEIGHT). Finally, the form is displayed with the Show subroutine.

The next line of code calls a subroutine (that I wrote) called InitDirect3D, which I'll show you in a minute. The next two lines are very interesting. GetBackBuffer is a function that returns a reference to the back buffer, which is handled automatically by Direct3D according to the settings you specified for the presentation parameters. Next, you see a call to LoadSurface with the filename for a bitmap file. That is a custom function that I wrote just for loading a bitmap and returning it as a Direct3DSurface8 object. If you are confused at this point, don't worry—I realize it's all new information and it is explained again as you move along from one chapter to the next. I don't expect you to remember anything after just reading about it one time, but prefer to use repetition to teach something new.

Initializing Direct3D

Next comes the InitDirect3D subroutine, as promised. This subroutine has some error-checking code, so it displays an error message in a message box if an error occurs while initializing Direct3D (another reason to stick with windowed mode while working on a game, because you will not see a message box when the game is running full screen). As you can see, it's a lot easier to sneak in error handling when a section of code is stuffed into a separate subroutine or function like this case. If you look at the code line by line, you realize it's exactly the same code you saw in the previous program example, but it now includes all of the error-handling as well, so the program actually displays an error message rather than just crashing when there's a problem. The code here also makes use of the constants you saw at the top of the program listing.

```
Public Sub InitDirect3D( _
    ByVal hwnd As Long, _
    ByVal lWidth As Long, _
    ByVal lHeight As Long, _
    ByVal bFullscreen As Boolean)

    'catch any errors here
    On Local Error GoTo fatal_error

    'create the DirectX object
    Set dx = New DirectX8

    'create the Direct3D object
    Set d3d = dx.Direct3DCreate()
    If d3d Is Nothing Then
        MsgBox "Error initializing Direct3D!"
        Shutdown
    End If

    'tell D3D to use the current color depth
    d3d.GetAdapterDisplayMode D3DADAPTER_DEFAULT, dispmode

    'set the display settings used to create the device
    Dim d3dpp As D3DPRESENT_PARAMETERS
    d3dpp.hDeviceWindow = hwnd
    d3dpp.BackBufferCount = 1
    d3dpp.BackBufferWidth = lWidth
```

```
    d3dpp.BackBufferHeight = lHeight
    d3dpp.SwapEffect = D3DSWAPEFFECT_COPY_VSYNC
    d3dpp.BackBufferFormat = dispmode.Format

    'set windowed or fullscreen mode
    If bFullscreen Then
        d3dpp.Windowed = 0
    Else
        d3dpp.Windowed = 1
    End If

    'chapter 9
    d3dpp.MultiSampleType = D3DMULTISAMPLE_NONE
    d3dpp.AutoDepthStencilFormat = D3DFMT_D32

    'create the D3D primary device
    Set d3ddev = d3d.CreateDevice( _
        D3DADAPTER_DEFAULT, _
        D3DDEVTYPE_HAL, _
        hwnd, _
        D3DCREATE_SOFTWARE_VERTEXPROCESSING, _
        d3dpp)

    If d3ddev Is Nothing Then
        MsgBox "Error creating the Direct3D device!"
        Shutdown
    End If

    Exit Sub
fatal_error:
    MsgBox "Critical error in Start_Direct3D!"
    Shutdown
End Sub
```

Loading a Bitmap File

Now you come to perhaps the most difficult part of the program: the code that loads a bitmap file into a Direct3D surface object. This is a pretty advanced topic for just the second chapter, don't you think? Well, like I said before, I want to keep the discussion challenging while ramping up the difficulty level little by little. (This actually mirrors the leveling up of an RPG character, if you think about it!)

The LoadSurface function accepts a filename parameter and returns a reference to a surface object that you must declare first, before calling the function. Remember, here is how I defined the variable:

```
Dim surface As Direct3DSurface8
```

Here is the code that actually calls the LoadSurface function, which you may recall was located in Form_Load:

```
'load the bitmap file
Set surface = LoadSurface(App.Path & "\sky.bmp")
```

When you take a look at the code that actually loads a bitmap file, it's rather simple because you can use the LoadSurfaceFromFile function. The only drawback is that you have to create the surface in memory before loading the bitmap file, because the surface must exist first. That complicates things! If all you had to do was call the LoadSurfaceFromFile function, it would be very simple to load a bitmap file into a surface. That is not the case, so it's good that I have put this code inside a function. Thanks to this function, you can load a bitmap file into memory as a Direct3D surface, with just a single line of code (with error handling).

```
Private Function LoadSurface(ByVal filename As String) As Direct3DSurface8
    On Local Error GoTo fatal_error
    Dim surf As Direct3DSurface8

    'return error by default
    Set LoadSurface = Nothing

    'create the new surface
    Set surf = d3ddev.CreateImageSurface(SCREENWIDTH, SCREENHEIGHT, dispmode.Format)
    If surf Is Nothing Then
        MsgBox "Error creating surface!"
        Exit Function
    End If

    'load surface from file
    d3dx.LoadSurfaceFromFile _
        surf, _
        ByVal 0, _
        ByVal 0, _
        filename, _
        ByVal 0, _
        D3DX_DEFAULT, _
        0, _
        ByVal 0
```

```
    If surf Is Nothing Then
        MsgBox "Error loading " & filename & "!"
        Exit Function
    End If

    'return the new surface
    Set LoadSurface = surf

fatal_error:
    Exit Function
End Function
```

Drawing the Bitmap

Okay, the hard part is done and there's just some minor code left to be written to get this program finished. The last bit of code includes the Form_Paint event (which is run anytime the form window changes) that displays the image after it has been loaded. The Form_Key-Down and Form_QueryUnload events, with the help of Shutdown, clean up when you try to end the program.

One thing that requires some explanation here is the CopyRects subroutine. This is used to copy one surface onto another surface, and is quite versatile. It allows you to specify the exact rectangle to copy from as well as the exact rectangle to copy to within the destination surface. CopyRects is the workhorse for Direct3D surfaces.

```
Private Sub Form_Paint()
    'copy the bitmap image to the backbuffer
    d3ddev.CopyRects surface, ByVal 0, 0, backbuffer, ByVal 0

    'draw the back buffer on the screen
    d3ddev.Present ByVal 0, ByVal 0, 0, ByVal 0
End Sub

Private Sub Form_KeyDown(KeyCode As Integer, Shift As Integer)
    If KeyCode = 27 Then Shutdown
End Sub

Private Sub Form_QueryUnload(Cancel As Integer, UnloadMode As Integer)
    Shutdown
End Sub
```

```
Private Sub Shutdown()
    Set surface = Nothing
    Set d3ddev = Nothing
    Set d3d = Nothing
    Set dx = Nothing
    End
End Sub
```

Level Up

Congratulations, your character has gained a level! This chapter was very important to your understanding of how to interface with DirectX from Visual Basic. You learned some critical concepts, such as how to initialize the DirectX and Direct3D objects and how to create a surface in memory that can hold a bitmap file. This chapter provided you with two reusable subroutines called InitDirect3D and LoadSurface that come in handy in future chapters.

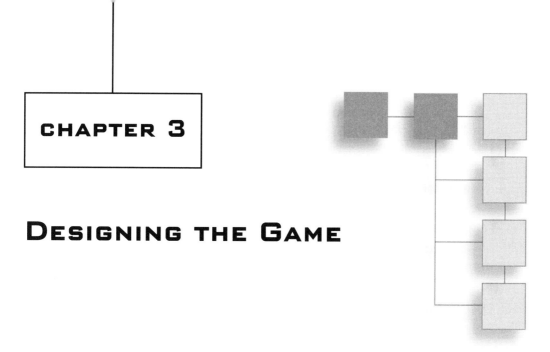

CHAPTER 3

Designing the Game

Y ou might think it strange to break the game design coverage pace set in the previous chapter, but that is exactly what this chapter is about, and for a good reason. Designing a game is no simple task that should be thrown together after the source code has been nearly completed. The design should direct what code gets written and what the game world looks like.

Here is a breakdown of the major topics in this chapter:

- Designing the RPG world
- The player's character (PC)
- The non-player characters (NPCs)
- Weapons and armor
- Magic
- Communication
- Combat

The Quest-Based Storyline

You can learn a lot about your subconscious motivations and creative impulses by designing a game with pencil and paper. I get so much enjoyment out of the design process that my enthusiasm gets the best of me and I want to jump into the code and start writing the game! At the same time, I enjoy drawing even though I'm not a very good artist. (I can't draw people or living creatures at all, so I don't even try.)

note

For a complete discussion of how to design a role-playing game, see *Swords & Circuitry: A Designer's Guide to Computer Role-Playing Games* by Neal and Jana Hallford. I also recommend *Character Development and Storytelling for Games* by Lee Sheldon if you are interested in learning how to create realistic storylines and characters for your games.

It's important to put as much on paper as possible before you start writing source code. It is good to get started on the artwork for a game while doing the design, as that helps you realize what is possible and somewhat helps with the creative process. If you start working on a game without any design at all, at worst it ends up being left unfinished, at best it is a clinical game (meaning it is functional but lacks substance).

Celtic Crusader is based in 9th-century Ireland, a country occupied by Vikings. The Vikings were not just barbarous raiders, although this game's story is about Viking occupation in Ireland and generally depicts Vikings as the bad guys. The Viking civilization was spread across a much wider area than even the Roman Empire, although it was not as strong and not based entirely on military conquest. The Vikings were explorers and traders who settled lands, such as Iceland and Greenland, that had never before been visited by humans. Although humans had migrated to North and South America at around this time, the Vikings are also credited as being the first Europeans to discover and settle North America. (Actually, the Viking settlers in Greenland were the first Canadians.)

The storyline is usually not as important as are the quests, which is what drives the story forward. Your character does not have a specific goal, because nothing in life is that clearly defined. Instead, the game develops while your character develops, mainly by fighting animals and fantasy creatures, as well as the occasional Viking raiding party. Your character's attributes determine how good he is in combat. (See "The Player's Character [PC]" section later in this chapter.) The quests in the game are based on events in certain parts of the map, which I explain next.

note

Celtic Crusader will not be a fully-featured RPG, since that would require much more work than is possible in this book. But by the end of this book, you will have a very functional and customizable RPG engine that you may use as a basis to implement the concepts presented in this chapter.

Designing the RPG World

The game world in Celtic Crusader is based on the island country of Ireland. I chose this land because it has a rich mythology going back over 2,000 years, providing a huge pool of possible plot elements for the storyline and subquests in a game. I had thought of basing the game on ancient America, designing a game around the Mayan or Incan civilizations, but decided to go with Ireland because it is easier to design a smallish game story around an island. That also makes it possible to set boundaries on the game map limiting the player's movement (as opposed to putting mountains or some sort of no-man's land at the boundary of a land-locked game world).

There is a lot to be said for a randomly generated world, or a world based on a completely fictional land with no historical basis, because that allows you (the game's designer) to let loose with your imagination to create a world that does not influence, nor is affected by, the "real world." Generating a random world is definitely possible, but I don't like the random factor because it prevents me from designing the game around real locations in the world. Celtic Crusader has characters that are from specific towns based on character class, and I want those towns to be real places on the map, not just generated locations in a random world. The goal is to build a game that has a lot of replay value by offering strong character development rather than anonymous random combat. The fact of the matter is, most people love a good story. Giving your game a good story with believable characters makes it far more fun to play than a randomly generated world, even if the same characters appear in that fictional world.

Map of the World

Figure 3.1 shows the map of the world in Celtic Crusader as a traditional hand-drawn illustration. This rough sketch represents Ireland in the 9th century when the Vikings invaded England and Ireland from their empire in Norway, Denmark, and Sweden.

This map shows Viking towns (a V inside a square), Irish towns (an I inside a circle), and ruins (an R inside a triangle), to give you an idea about how quests are based on the game world itself rather than by some random quest-generation system. In reality, I have taken some creative liberties with the true historical significance of the towns shown in this map. The Irish "towns" were, in reality, monasteries that the Vikings either did not discover or did not plunder for one reason or another. The ruins shown on the map are, in fact, monasteries that the Vikings had plundered (by stealing all gold, silver, and valuables they could find). I thought the idea of a plundered monastery lent itself well to a ruin (filled with evil creatures). The ruins in Celtic Crusader are based somewhat on historical fact (which I believe really helps with the story), with the idea being that the plundered monasteries, by becoming ruins, have been invaded by vile monsters that are not generally found elsewhere in the game.

The ruins are basically a training ground where the player's character gains experience, goes up in levels, and acquires gold to buy better equipment in the towns. The goal with this game engine is to have certain parts of the map cause a new map to load, with the player inserted into a certain part of the new map. However, I have found that this is a very

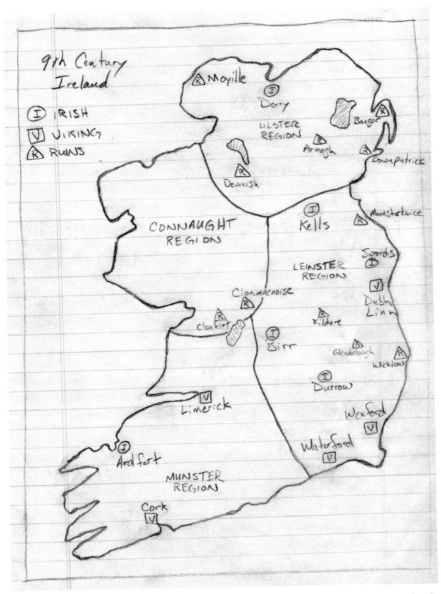

Figure 3.1 Hand-drawn illustration of the world in Celtic Crusader, based in Ireland.

difficult thing to do without causing the source code to grow in complexity (and I want to keep this game on the simple side). Therefore, the towns in the game world are represented on the map itself rather than as a *warp* type of system that enters and exits the towns. I really like this idea better because it keeps the suspense of disbelief going.

note

Suspense of disbelief is a term that describes one's immersion in a fictional setting. You may have experienced this while reading a good book or while playing a good game: You lose track of the real world around you and become totally immersed in the book or game. This is a very good thing and you should strive to achieve it with your game. Anything that takes away the player's suspense of disbelief should be removed from the game. A clunky user interface, a difficult combat system, an overload of information on the screen all lead to ruining the player's immersion.

By taking the hand-drawn map and scanning it into the computer, I have been able to clean it up and turn it into a digital version of this game's world. That world is shown in Figure 3.2.

My goal is to teach you how to create an RPG as well as an RPG game engine that you can customize for your own vision and imagination for a game. I want to give you just enough to get the job done, avoiding doing everything for you, so you are motivated to improve the game.

While you're working on a game like this, always consider ways to make whatever you're working on reusable. If you are constructing a player creation screen, think of ways to make the screen dynamic and flexible, without hard-coding anything specific. It is a good idea to keep things concrete and solidly built in the game, but not to the point where it's impossible to modify later. If you have buttons on the screen that the player needs to click with the mouse, make those buttons easy to move around: Use constants at the top of the source code for that particular screen. Another option is to make everything in your game *skinnable*. You know, skins are all the rage in user interfaces today, and most music players for your PC support skinning. This is a process where the program controls can be repositioned and the images used to represent those controls can be modified—with some fantastic results. Why not take that excellent design methodology with you in the design of a game and make it totally customizable by storing skins and settings in files outside of the source code for the game? This excellent concept may be beyond the scope of this short book, but I want you to keep it in mind while you are working.

Figure 3.3 shows my design for the scrolling game world. The player's sprite remains in the center of the screen at all time, with the world scrolling underfoot. With this design in mind, the map has to be laid out so there is room around the borders for the player to reach the edge of the map. In other words, when the player reaches the ocean, the map needs to have ocean squares going out a little so the player can walk right up to the seashore. I explain how this works more in Chapter 5, "Level Editing with Mappy." The eight-way scrolling of the map is perfect for the sprites in this game, which have been rendered with animation in eight directions.

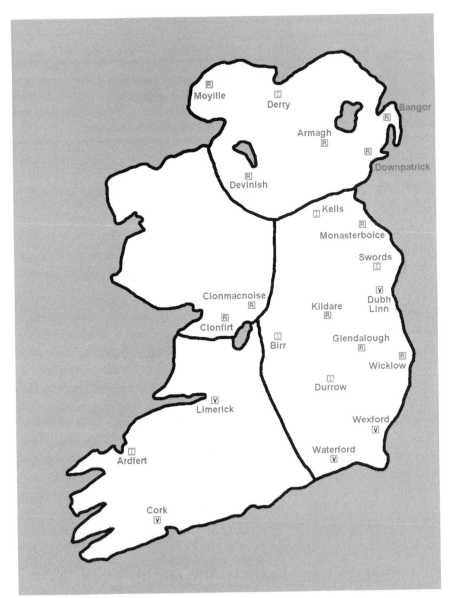

Figure 3.2 The hand-drawn map has been scanned and converted to a digital map.

Regions

There are four provinces, or regions, in the version of Ireland represented in this game: Leinster, Munster, Connaught, and Ulster. It is not crucial, but I have always found that a background story and historical depth make a game far more compelling for the player,

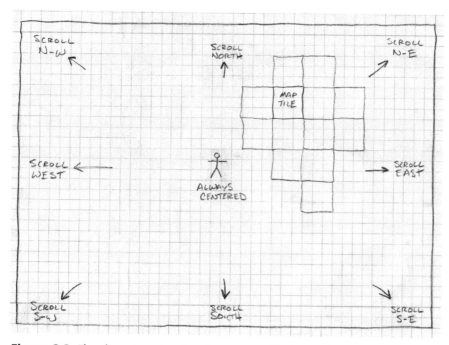

Figure 3.3 The player is centered on the screen, with the scrolling tile-based world.

greatly improving the sense of immersion in the game world. A game is not just backgrounds, sprites, and collision detection (something you will learn about in Chapter 14), and players expect much more depth to an RPG than they expect from an arcade game. One aspect of the Ultima series that made it so popular is the wealth of historical information provided to the player within the game (usually through dialog with NPCs). You want to create the illusion that the player is just one person in a huge, populated world that goes on with or without you.

Leinster Region

Leinster region, located on the east side of Ireland is where most of the fighting takes place between the native Irish people (who are, admittedly, descended from Anglo-Saxons in the first place, never mind that the Celts are long gone . . .) and the Viking invaders who created three settlements: Dubh Linn, Wexford, and Waterford. Leinster, shown in Figure 3.4, borders all three of the other regions.

The Irish monastery towns include Kells, Swords, Birr, and Durrow. There are also some ruins (pillaged monasteries) in this region: Monasterboice, Kildare, Glendalough, and Wicklow. This region produces the most axe-bearing warriors and sword-wielding paladins in the world.

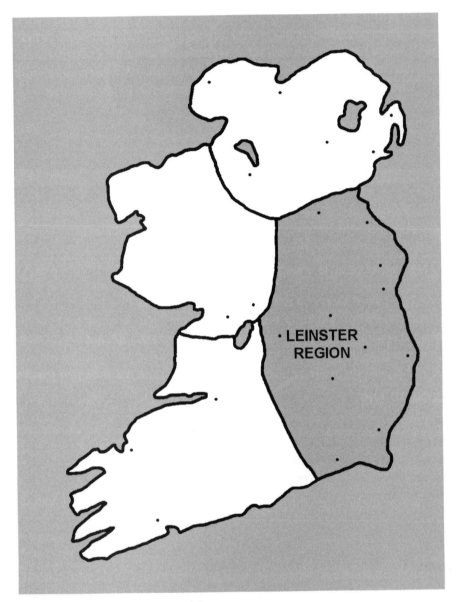

Figure 3.4 The Leinster region of the map.

Munster Region

The Munster region of Ireland, located in the southwest, is adjacent to Leinster and Connaught. See Figure 3.5.

Munster is the second strongest region of Viking occupation on Ireland with the two Viking settlements of Limerick and Cork. While there are no ruins in this region at all,

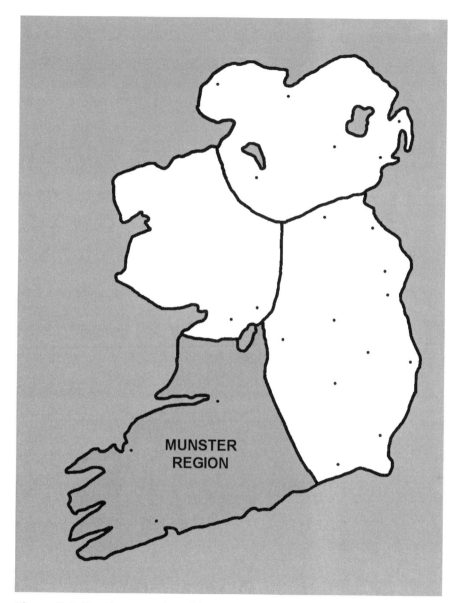

Figure 3.5 The Munster region of the map.

there is one Irish monastery town called Ardfert, which is famous for producing skilled archers (known by the character class scout), the likes of which have fought against the Vikings during their initial invasion and occupation. The Vikings have never learned about the secret bow craft of Ardfert, so many patriotic archers are still trained there.

Ulster Region

Ulster region, located on the north side of Ireland, is the location for most of the island's religious artifacts; its inhabitants practice the ancient art of mastering the natural world. Ulster, shown in Figure 3.6, was devastated by the Vikings during their initial invasion, with many mages killed while trying to protect their monasteries. There were vast arrays

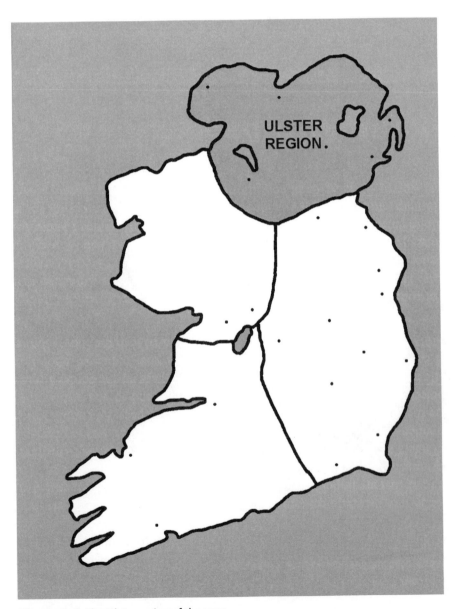

Figure 3.6 The Ulster region of the map.

of gold and silver artifacts given to the mages of Ulster as offerings throughout the generations. Despite mastery of the natural world, Ulster mages were peaceful in nature and abhorred violence of any kind, even in one's defense. As a result, the mages of Ulster were defenseless against an unknown enemy that brought brutality to the region, plundering the monasteries of Moyille, Devinish, Armagh, Downpatrick, and Bangor, leaving them in ruins. Only Derry remains unscathed by the plundering.

The tenants of Derry, the last vestige of Celtic mages left alive, have been forced to abandon their prior unity with the natural world, and focus their attention on combat in order to drive out the Viking invaders. Mages of Derry are masters of the staff in hand-to-hand combat and able to wield some of the unseen forces of the world to aid them in battle.

Connaught Region

The Connaught region, shown in Figure 3.7, is located on the western side of Ireland. Connaught was once a vast grazing land for cows, sheep, and goats, with its wide-open plains and plentiful feeding ranges. Connaught is not a widely settled region, though, and the Viking invasion rallied those few living in Connaught to the battle in defense of the land. The result is that forests have grown into Connaught from the south, and it is mainly a breeding ground for evil creatures and a hiding place for criminals.

Two monasteries in southern Connaught—Clonmacnoise and Clonfirt—were pillaged by the Vikings, who left them in ruins. The inhabitants of these two ruins are a constant nuisance to the hard-working citizens of Birr, located nearby in Leinster region.

The Player's Character (PC)

One of the most enjoyable aspects of playing an RPG is creating your very own custom character to use in the game. This is why true RPGs have more depth and more replay value than games featuring a specific set of characters (as in the Zelda series). Since player character creation is so much a part of the experience, it's important to design the character creation screen with as much versatility as possible so the player can create his or her own persona for the game.

Celtic Crusader is taking shape as an old-school RPG, and will eventually allow you to design your own character from scratch. The game should allow your character to interact within the confines of the main storyline of the game (as well as within the subquests). Figure 3.8 shows one possible design for a character creation screen.

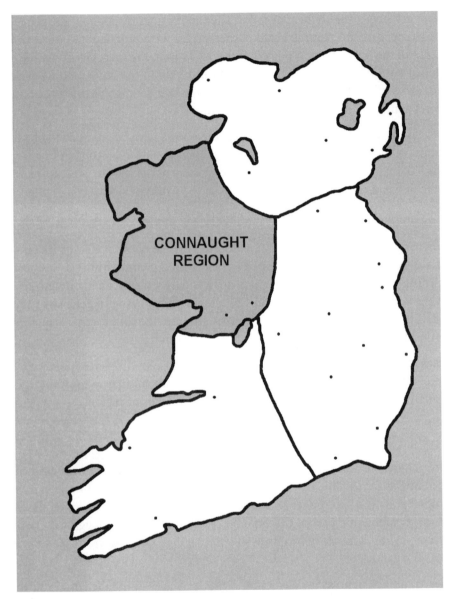

Figure 3.7 The Connaught region of the map.

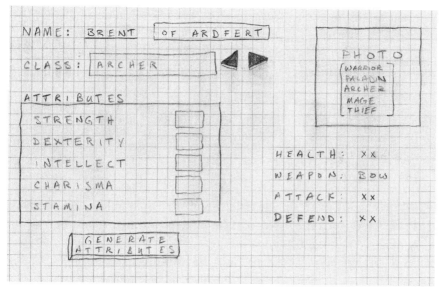

Figure 3.8 The design for the character creation screen.

Character Attributes

All characters (including non-player characters and monsters) in the game have the same set of attributes in order to make combat possible: Strength, dexterity, intellect, charisma, and stamina.

Strength

Strength represents the character's ability to carry a weight and swing a weapon, and is generally good for the warrior and knight classes, which carry hand-to-hand combat weapons such as axes and swords. The strength attribute is used to calculate the attack value for the character (meaning, the amount of damage the player inflicts on enemies with each swing of a weapon). Each time the character attacks, a dice roll (which is a random number in code) against the attack value determines whether the attack succeeds. If the attack is a hit, then the weapon's damage value is used to inflict damage against the opponent.

Suppose your character has an attack value of 12, which is calculated using the character's strength (mainly, although you may include dexterity in a custom calculation to make the game more interesting). Typical "attack rolls" are done with a 20-sided die. In a Visual Basic program, you can simulate the roll of dice using the Rnd function, which returns a decimal value from 0 to 1.0. You can use `Rnd` to write a random-number function that returns integer (whole) numbers:

```
Public Function Random(ByVal lMax As Long)
    Random = Int(Rnd * lMax)
End Function
```

So, if you wanted to roll against the attack value, you might do so like this:

```
If Random(20) > Attack_Value Then ...
```

Dexterity

Dexterity represents the agility of the character, the ability to manipulate objects (like a weapon), and the skill with which the player uses his or her hands in general. A very low dexterity means the character is clumsy, while a very high dexterity means the character can manipulate complicated devices and perform fast, complex actions. Use of any weapon (such as sword, mace, or even a bow) is improved with a high dexterity.

Intellect

Intellect represents the character's ability to learn, remember things, and solve problems. The mage class requires a very high intellect, while relatively low intellect is common in fighter classes where brute force is more important than mental faculties.

Charisma

Charisma represents the character's attractiveness and appearance, and generally affects how others respond to the character. A character with very high charisma attracts others, while very low charisma shuns others. Knights usually have very high charisma, reflecting their heroic stature.

Stamina

Stamina represents a character's endurance, or the ability to continue performing an activity for a long period of time. A very high stamina provides a character with the ability to engage in lengthy battles without rest, while a character with low stamina tires quickly (and likely falls in battle).

Character Status

When the character is actually in the game, you want the player to be able to view the information about his or her character by bringing up some sort of status screen, as is the norm with most RPGs. Figure 3.9 shows an example screen that I designed to show the player's stats in a "pop-up" window over the game screen. The window shows information about the player in the game, such as attributes, equipment, health, gold, and so on.

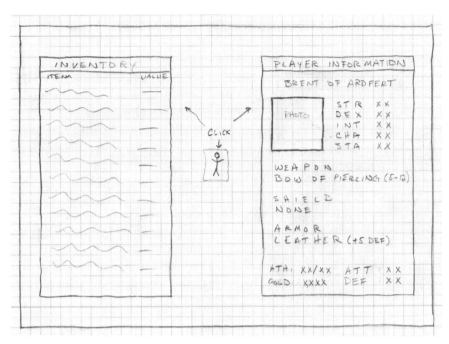

Figure 3.9 The design for the in-game player information screen.

This screen design also has one possible way of handling inventory management in the game. Since inventory is such a huge and complex issue, I've had to scrap the idea at this point and make the game simpler—or else it would never have made it into this book! Instead of a complex inventory system in the game, the player just picks up gold and uses it to upgrade weapons and armor in the towns. I'm a little disappointed at this, but inventory is unbelievably difficult to deal with in an RPG. While it is essential for some game designs, I've scaled down my aspirations for Celtic Crusader in the interest of getting the game done. In reality, my experience has shown that this is a justified decision because most inventory management is used just to sell weapons and items found in the world, with the sole purpose of equipping the character with better gear. This shortened method skips the steps required to pick up and sell items.

There is yet a third reason for skipping this part of the game: It's just not realistic. I've played games where inventory was so time consuming and required so much micromanagement that it absolutely ruined my suspension of disbelief while playing the game. Realistically, if you are a soldier of one class or another, do you have the strength to carry 100 swords, shields, and suits of armor while also carrying 1,000 arrows and 250 rings? Some RPGs *are* that ridiculous. A limited form of inventory management is definitely needed, though, so I suggest making that a serious first upgrade to the game if you want to make it better.

I like how Peter Molyneux designed an intuitive inventory system for the game Fable. In Fable, your character can carry quite a lot of stuff, because there is a fascinating aspect of this game that allows you to become a trader, making money by buying and selling goods. But with respect to combat gear, the game automatically recognizes "suits" of related armor items so you can auto-equip all related items of armor at once. I could literally go on for pages describing this amazing game. One thing that caused me to fall off my seat with laughter was what happened to my character when I equipped him with a very heavy hammer weapon. The game accurately modeled the character *dragging* the hammer behind him, and he was barely able to swing it!

Character Classes

Each character class comes from a certain part of the world, where it is assumed that the raw materials and skills are available for that class. For instance, sword-wielding paladins come from the Irish towns within the region of Leinster. There is no real reason for this historically, but I just like the idea of certain character classes coming from different parts of the world.

Table 3.1 shows the character classes and their home regions. The two fighter classes—warrior and paladin—both originate in Leinster. In reality, a character might be born anywhere, but is located in one of the towns in a certain region when the character is created. In the context of the game, creating a character means simply that you, as the player, are finding and assuming the identity of someone in the fictional world (or rather, of whom you are taking control).

Table 3.1 Character Classes and Their Home Regions

Character Class	Region
Warrior	Leinster
Knight	Leinster
Thief	Connaught
Scout	Munster
Mage	Ulster

Note that there are no Irish towns in the region of Connaught (only two ruins), so no characters can originate from this region. This is generally going to be a chaotic region ruled by anarchy, populated with thieves, cutthroats, and evil creatures aplenty.

The character attribute modifiers for each class are based on a fixed set of 15 points distributed among the attributes to reflect that class' strong and weak characteristics. If you add the modifiers together they equal 15, no matter the class, so there is no numerical advantage of one class over another. These base attributes are essential to defining each class. You should feel free to change this numerical basis for your own vision of this game. Just be sure to start off the base character classes with low "stats" because you don't want the player to become too strong early in the game.

Warrior Class

Warriors originate in the Leinster region due to the ongoing conflict with the Vikings, which have the strongest presence here of all Ireland. (There are three Viking settlements: Dubh Linn, Wexford, and Waterford.) It does make sense, if you think about it, because where there is the greatest conflict there is likely to be the most surplus of weapons available. A character in this region should be able to find a weapon and begin training—and there is the added possibility that a character was formerly an Irish patriot in a defeated and disbanded army. Figure 3.10 shows an example of a concept drawing of a Viking warrior.

Warriors can wield any type of heavy weapon but are basically limited by the available artwork, meaning that the warrior in this game carries an axe. Warriors have the attribute modifiers detailed in Table 3.2.

Table 3.2 Warriors' Attribute Modifiers

Attribute	Modifier
Strength	+8
Dexterity	+4
Intellect	−3
Charisma	0
Stamina	+6

Figure 3.10 An artistic concept drawing of a Viking warrior (courtesy of Eden Celeste).

Knight Class

Knights (frequently called "Paladins" in RPGs) are holy warriors who pledge their loyalty to God and country, so to speak, although this has been fantasized in literature and fantasy gaming to mean that knights have certain magical capabilities (notably the ability to heal others). It is generally accepted that a knight in an RPG should always defend good and fight against evil. You should never have an evil knight (otherwise, you should just create a character from another class), although it might be possible to have a "dark knight" who has become corrupted, which is an interesting story element.

Figure 3.11 shows an example of a concept drawing of a dark knight. You can see from this single drawing that concept artwork is extremely valuable, as it helps to fully realize the potential of the game and gives the sprite artist an example of what the sprite should look like. When you have 100+ frames of animation for a sprite, you want to be sure that it is correct on the first frame because animation is very difficult to modify after the artist has completed the work.

Figure 3.11 An artistic concept drawing of a dark knight (courtesy of Eden Celeste).

In this game, I loosely define a knight as a sword-wielding character, or swordsman for short. Knights are well-rounded characters, with the character attribute modifiers in Table 3.3.

Table 3.3 Knights' Attribute Modifiers

Attribute	Modifier
Strength	+6
Dexterity	+4
Intellect	−3
Charisma	+5
Stamina	+3

Thief Class

The thief is a classic character class in RPGs because this type of character sort of fills in the gap between the very powerful warrior/knight classes and the scout (archer). A thief typically carries a small dagger or a club and is skilled at opening locks (such as locked doors and treasure chests). A thief is not strong enough to be a powerful warrior or knight nor is skilled with a bow or trained in the art of magic; a thief is sort of an odd character that has a different set of skills based on stealth.

Thieves generally come from Connaught and are found lurking in the corners and alleys of Birr and Limerick, though they tend to travel quite often, following merchant caravans from one region to another. As a result, a thief character may be from any Irish or Viking town. Table 3.4 shows the attribute modifiers for the thief class.

Table 3.4 Thieves' Attribute Modifiers

Attribute	Modifier
Strength	−1
Dexterity	+7
Intellect	+3
Charisma	+1
Stamina	+5

Scout (Archer) Class

Scouts are common in the land of Ireland since the bow is the most common hunting weapon throughout the world. However, the military-caliber archer is only found in one place: the forest-encroached Irish town of Ardfert, the only unscathed Irish settlement in the region of Munster. The craft of building bows and carving straight arrows may be found throughout the land, but the craft of building armor-piercing knight arrows and multistring compound bows is now limited exclusively to Ardfert.

Table 3.5 Scouts' Attribute Modifiers

Attribute	Modifier
Strength	+3
Dexterity	+8
Intellect	−2
Charisma	+1
Stamina	+5

The skilled archers of Ardfert are themselves as skilled in bowcraft as they are in warcraft, often recruited by Irish militia at the outlying towns and by rebel factions still fighting against the Vikings. The attribute modifiers for the scout class are given in Table 3.5.

Mage Class

The mages of Ulster region were once peaceful caretakers of Ireland's monasteries, turning their attention to a mastery of the natural world, including the use of healing herbs and in cultivating gardens. The invasion of the Vikings and subsequent pillaging of monasteries left many of the mages slaughtered, and those remaining fled to the few monasteries there were not discovered by the Vikings. Those who were left refocused their attention on combat techniques that they observed in the natural world, that, along with their mastery of unseen forces, makes the mages of Ulster skilled in hand-to-hand combat as well as in using magic. In addition, mages still know the art of healing.

Figure 3.12 shows an artist's concept drawing of a female mage character. What is the most significant thing that you notice about the concept drawings? They are hand-drawn, often in pencil, and scanned, rather than edited in a graphic editor program. Even if you have some fantastic character models already available for your game (that you plan to render into animated sprites), your game will still benefit greatly from hand-drawn concept renditions of each character. Table 3.6 reveals the attribute modifiers for the mage class.

Table 3.6 Mages' Attribute Modifiers

Attribute	Modifier
Strength	−6
Dexterity	+3
Intellect	+9
Charisma	+4
Stamina	+5

Figure 3.12 An artistic concept drawing of a female mage (courtesy of Eden Celeste).

The Non-Player Characters (NPCs)

Non-player characters (NPCs) represent everyone in the world other than the player's character (and the party in a game with more than one person playing, as in multiplayer games). NPCs are usually controlled by the game itself using a scripted or behavioral subroutine. The NPCs might be common townsfolk walking around the towns, doing their work and conducting business. NPCs might also be enemies, opposed to the player's character, who attack the PC on sight. Most of the time, fantasy creatures and monsters are not called NPCs because they are just obstacles that the player must overcome to complete a quest, and generally help build the PC's experience to level up and increase his skills.

The NPCs in Celtic Crusader follow a simple predefined path in the towns and do not venture outside the towns in which they are placed. This is accomplished by having them move around only within a limited range from their starting points. So, if the town of Durrow is located at a certain x,y position on the map, then the game generates a certain number of NPCs and places them at the same location identified as that town (along with a small random value, so they aren't all bunched up). The NPCs then move about in random directions and distances within a close proximity to their original starting points. In many cases, NPCs walk back and forth between two points on the map.

This rather simplistic behavior produces a surprisingly realistic town, and you can always insert some NPCs with more advanced behavior necessary to complete a certain quest. But most of the NPCs simply move around in this simple manner and make themselves available to the PC for dialog. Each NPC is provided with a simple set of responses to dialog that the player can choose to engage in (by walking up to an NPC and hitting a button).

The player is unable to attack non-combat NPCs, because the game simply does not have the capability at this point to cause the townsfolk to react to attack, but this is a good idea for a future upgrade to the game. As you will see in the second half of this book, there are a lot of concepts that must be covered in a short time and in a limited amount of space, so I cannot fully develop the idea of populating the towns and furthering the storyline. However, you will learn enough from the continual upgrades to the Celtic Crusader game project in each chapter to fully develop an interactive game world.

Weapons and Armor

The standard weapons are very weak in combat while the player is just getting started in the first few levels. This is balanced by the levels of creatures and enemy NPCs that the player encounters in the early stages. As the player increases in experience and goes up in levels, the foes are equally challenging to keep the player on edge all the time and to keep the good players from finishing the game too quickly.

The player should be able to equip a standard weapon, shield, and armor, and automatically swap gear when better items are found (which is not a significant part of the game, so it is not strongly emphasized). Table 3.7 shows the standard weapons that may be used by each character class.

Magic

Magic is a huge part of most RPGs and adds a lot to the character development aspects of a game. However, I have played many games that emphasize way too much magic, to the point of almost abandoning traditional weapons for offense and defense. In my

Table 3.7 Standard Weapons by Class

Character Class	Standard Weapon
Warrior	Axe
Knight	Sword
Thief	Club
Scout	Bow
Mage	Staff

opinion, magic should be downplayed as much as possible because it ruins the story. When there are hundreds of available magic spells that a character can learn, it tends to become the whole focus of the game play, and that's a shame! The game shouldn't be totally about character development and becoming the most powerful wizard in the world, although that is exactly what happens with some games. I want a more limited form of magic, and must admit that I'm tempted to leave it out altogether because it can be quite complex.

One way to handle magic is by treating spells as animated projectile sprites with embedded damage modifiers that cause things to happen to the target. For instance, arrows fired by the scout do damage based on the scout's character attack value, which is affected by the quality of the character's bow and skill. Several factors determine the possible amount of damage that an arrow can inflict on an opponent, if the opponent doesn't block the attack. (A strong defense value causes the arrow to miss entirely in some attacks.)

The amount of magic that can be used in an RPG is greatly dependent upon the available artwork to render magic spells used as weapons (such as fireball). It is better to start off with a limited magic system that allows the mage classes (which you might subclass into cleric, wizard, and so on) to heal themselves and others, as well as to enchant weapons. It is very common for magic in an RPG to grow in usage and depth as the game develops from one sequel to the next. Don't assume that you absolutely must get every single idea into the game on your first attempt. It's fun to leave room for growth, and players enjoy the new features of follow-up games in the series.

You might also consider the possibility of marketing a game as shareware, where you freely give away a limited version of the game (which may, for instance, just provide one character class), and then ask fans to pay for the full version which would have a full assortment of magic spells and other important features.

Communication

The communication system in the game is absolutely critical—although I could probably say the same thing for every major topic of this chapter. The fact is, without any dialog or communication, it is just a hack 'n' slash game. Granted, such games are popular and have a lot of fans, but my goal with Celtic Crusader is to build a simple RPG engine that works well enough, but provides room for a lot of customization and improvement (on your part). I don't want to fix the game to a specific goal (such as defeating a certain boss character), although that is certainly a goal that might be put into the game as one way to win.

Dialog in most games takes place at the bottom of the screen where messages are printed out and where the player can choose what to say to the NPCs. Some games feature dialog that appears over the characters. A nice feature to add to the dialog system is recorded voice acting, although if poorly presented, this can actually take away from the suspension of disbelief. (Always be careful not to do that!) It is sometimes better to just leave the player with his or her imagination, as many RPG fans regularly read fantasy books.

Combat

The combat in Celtic Crusader takes place in real time using the same scrolling map game engine used for walking around and communicating with NPCs. The combat system is more challenging when programming NPCs to react realistically to the dynamic environment than to combat itself. The basis for combat is an engagement of weapons using a custom subset of animated sprite frames showing the swinging of a weapon or shooting of an arrow.

When an attack takes place, the player's attack value (which is derived from the player's strength and character level) is compared to the opponent's defense value (which is based on strength, shield, and armor), and the result is added to a randomly generated number. If the final result is positive, then the attack succeeded; otherwise, the attack missed. On a successful attack, the amount of damage done by the weapon is rolled (usually a range, like 5 to 12) and that is how much damage the target takes. The damage reduces the health points of the player or NPC, and the target is killed if health drops below 0.

Level Up

Although game design should be considerably more complete than the partial design provided in this chapter, I think you now have a good idea about how to get started with your own game designs. Drawing what you think each screen should look like and brainstorming gameplay ideas ahead of time makes the game far more interesting when you start writing the source code that actually makes the game work. Without a solid design up front, you are destined to give up on the game before it is finished. In contrast, you will become more and more enthusiastic about the game as you complete the design of each part of the game, because the process opens your mind to the possibilities. This chapter explored just some of the primary aspects of the Celtic Crusader game, giving you a basic idea about how to design a game.

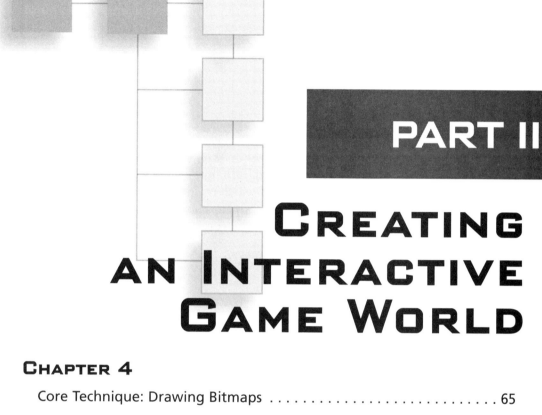

PART II

CREATING AN INTERACTIVE GAME WORLD

P art II focuses on the game world, with emphasis on how to create the world using a map editing program called Mappy, and several chapters devoted to displaying the game world on the screen. First, you learn how to load a Mappy level and perform horizontal and vertical scrolling, each of which is a suitable subject for a complete game in and of itself. The last chapter in Part II explains how to create the scrolling game world used in Celtic Crusader. The following chapters make up Part II:

- Chapter 4: Core Technique: Drawing Bitmaps
- Chapter 5: Level Editing with Mappy
- Chapter 6: The Basics of Tile-Based Scrolling
- Chapter 7: Scrolling the Game World
- Chapter 8: Advanced Scrolling Techniques

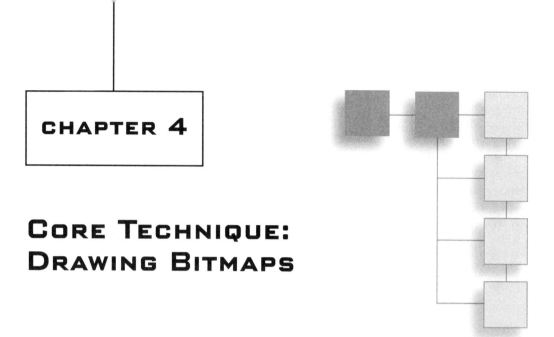

CHAPTER 4

CORE TECHNIQUE: DRAWING BITMAPS

The core of a 2D game of any kind is the basic bitmap image. Bitmaps come in a variety of file formats with a myriad of resolutions and color depths. This chapter teaches you the core technique of how to manipulate bitmaps in preparation for the tile-based scrolling chapters that follow (with the ultimate goal of displaying the scrolling game world of Celtic Crusader). You have already had some exposure to these bitmap routines in Chapter 2, "Your First DirectX Program," when you learned how to create a Direct3D surface in memory, load a bitmap file into the surface, and then draw it on the screen. I take you beyond that basic skill by showing you how to grab individual tiles out of a larger bitmap image and draw those tiles anywhere on the screen with precision control over the process.

Here is a breakdown of the major topics in this chapter:

- Understanding bitmaps and tiles
- Drawing a portion of a source bitmap

Understanding Bitmaps and Tiles

There's a lot more to creating a tile-based scrolling game world than simply loading a huge bitmap file of the world and drawing it on the screen. Not only is that terribly inefficient—because you can't reuse the same tiles over and over—but it is almost impossible to modify the map of the world without editing the actual pixels on the bitmap image.

What Is a Tile?

The concept of *tiling* means that you create a larger image by assembling smaller images (or tiles) in a pattern that results in the final image you want. Most often, a world map for a game uses a lot of the same images for the ground terrain, like dirt paths, grassy plains, rivers, roads, and so on. You can actually construct a huge game world with just a handful of tiles. The trick is to store the tiles in a bitmap file in a certain order, so your program can reference the tiles by number.

For instance, suppose you want to make a road. Let's ignore the whole process of loading the map and drawing it on the screen for a moment, and just talk about one small part of a game world that is yet to be created. I want to make a road that is the center of a town (such as Durrow, for instance). If I want to draw the road and just store it in a bitmap file, that bitmap might look something like Figure 4.1.

You know, you might just get away with making a game using one gigantic bitmap file for the world, especially if you break up the world into a sort of grid where the game loads the next screen when the player reaches one of the four edges. The end result, though, is an inflexible game that requires a lot more work on your part to construct, and any changes you want to make to the world require editing the bitmaps rather than just using a map editor program (like Mappy, which is covered in the next chapter) and reassembling the tiles like a huge puzzle. Actually, a tiled floor is a more appropriate analogy to a tile-based world, and that is the origination of the term.

note

A similar technique is used in Part III, "The Player's Character (PC)," for the discussion of loading and drawing transparent, animated sprites (although sprites are based on Direct3D textures rather than surfaces, as you will learn in Chapter 9).

Figure 4.1 An example bitmap of a road.

Tiling the Road

The tiles used to make the road image are shown in Figure 4.2. As you can see, a fairly large map was created using just four tiles. This is a very typical example of what you can do with just a handful of tiles. Where map editing gets a little more complex is when you add things like buildings, houses, trees, and other objects to the game world, which requires a little extra work (although you still use the map editor program).

The actual source for the tiles seen here is a bitmap file shown in Figure 4.3. This file has 16 tiles that can be used to fill in the road for a town or for any other purpose (although cobblestone was difficult to build, so it would be unrealistic to have a road like this going across the whole country).

note

> If you are surprised by how quickly I'm moving along in this chapter already, it's just because there's a lot of rudimentary information that you don't need to program an RPG in Visual Basic. I covered an enormous amount of information and went into excruciating detail about every single aspect of loading and handling bitmaps in my previous book, *Visual Basic Game Programming with DirectX* (which is based on the same exact technology you're seeing in this book: DirectX 8). In my opinion, it's more fun to learn specific skills that are directly related to a game project than to cover an enormous amount of theory without much return on the investment of time (both in writing the material, as well as reading it), so I'm focusing on exactly what you need to create a tile-based game world at this stage.

| Tile #1
Grass | Tile #2
Intersection | Tile #3
N/S Road | Tile #4
W/E Road |

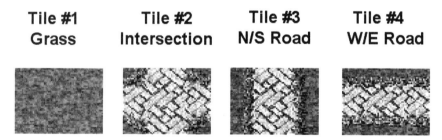

Figure 4.2 The complete set of road tiles.

Figure 4.3 This bitmap file is the source for the road tiles.

Tile-based scrolling is usually an advanced subject not even covered by some books of this type, but by covering it early on, we can move along together toward building an RPG fairly quickly. I just want to encourage you not to get frustrated if this seems to move along too quickly. I'd like you to experience what can be done with Visual Basic and DirectX first, and then overcome the shell shock as you learn. This is a better way to grasp the material than having a lot of information up front to which you have a hard time relating.

Drawing a Portion of a Source Bitmap

I'm going to reserve any more discussion of the tile-based world for the next two chapters. At the present time, you need some skill with handling bitmaps. Let's work on a program that shows you how to load a bitmap file and draw a portion of it on the screen. You then have some reusable code that comes in handy in the upcoming chapters on creating the game world.

Back in Chapter 2 you saw just how easy it is to load a bitmap file into a Direct3D surface and then draw it on the screen, so I don't need to go over that again, right? Instead, let's push the envelope a little and learn how to draw a *portion* of a bitmap image to the screen. This is the first important step toward creating a scrolling game world, so brace yourself!

Grabbing a Tile

Let's take a look at that `CopyRects` function again. Remember it is a *method* in the `Direct3DDevice8` object, in *object-oriented programming (OOP)* terminology. `CopyRects` has five parameters that I explain here so you have a complete understanding of how it works:

- `SourceSurface As Direct3DSurface8`. This first parameter specifies the source bitmap image (surface) containing the image that you want to draw on the screen.

- `FirstElementOfSourceRectsArray As Any`. The second parameter can be an *array* of rectangles that you want drawn in order, which is actually pretty cool if you think about it—you can draw a whole bunch of images on the screen using a single function call, as long as the tiles are all located in the same source image! You definitely look at this more fully in the next two chapters, and I hope this piques your curiosity. For the time being, I just show you how to draw a single image.

- `NumberOfRects As Long`. This parameter specifies the number of rectangles you want to draw in order, as specified in the rectangle array (the previous parameter).

- `DestinationSurface As Direct3DSurface8`. This specifies the destination surface where the image(s) are drawn, and can be any surface but is usually just the back buffer (which is, for all practical purposes, the same as *screen*).

- `FirstElementofDestPointArray As Any`. For every rectangle in the rectangle array (specifying portions of the source image to be drawn), you must provide a destination point to where that image will be copied. For one image, you can specify just a single point.

tip

If you don't fully understand `CopyRects` after finishing this chapter, don't worry. I use it quite a bit more in the next few chapters.

You already saw how to use `CopyRects` in Chapter 2 just to draw an entire bitmap to the screen. Now I'm going to show you how to use these advanced parameter options to specify a smaller portion of the bitmap to draw onto the screen. I have a really cool bitmap of a castle for this example (provided courtesy of Reiner's Tilesets; http://www.reinerstileset.de), shown in Figure 4.4.

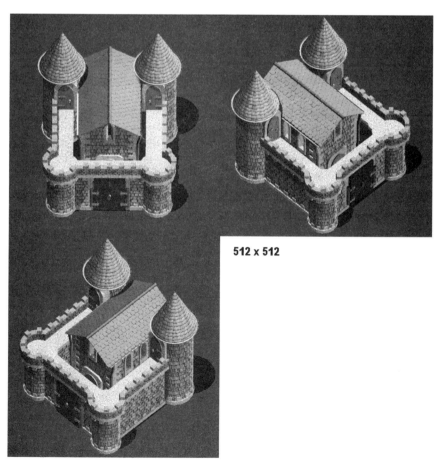

512 x 512

Figure 4.4 The castle bitmap containing three tiles.

The World Is a Big Place

A really simple way to make a game is to store every single tile in its own bitmap file. The problem with that is gross, terrible, heinous, grotesque, hideous inefficiency. Can you imagine how long it would take to start up the game when there are 15,000 bitmap files that have to be loaded? Let's just put it like this: The screensaver will kick in while the game is loading. Some games might have worked that way in the old days (remember Pac-Man?), but that's not an option in the 21st century. We're supposed to be sending a manned mission to Mars sometime soon, so we shouldn't be writing bad games—it's embarrassing. You know, it will take about nine months for a ship to reach Mars, so odds are the crew will be playing a lot of video games on the way . . . food for thought!

tip

Artwork is *everything* in an RPG. There's no point even getting started on the game until you have all the artwork you're going to need. Reiner's Tilesets provided all of the graphics you see in this book, and you can use the same tiles and sprites for your own games by visiting http://www.reinerstileset.de. (Both English and German versions of the site are available.)

Okay, we've settled the reason why tiled bitmaps are necessary, so what about drawing one of those castles? That castle bitmap was designed to work in a regular tiled game world or an isometric game world, which is why you see two images at an odd angle (which looks great in an isometric game, but we're focusing on the rectangular orientation).

That second parameter of CopyRects requires the most attention. It's calling for the *first element* of a source rectangle array, which means you can have a huge array of rectangles specifying the position of tiles in a bitmap image, and you can jump to any tile in the array you want to draw—and the number of images to draw is specified in the third parameter. First, you have to create this rectangle array. It doesn't have to be an array at all right now, as you can just create a single rectangle variable and use that as the start of the rectangle array. (Just remember this is a very important subject in the coming chapters!) Take a look:

```
Dim sourceRect As DxVBLibA.RECT
```

DxVBLibA is the root of the DirectX Type Library containing a lot of structures, classes, and constants you use to write DirectX code. The RECT is a structure that looks like this:

```
Public Type RECT
    left As Long
    top As Long
    right As Long
    bottom As Long
End Type
```

caution

I strongly suggest using windowed mode while you are writing Direct3D code. When there is an error (and there will be a *lot* of them, guaranteed!), you have a hard time breaking out of full-screen mode to deal with the error. You wind up having to open Task Manager (Ctrl+Alt+Del) and then kill the program, which also shuts down Visual Basic. Doh!

You don't need to add this RECT Type to your program because it's already included in DxVBLibA. How you use it is the important thing. Let's say I want to grab the first castle image in castle.bmp. The castle is 512 × 512 pixels in size, so I want to specify a rectangle that looks like this:

```
sourceRect.left = 0
sourceRect.top = 0
sourceRect.right = 511
sourceRect.bottom = 511
```

That takes care of the rectangular shape of the source image. What comes next is the destination point. POINT is another Type included in DxVBLibA, and you can create a point like this:

```
Dim point1 As DxVBLibA.POINT
```

The POINT structure has a format that looks like this:

```
Public Type POINT
    x As Long
    y As Long
End Type
```

Therefore, you can specify a point for the position on the destination surface where you want to draw the image:

```
point1.x = 25
point1.y = 25
```

This specifies a position of (25,25) on the screen where the image is drawn. This brings us to the last part of this process: actually calling CopyRects to do the drawing. By using parameters, you can write a reusable DrawTile function that uses its own RECT and POINT types to keep your code looking clean. Here is the actual CopyRects call:

```
d3ddev.CopyRects source, sourceRect, 1, backbuffer, point
```

Note that I told it to copy one item in the rectangle array, sourceRect, and to use point to specify where on the back buffer to draw the image. I think this makes more sense if you see a whole procedure handling the details automatically based on parameters that you pass to it. DrawTile has a lot of parameters because I prefer to use simple data types instead of things like RECT and POINT in my own code. This DrawTile subroutine therefore creates its own types to take care of that for me. The code is a little bit longer than you might expect for a subroutine that just draws an image, but remember this is a very useful routine that can draw any tile from a source surface to the screen.

```
Private Sub DrawTile( _
    ByRef source As Direct3DSurface8, _
    ByVal sourcex As Long, _
    ByVal sourcey As Long, _
    ByVal width As Long, _
    ByVal height As Long, _
    ByVal destx As Long, _
    ByVal desty As Long)

    'create a RECT to describe the source image
    Dim sourceRect As DxVBLibA.RECT
    'set the upper left corner of the source image
    sourceRect.left = sourcex
    sourceRect.top = sourcey
    'set the bottom right corner of the source image
    sourceRect.right = sourcex + width
    sourceRect.bottom = sourcey + height

    'create a POINT to define the destination
    Dim point1 As DxVBLibA.point
    'set the upper left corner of where to draw the image
    point1.x = destx
    point1.y = desty

    'draw the source bitmap tile image
    d3ddev.CopyRects source, sourceRect, 1, backbuffer, point1

End Sub
```

The Rest of the DrawTile Program

In addition to the DrawTile routine you just saw, type the following code into a new Visual Basic project to demonstrate how to draw a portion of a bitmap, your first step toward building a tile-based game world! As a reminder, you must include a reference to the Visual Basic Type Library. You do this by opening the Project menu, selecting References, and then checking the item called DirectX 8 for Visual Basic Type Library from the list. Figure 4.5 shows the output of the DrawTile program.

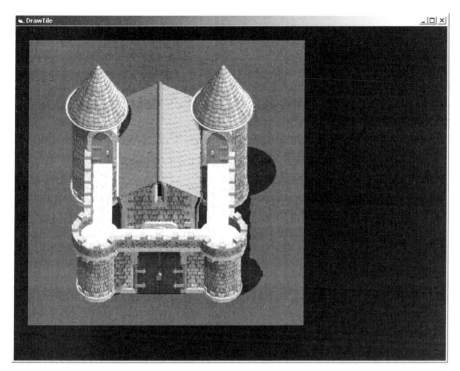

Figure 4.5 The DrawTile program.

tip

Remember to include the DirectX 8 for Visual Basic Type Library in all of your Visual Basic projects.

Now here's the rest of the code for the DrawTile program (in addition to the DrawTile procedure, provided earlier, that you also need to include in this program).

```
'--------------------------------------------------------
' Visual Basic Game Programming for Teens
' Chapter 4 - DrawTile program
'--------------------------------------------------------

'make sure every variable is declared
Option Explicit
'make all arrays start with 0 instead of 1
Option Base 0
```

```
'customize the program here
Const SCREENWIDTH As Long = 800
Const SCREENHEIGHT As Long = 600
Const FULLSCREEN As Boolean = False
Const C_BLACK As Long = &H0
Const C_RED As Long = &HFF0000

'the DirectX objects
Dim dx As DirectX8
Dim d3d As Direct3D8
Dim d3dx As New D3DX8
Dim dispmode As D3DDISPLAYMODE
Dim d3dpp As D3DPRESENT_PARAMETERS
Dim d3ddev As Direct3DDevice8

'some surfaces
Dim backbuffer As Direct3DSurface8
Dim castle As Direct3DSurface8

Private Sub Form_Load()
    'set up the main form
    Form1.Caption = "DrawTile"
    Form1.AutoRedraw = False
    Form1.BorderStyle = 1
    Form1.ClipControls = False
    Form1.ScaleMode = 3
    Form1.width = Screen.TwipsPerPixelX * (SCREENWIDTH + 12)
    Form1.height = Screen.TwipsPerPixelY * (SCREENHEIGHT + 30)
    Form1.Show

    'initialize Direct3D
    InitDirect3D Me.hwnd, SCREENWIDTH, SCREENHEIGHT, FULLSCREEN

    'get reference to the back buffer
    Set backbuffer = d3ddev.GetBackBuffer(0, D3DBACKBUFFER_TYPE_MONO)

    'load the bitmap file--castle.bmp is 1024x1024
    Set castle = LoadSurface(App.Path & "\castle.bmp", 1024, 1024)

End Sub
```

```
Public Sub InitDirect3D( _
    ByVal hwnd As Long, _
    ByVal lWidth As Long, _
    ByVal lHeight As Long, _
    ByVal bFullscreen As Boolean)

    'catch any errors here
    On Local Error GoTo fatal_error

    'create the DirectX object
    Set dx = New DirectX8

    'create the Direct3D object
    Set d3d = dx.Direct3DCreate()
    If d3d Is Nothing Then
        MsgBox "Error initializing Direct3D!"
        Shutdown
    End If

    'tell D3D to use the current color depth
    d3d.GetAdapterDisplayMode D3DADAPTER_DEFAULT, dispmode

    'set the display settings used to create the device
    Dim d3dpp As D3DPRESENT_PARAMETERS
    d3dpp.hDeviceWindow = hwnd
    d3dpp.BackBufferCount = 1
    d3dpp.BackBufferWidth = lWidth
    d3dpp.BackBufferHeight = lHeight
    d3dpp.SwapEffect = D3DSWAPEFFECT_COPY_VSYNC
    d3dpp.BackBufferFormat = dispmode.Format

    'set windowed or fullscreen mode
    If bFullscreen Then
        d3dpp.Windowed = 0
    Else
        d3dpp.Windowed = 1
    End If
```

```
    'chapter 9
    d3dpp.MultiSampleType = D3DMULTISAMPLE_NONE
    d3dpp.AutoDepthStencilFormat = D3DFMT_D32

    'create the D3D primary device
    Set d3ddev = d3d.CreateDevice( _
        D3DADAPTER_DEFAULT, _
        D3DDEVTYPE_HAL, _
        hwnd, _
        D3DCREATE_SOFTWARE_VERTEXPROCESSING, _
        d3dpp)

    If d3ddev Is Nothing Then
        MsgBox "Error creating the Direct3D device!"
        Shutdown
    End If

    Exit Sub
fatal_error:
    MsgBox "Critical error in Start_Direct3D!"
    Shutdown
End Sub

Private Sub Form_Paint()
    'clear the background of the screen
    d3ddev.Clear 0, ByVal 0, D3DCLEAR_TARGET, C_BLACK, 1, 0

    'draw the castle bitmap "tile" image
    DrawTile castle, 0, 0, 511, 511, 25, 25

    'send the back buffer to the screen
    d3ddev.Present ByVal 0, ByVal 0, 0, ByVal 0
End Sub

Private Sub Form_KeyDown(KeyCode As Integer, Shift As Integer)
    If KeyCode = 27 Then Shutdown
End Sub

Private Sub Form_QueryUnload(Cancel As Integer, UnloadMode As Integer)
    Shutdown
End Sub
```

```
Private Sub Shutdown()
    Set castle = Nothing
    Set d3ddev = Nothing
    Set d3d = Nothing
    Set dx = Nothing
    End
End Sub
```

I've saved LoadSurface for the end so I can explain a change that I made to it. The original LoadSurface subroutine that you saw in Chapter 2 just used the SCREENWIDTH and SCREEN-HEIGHT constants for the resolution of the surface to be created. Instead of using those constants, I've modified the routine so it accepts the width and height values as parameters. This will make LoadSurface far more useful as you start working with bitmaps for tiles and sprites.

```
Private Function LoadSurface( _
    ByVal filename As String, _
    ByVal width As Long, _
    ByVal height As Long) _
    As Direct3DSurface8

    On Local Error GoTo fatal_error
    Dim surf As Direct3DSurface8

    'return error by default
    Set LoadSurface = Nothing

    'create the new surface
    Set surf = d3ddev.CreateImageSurface(width, height, dispmode.Format)
    If surf Is Nothing Then
        MsgBox "Error creating surface!"
        Exit Function
    End If
```

```
        'load surface from file
        d3dx.LoadSurfaceFromFile _
            surf, _
            ByVal 0, _
            ByVal 0, _
            filename, _
            ByVal 0, _
            D3DX_DEFAULT, _
            0, _
            ByVal 0

        If surf Is Nothing Then
            MsgBox "Error loading " & filename & "!"
            Exit Function
        End If

        'return the new surface
        Set LoadSurface = surf

    fatal_error:
        Exit Function
    End Function
```

Level Up

This chapter is a significant step toward building the complete tile-based game world for Celtic Crusader. You learned a core technique of grabbing a tile out of a larger bitmap image and drawing it to any location on the screen. You also learned in the process how the powerful CopyRects procedure has the ability to draw many tiles with a single call to the procedure—something that comes in very handy in the next few chapters. The next step is to actually become familiar with Mappy, the map-editing program that uses tiles to construct a game level. You learn how to create a small game world with Mappy in the next chapter and then learn how to use that level in a program in the following chapter. You are right on track!

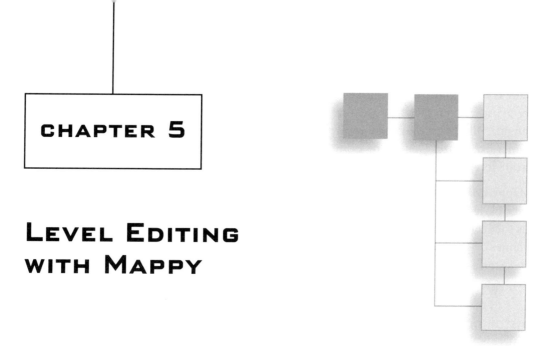

CHAPTER 5

LEVEL EDITING WITH MAPPY

T he game world defines the rules of the game and presents the player with all of the obstacles that must be overcome to complete the game. Although the world is the most important aspect of a game, it is not always given the proper attention when a game is being designed. This chapter provides an introduction to world building, or more specifically, map editing. You learn to create the game world for Celtic Crusader, as well as levels for your own games, using an excellent program called Mappy.

Here is a rundown of the major topics in this chapter:

- Installing Mappy
- Creating a new map
- Importing the source tiles
- Editing the tile map
- Saving the map file as FMP
- Saving the map file as text
- Using layers

Creating the Game World

Mappy is a powerful map editing program created by Robin Burrows. Mappy is *freeware*, so you can download and use it to create maps for your games at no cost, although the pro version has additional features. If you do find Mappy as useful as I have, I encourage you to send the author a small donation to express your appreciation for his hard work. The home page for Mappy is http://www.tilemap.co.uk. You can purchase the pro version of Mappy from this web site for a small amount.

Why is Mappy so great, you ask? First of all, it's easy to use. In fact, it couldn't be any easier to use without sacrificing features. Mappy supports maps made up of the standard rectangular tiles, as well as isometric and hexagonal tiles! Have you ever played hexagonal games like Panzer General or isometric games like Age of Empires? Well, Mappy lets you create levels similar to the ones used in these games.

Mappy has been used to create many retail (commercial) games, some of which you may have played! I personally know of several developers who have used Mappy to create levels for retail games for Pocket PC, Game Boy Advance, Nokia N-Gage, and wireless (cell phones). MonkeyStone's Hyperspace Delivery Boy (created by Tom Hall, John Romero, and Stevie Case) for Pocket PC and Game Boy Advance is one example. Suffice it to say, Mappy is a great map editor that I explain how to use in this chapter.

Installing Mappy

Mappy is included on the CD-ROM that accompanies this book, in the \mappy folder. You can run Mappy directly without installing it, although I recommend copying the mapwin.exe file to your hard drive. Mappy is so small, at 514 KB, that it's not unreasonable to copy it to any folder where you may need it. (If you want to check for a newer version of Mappy, the home site is located at http://www.tilemap.co.uk. In addition to Mappy, sample games are available for download.) If you do copy the executable without the subfolders, INI file, and so on, you miss out on the scripts and settings, so you may want to copy the whole folder containing the executable file to your hard drive.

Creating a New Map

Now let's fire up Mappy and create a new map.

1. Locate mapwin.exe and run it.

   When first run, Mappy comes up with two blank child windows. See Figure 5.1.

2. Open the File menu and select New Map to bring up the New Map dialog shown in Figure 5.2.

   As the New Map dialog shows, you must enter the size of each tile in your tile image file. The tiles used in Celtic Crusader vary, but most of the ground tiles are 64 × 48 pixels, so I have typed in 64 in the width box and 48 in the height box.

3. Next you must enter the size of the map.

   The default 100 × 100 map is large—probably too large to be useful as a good example at this point, although the entire island of Ireland needs to be much bigger than that. Let's use the default map size for now. Of course you can use any size you want for the map.

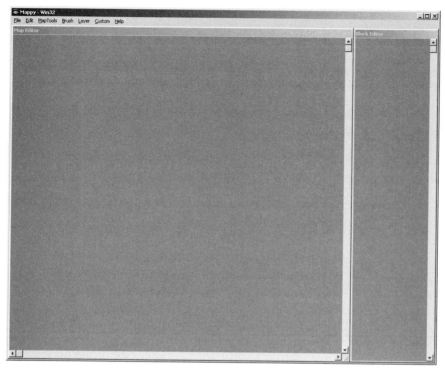

Figure 5.1 Mappy is a simple and unassuming map editor.

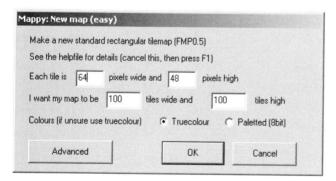

Figure 5.2 The New Map dialog in Mappy is used to configure a new game level.

tip

Mappy allows you to change the map size after it has been created (using MapTools, Resize Map), so if you need more tiles in your map later, it's easy to enlarge. Likewise, you can shrink the map, and Mappy has an option that lets you choose what portion of the map is cropped.

4. If you click the Advanced button on the New Map dialog you see the additional options shown in Figure 5.3.

   These options allow you to select the exact color depth of the source tiles (8-bit through 32-bit), the map file version to use, and dimensions for nonrectangular map tiles (such as hexagonal and isometric).

5. When you click the OK button, a new map is created and filled with the default black tile (tile #0).

   At this point, you must import the tile images that you want to use in the map (which is what the next section details). This is where things really get interesting, because you can use multiple image files containing source artwork; Mappy combines all the source tiles into a new image source with correctly positioned tiles. (Saving the tile bitmap file is an option on the Save As dialog.) Mappy looks like Figure 5.4.

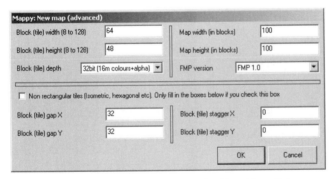

Figure 5.3 The advanced options in the New Map dialog.

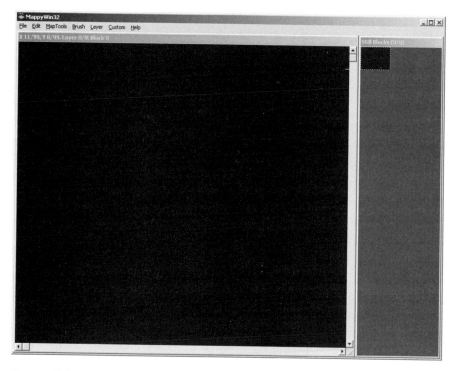

Figure 5.4 A new map is ready to be edited, but first some tiles are needed.

Importing the Source Tiles

Here's where you import the tile images that you want to use in the map.

1. Open the File menu and select Import. See Figure 5.5.

   The Open File dialog appears, allowing you to browse for an image file, which may be BMP, PCX, PNG, or MAR/P (map array file—something that can be exported by Mappy). I have used the same bitmap file you saw in the last chapter containing a cobblestone street and grass, and called it maptiles.BMP here.

After choosing this file, Mappy imports the tiles into the tile palette shown in Figure 5.6. Recall that you specified the tile size when you created the map file; Mappy used the dimensions provided to automatically read in all of the tiles automatically.

You must make the image resolution reasonably close to the edges of the tiles, but it doesn't need to be perfect—Mappy is smart enough to account for a few pixels off the right or bottom edges and move to the next row. In other words, once you create a map with a specified tile size, you *must* use tiles of that size for the entire map, as there is no way to have a tile map with differently sized tiles (which would screw up the drawing process, anyway).

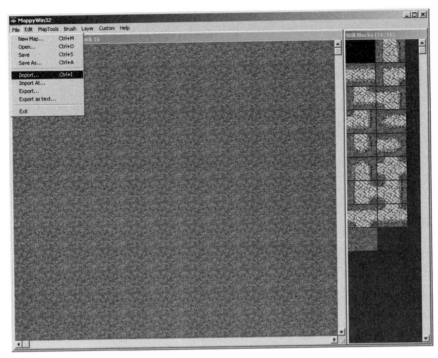

Figure 5.5 The Import option on the File menu.

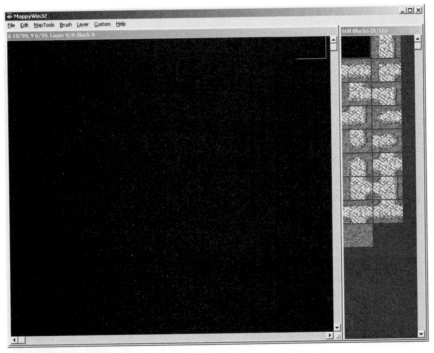

Figure 5.6 The tiles have been imported into Mappy's tile palette.

You can import tiles another way that I find even more useful than the Import feature: It is in the MapTools menu under Useful Functions. Look for an option called Create Map from Big Picture and select it, as shown in Figure 5.7.

This brings up the standard File Open dialog, which shows the available image files. I have changed the dialog display to show thumbnails rather than a list of files, as shown in Figure 5.8.

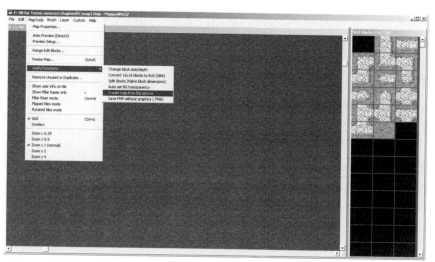

Figure 5.7 Locating the Create Map from Big Picture option.

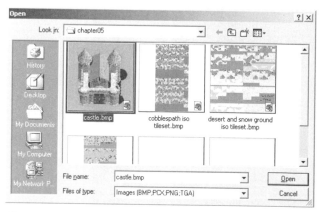

Figure 5.8 Importing an entire bitmap image, which is broken up into tiles.

2. Select the bitmap file to use and click Open.

A dialog box appears, asking if you would like to remove duplicate graphics and blocks. You should *always* do this, because it is the one way I know to clean up the tile palette after several bitmaps have been imported into the palette. After you work with it for a while, there are usually a lot of duplicate tiles after importing large images. This feature optimizes the palette and removes duplicates.

After Mappy has imported the image into the tile palette, the result is shown in Figure 5.9. Note how Mappy automatically adds new tiles to the end of the list so the current map is not affected. In contrast, the Import command from the File menu overwrites the palette! You want to use the Create Map from Big Picture option most of the time.

Editing the Tile Map

You can now create a map with the available tiles. I'd like to show you a convenient feature that I use often. I like to see most of the level on the screen at once to get an overview. Mappy lets you change the zoom level of the map editor display.

1. Open the MapTools menu and select one of the zoom levels to change the zoom.

2. Select a tile from the tile palette and use the mouse to "draw" that tile on the map edit window to see how the chosen zoom level appears.

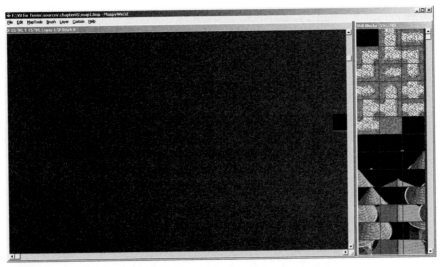

Figure 5.9 The castle image has been imported as a series of tiles.

I frequently use 0.5 (1/2 zoom), shown in Figure 5.10. Until you have added some tiles to the map window, you won't see anything happen after changing the zoom.

Now let me show you a quick shortcut for filling the entire map with a certain tile.

1. Select a neutral tile that is good as a backdrop, such as the grass, dirt, or stone tile.

2. Open the Custom menu. This menu contains scripts that can be run to manipulate a map.

   You can write your own scripts if you learn the Lua language. Visit http://www.lua.org for more information.

3. Select the script called Solid Rectangle (see Figure 5.11) to bring up the dialog shown in Figure 5.12.

4. Modify the width and height parameters for the rectangle (such as 10,10).

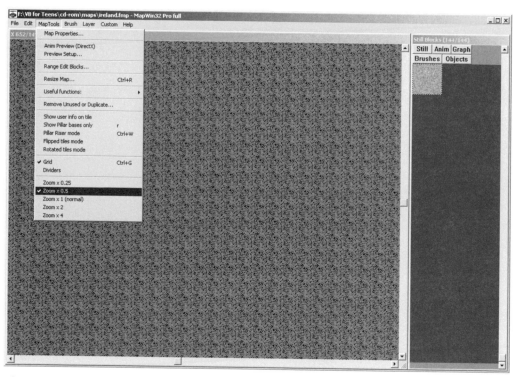

Figure 5.10 Changing the zoom level of the map editor window.

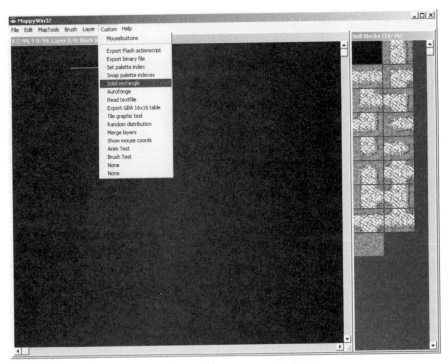

Figure 5.11 Filling a region of the map with a specified tile.

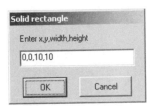

Figure 5.12 Specifying the range of map tiles to be filled in with the selected tile.

5. Click OK and the map is filled with the currently selected tile, as shown in Figure 5.13.

Selecting a different tile and filling in the whole map results in what you see in Figure 5.14.

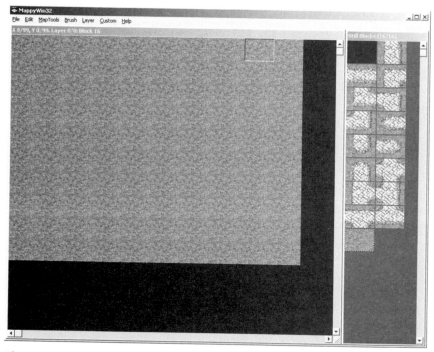

Figure 5.13 The Solid Rectangle script fills a region of the map with a tile.

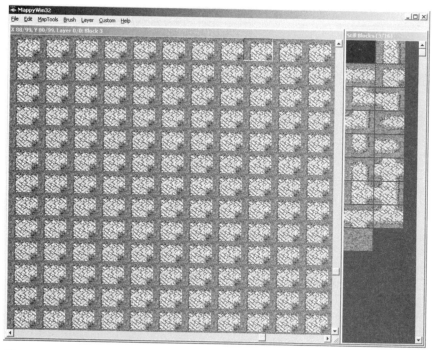

Figure 5.14 Filling in the whole map with a specific tile.

Go ahead and play around with Mappy to gain familiarity with it. You can erase tiles with the right mouse button and select tiles in the palette with the left button. You can use the keyboard arrow keys to scroll the map in any direction. (This is very handy when you want to keep your other hand on the mouse for quick editing.) Try to create an interesting map; I show you how to save the map in two different formats that you use in the following sample programs.

Saving the Map File as FMP

Have you created an interesting map yet that can be saved? If not, go ahead and create a map, even if it's just a hodge-podge of tiles. Don't be afraid to save a *lot* of different files. Disk space is cheap, but your imagination is valuable. I show you how to save the map file first and then you export the map to a text file and try to use it in sample programs later on. For now, open the File menu and select Save As to bring up the Save As file dialog shown in Figure 5.15.

You want to save your source maps in the default Mappy format for safe keeping, even if you plan to export the file for use in Visual Basic. Unfortunately, there's no simple way to load an FMP file directly in Visual Basic, and I don't have the space to cover it in this book, so use the simpler export format. Type a map file name such as map1.fmp and click Save.

note

Always keep backup copies of your original source map files.

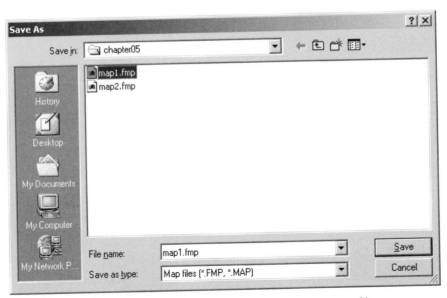

Figure 5.15 The Save As file dialog in Mappy is used to save a map file.

Saving the Map File as Text

Now that you have saved the new level in the standard Mappy file format, I'd like to show you how to export the map to a simple text file that can be pasted into a program. The result is an array in text format that can be easily modified to work in Visual Basic.

1. Open the File menu and select Export.

   Do not select Export As Text at this time. That is an entirely different option used to export a map to accommodate multiple layers, which is something that you do shortly; at the moment, start with just a simple map export. (You need to use Export As Text in order to support transparent layers, which you learn more about later in this chapter.)

2. Select Export to bring up the Export dialog shown in Figure 5.16.

   You can explore the uses for the various formats in the Export dialog when you have an opportunity; I explain the one option you need to export the map data as text.

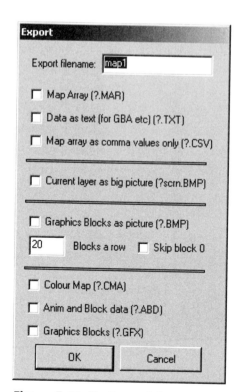

Figure 5.16 The Export dialog in Mappy lets you choose options for exporting the map.

3. You want to select the third checkbox from the top: Map Array as Comma Values Only (?.CSV).

If you want to build an image containing the tiles in the proper order as they were in Mappy, then you can also select the Graphics Blocks as Picture (?.BMP) checkbox. I strongly recommend exporting the image. For one thing, Mappy adds the blank tile that you may have used in some parts of the map; Mappy also numbers the tiles consecutively, starting with this blank tile unless you check the option Skip Block 0. (I suggest leaving it *unchecked.*) You should be able to normally just leave the default of 20 in the Blocks a Row input field, but feel free to change it if you wish.

For our purposes, both the CSV and BMP files are needed to properly draw the map in Visual Basic. The CSV file is dumped into a Visual Basic module file, while the bitmap file is loaded at runtime.

4. Click OK to export the map.

The Saved Bitmap File

Mappy outputs the map with the name provided in the Export dialog as two files: map1.BMP and map1.CSV. (Your map name may differ.) Microsoft Excel recognizes the CSV format, but there is no point loading it into Excel (if you have Microsoft Office installed). Instead, rename the file to map1.txt and then open it with Notepad or another text editor. You can now copy the map data text and paste it into a source code file, and you have the bitmap image handy as well. The resulting bitmap file is shown in Figure 5.17 (with the cobblestone and castle tile sets).

You know, with the ability to export the tiles from Mappy, there's nothing you can't do with this wonderful program. You can import all kinds of weird tiled bitmaps into your world and let Mappy generate one big bitmap file, which you can use in your program. So, you don't need to worry about loading all of your source tiles—just a single bitmap file.

Figure 5.17 The bitmap file generated by Mappy.

The Saved Data File

Mappy creates a text file filled with tile values separated by commas and looks something like Figure 5.18.

The real question is how you use this text file in a Visual Basic program. That's a logical question at this point in the chapter. However, I'm going to defer the discussion until the next chapter, which is focused entirely on displaying the map in a Visual Basic program. My goal here is just to introduce you to Mappy and help you to get familiar with it.

Advanced Map Editing Techniques

I've been holding back, anticipating some advanced techniques while going over the basics of using Mappy. Now I can't wait any longer; I just have to show you this stuff right now! Mappy doesn't look very feature rich by default, but a couple of relatively unknown secrets make it very powerful. Now, check this out. You can set up one of the layers as the background and then do all of your drawing on a "top" layer without affecting the background. You can draw, erase—everything—and the layer underneath remains untouched.

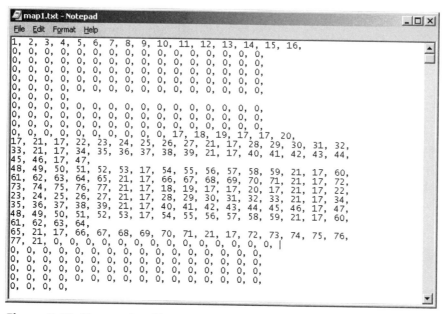

Figure 5.18 The map data file generated by Mappy.

Using Layers

Layering is a powerful feature of Mappy that becomes even more interesting when you load a Mappy data file directly in your game (something that is not possible here, unfortunately, due to no Visual Basic library for Mappy). A layer is just a tile map that exists above or below other tile maps in a multi-layer fashion. For the purpose of creating an RPG world, layers are helpful when designing the world map, and the layering isn't needed after the map has been saved, although it's extremely helpful while working on the map.

1. To add another layer to the map, open the Layer menu and select Add Layer, as shown in Figure 5.19.

2. Next, go back into the Layer menu and check the option called "Background Colored" option so the background layer will be darkened. This makes it easier to identify your foreground layer work.

3. Open Layer again and select the option "Onion Skin" to bring up the Onion Skin dialog box, shown in Figure 5.20. This allows you to view the background layer while working on other layers.

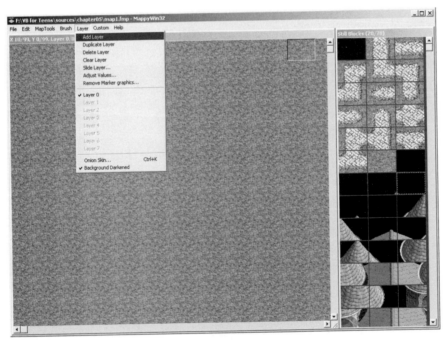

Figure 5.19 Adding another layer to the map in Mappy.

Transparency

An important consideration that I should mention is the topic of transparency. Mappy lets you draw transparent layers over the background layer, with some spectacular results. Take a look at Figure 5.21 showing tiles being drawn with Onion Skin enabled on the background; the top layer is being drawn transparently.

Figure 5.20 Enabling the Onion Skin feature.

Mappy understands the transparency of a source image if you set the transparent color to pink—that is, a color with a Red/Green/Blue combination of (255,0,255). If you are using a graphic editor like Pro Motion or Paint Shop Pro, you can edit a color's RGB directly. What you want to do is create a pink color with values of (255,0,255) and then perform flood fill anywhere on the bitmap that you want to have come up transparently in Mappy (and in your game world).

To add the castle to Mappy's tile palette, I cropped the castle bitmap you saw in the previous chapter (with the two extra isometric views of the castle), showing just the single

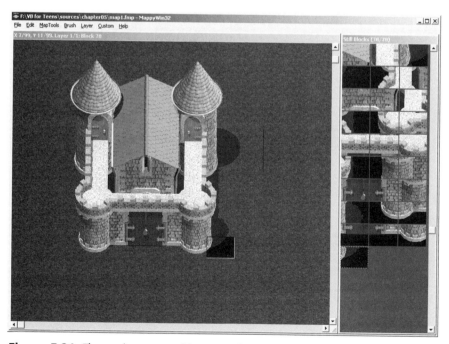

Figure 5.21 The castle re-created in Mappy from the source tiles.

rectangular castle. Then I made the surrounding pixels around the castle pink so it would show up transparently in Mappy. (See Figure 5.22.) Don't worry about blank space around the source bitmaps. Mappy optimizes the tile palette, removing any duplicate blank tiles. (That's a nice feature, isn't it?)

Combining Layers

Using the techniques you've learned here, you should be able to fill the background layer with a common tile and then do the "real work" on another layer so you don't have to constantly go back and fix background tiles that get messed up while building your world. In fact, feel free to create several layers if it makes the work easier on you. You might have one layer just for towns and roads, with another layer for mountains and rivers, with yet another layer for roads and bridges. Do whatever works for you.

Figure 5.22 The source bitmap for the castle with transparent (pink) color around the edges.

The time comes when you're finished and need to export the map for use in your game. What can you do with all the layers? First of all, save the map in the standard Mappy format so you can edit the map at any time. You want to export the map when you need to dump it into Visual Basic for use in the game.

There is an imperfect option that I want to at least bring to your attention, even if it isn't the ideal solution. The Custom menu contains scripts that you can run to do various things to your map. One such script is called Merge Layers. This script works well for some types of maps, but the only problem is that the additional layers lose their transparency, as shown in Figure 5.23.

The ideal solution to transparency, as it turns out, is only the rendering of objects transparently *within your program*, I'm afraid. There is no way to export the entire map with all layers merged together while also retaining transparency. Therefore, a lot of attention is given to drawing the background tiles as well as to drawing a transparent layer from a Mappy file in Celtic Crusader (and any other game you plan to write).

A simpler option is to modify the tiles used in the upper layers so that rather than being transparent, these tiles have the background tile integrated (and lined up so it appears seamless). This very good approach would certainly make the map editing much smoother, although it requires more up-front work to edit the images. As it turns out, a lot of stuff needs to be drawn transparently in the game anyway, such as trees, and of

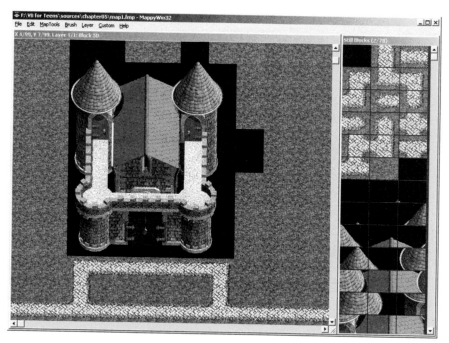

Figure 5.23 Merging the layers results in a loss of transparency.

course all of the *non-player characters (NPCs)* and animals in the game, so adding that extra step to draw the transparent portions of the map may be necessary.

Transparency is a subject that has to wait for Part III, as it is too soon to delve into Direct3D textures and sprite handling at this stage.

Level Up

This chapter moved rather quickly through a brief Mappy tutorial, which should have provided you with at least a working understanding of how Mappy can be used to create and edit game maps. I did not go into great detail in this chapter because the next two chapters are also devoted to the creation of the game world through the use of Mappy and Visual Basic source code.

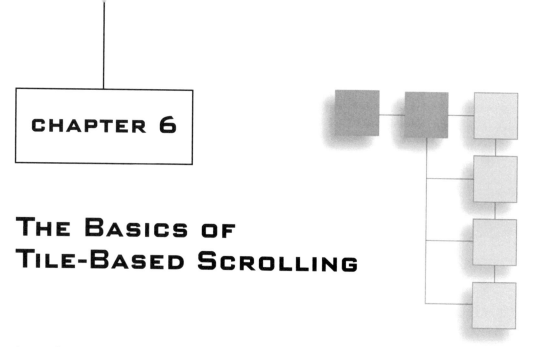

CHAPTER 6

THE BASICS OF TILE-BASED SCROLLING

This chapter is the first lesson on the game programming subject of scrolling a tile-based background. You will learn some of the basic techniques used in tile-based scrolling and will write a sample program that demonstrates the first of several techniques covered in the next two chapters on scrolling. This chapter continues the focus on the tile-editing program Mappy as the primary tool used to create tile-based maps and the associated tile bitmaps used to construct the game world.

Here is a breakdown of the major topics in this chapter:

- Introduction to scrolling
- Scrolling a large Mappy-generated bitmap

Introduction to Scrolling

What is scrolling? In today's gaming world, where 3D is the focus of everyone's attention, it's not surprising to find gamers and programmers who have never heard of scrolling. What a shame! The heritage of modern games is a long and fascinating one that is still relevant today, even if it is not understood or appreciated. The console industry puts great effort and value into scrolling, particularly on handheld systems, such as the Game Boy Advance. Given the extraordinary sales market for the GBA, would you be surprised to learn that more 2D games may be sold in a given day than 3D games?

Scrolling is the process of displaying a small window of a larger virtual game world. There are three types of scrolling:

- Loading a large tile-based bitmap image
- Creating a large bitmap out of tiles at runtime
- Drawing tiles directly on the screen (the most advanced method)

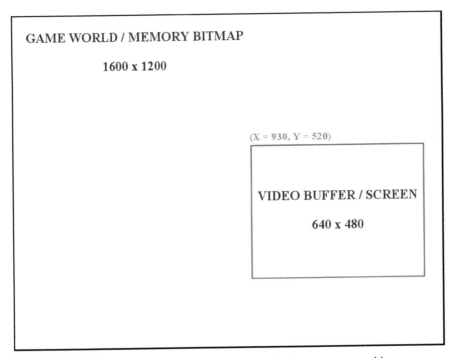

Figure 6.1 The scroll window shows a small part of a larger game world.

Figure 6.1 illustrates the concept of scrolling, which, in essence, involves the use of a large game world of which only a small portion is visible through the screen at a time.

The key to scrolling is having something in the virtual game world to display in the scroll window (or the screen). Also, I should point out that the entire screen need not be used as the scroll window. It is common to use the entire screen in scrolling-shooter games, but role-playing games (RPGs) often use a smaller window on the screen for scrolling, using the rest of the screen for gameplay (combat, inventory, and so on) and player/party information, as shown in Figure 6.2.

You could display one huge bitmap image in the virtual game world representing the current level of the game (or the *map*), and then copy a portion of that virtual world onto the screen. This is the simplest form of scrolling. Another method uses tiles to create the game world at runtime, which I cover in the next two chapters. First, you write a short program that demonstrates how to use bitmap scrolling, as this is an important first step to understanding the process—and, one might argue, a good enough method in and of itself for creating a scrolling game.

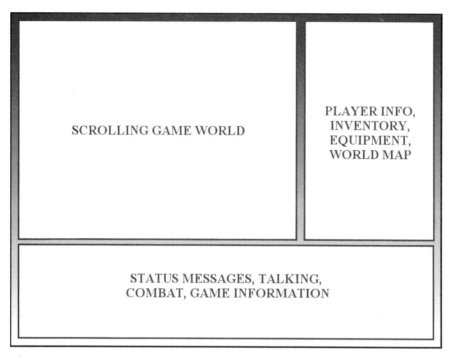

Figure 6.2 Some games use a smaller portion of the game screen for a scrolling window.

A Limited View of the World

I have written a program called ScrollScreen to show you. The \sources\chapter06 \ScrollScreen folder on this book's CD-ROM contains the gameworld.bmp file used in this program. Although I encourage you to write the program yourself, you may load the project file off the CD-ROM if you wish (or I should say, if you are feeling *lazy*). Figure 6.3 shows the testworld.bmp bitmap file.

When you run the ScrollScreen program, it loads the gameworld.bmp image into the virtual buffer (which is a Direct3D surface) and displays the upper-left corner in the 800×600 screen. You can change the resolution if you want, and I encourage you to try running the program in full-screen mode (by setting Fullscreen = True in the source code) for the best effect. The ScrollScreen program detects when the arrow keys have been pressed and then adjusts the game world's x and y position accordingly, which causes it to look like the image is scrolling.

Figure 6.4 shows the program running.

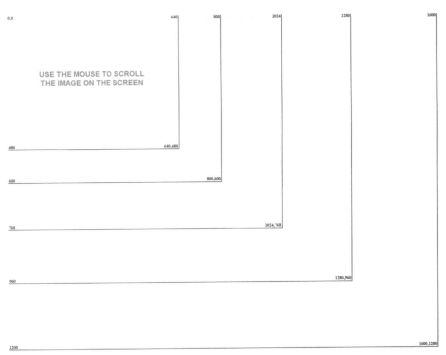

Figure 6.3 The testworld.BMP file is loaded into the virtual memory buffer for scrolling.

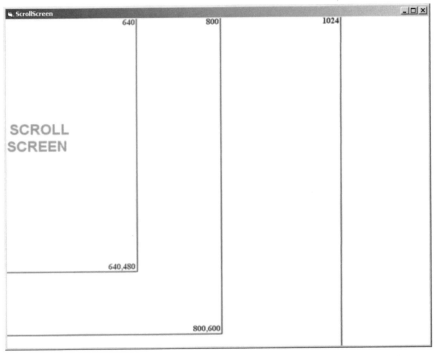

Figure 6.4 The ScrollScreen program demonstrates how to perform virtual buffer scrolling.

Scrolling a Large Mappy-Generated Bitmap

You can modify the gameworld.bmp file to display whatever you want, and it can be just about any size you want too (within reason). For instance, I took a map from Mappy and used the Export menu to save a giant bitmap image of the whole tile map, which works great for this example program. Figure 6.5 shows the Export dialog box in Mappy, where you can choose the Current Layer as Big Picture (?scrn.BMP) option to save the entire tile map as one large bitmap file.

When you use Mappy to generate a single large bitmap image of a map, it saves the map exactly as it appears inside the Mappy tile editor window, as you can see in Figure 6.6.

By modifying the source code in the ScrollScreen program (which is covered in the next section of this chapter), you can load a different bitmap file that is scrolled on the screen. Figure 6.7 shows the gameworld.bmp image being scrolled by this program.

Creating the ScrollScreen Program

The ScrollScreen program listing is coming up, so create a new project in Visual Basic so you can type it in. Make sure you add a reference to "DirectX 8 for Visual Basic Type Library," selecting Project, References to bring up the References dialog box.

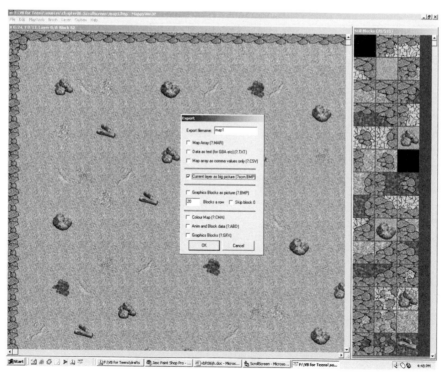

Figure 6.5 Exporting a Mappy map as one large bitmap image.

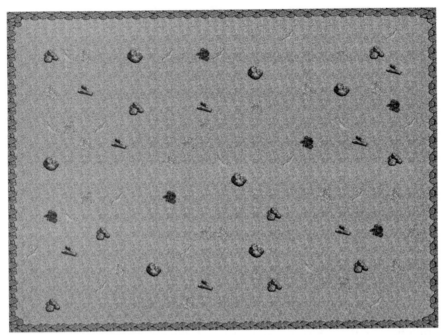

Figure 6.6 The Mappy-generated tile map has been saved as a single large bitmap image.

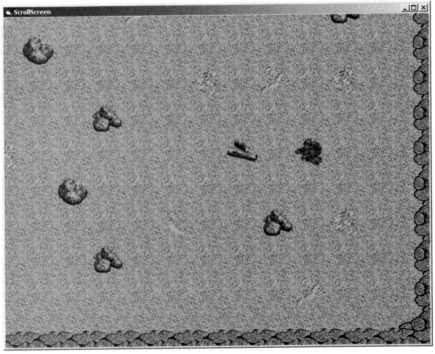

Figure 6.7 The ScrollScreen program running with a different map.

caution

Make sure you specify the correct width and height for the bitmap file that you use in this program (GAMEWORLDWIDTH, GAMEWORLDHEIGHT). Otherwise you are likely to get an Automation error as Direct3D tries to draw the image beyond the borders of the double buffer. You learn how to retrieve the bitmap dimensions directly from the bitmap file in Chapter 8, "Advanced Scrolling Techniques," but until then, it must be specified manually.

You can then type in the following source code into the code window for Form1. Copy the bitmap files out of the project folder on the CD-ROM (located in \sources\chapter06 \ScrollScreen) or create a large bitmap file for use by this program, as it works with any bitmap image as long as it's bigger than the program's screen resolution. I recommend generating a file with Mappy as explained in this chapter.

One of the interesting things you want to do with this program is experiment with different screen resolutions to see how the scrolling view changes based on the resolution. I also encourage you to use Mappy to create huge tile maps, which you can fill with tiles.

```
'--------------------------------------------------------
' Visual Basic Game Programming for Teens
' Chapter 6 - ScrollScreen program
'--------------------------------------------------------

Private Declare Function GetTickCount Lib "kernel32" () As Long

'make sure every variable is declared
Option Explicit

'make all arrays start with 0
Option Base 0

'customize the program here
Const SCREENWIDTH As Long = 800
Const SCREENHEIGHT As Long = 600
Const FULLSCREEN As Boolean = False
Const GAMEWORLDWIDTH As Long = 1600
Const GAMEWORLDHEIGHT As Long = 1152

'keyboard codes
Const KEY_LEFT As Integer = 72
Const KEY_RIGHT As Integer = 74
Const KEY_UP As Integer = 76
Const KEY_DOWN As Integer = 82
```

```
'the DirectX objects
Dim dx As DirectX8
Dim d3d As Direct3D8
Dim d3dx As New D3DX8
Dim dispmode As D3DDISPLAYMODE
Dim d3dpp As D3DPRESENT_PARAMETERS
Dim d3ddev As Direct3DDevice8

'some surfaces
Dim backbuffer As Direct3DSurface8
Dim gameworld As Direct3DSurface8

'scrolling values
Const STEP As Integer = 8
Dim ScrollX As Long
Dim ScrollY As Long
Dim SpeedX As Integer
Dim SpeedY As Integer

Private Sub Form_Load()
    'set up the main form
    Form1.Caption = "ScrollScreen"
    Form1.AutoRedraw = False
    Form1.BorderStyle = 1
    Form1.ClipControls = False
    Form1.ScaleMode = 3
    Form1.width = Screen.TwipsPerPixelX * (SCREENWIDTH + 12)
    Form1.height = Screen.TwipsPerPixelY * (SCREENHEIGHT + 30)
    Form1.Show

    'initialize Direct3D
    InitDirect3D Me.hwnd, SCREENWIDTH, SCREENHEIGHT, FULLSCREEN

    'get reference to the back buffer
    Set backbuffer = d3ddev.GetBackBuffer(0, D3DBACKBUFFER_TYPE_MONO)

    'load the bitmap file
    Set gameworld = LoadSurface(App.Path & "\testworld.bmp", _
        GAMEWORLDWIDTH, GAMEWORLDHEIGHT)

    'this helps to keep a steady framerate
    Dim start As Long
    start = GetTickCount()
```

```vb
    'main loop
    Do While (True)

        'update the scrolling viewport
        ScrollScreen

        'set the screen refresh to 40 fps (25 ms)
        If GetTickCount - start > 25 Then
            d3ddev.Present ByVal 0, ByVal 0, 0, ByVal 0
            start = GetTickCount
            DoEvents
        End If
    Loop
End Sub

Public Sub InitDirect3D( _
    ByVal hwnd As Long, _
    ByVal lWidth As Long, _
    ByVal lHeight As Long, _
    ByVal bFullscreen As Boolean)

    'catch any errors here
    On Local Error GoTo fatal_error

    'create the DirectX object
    Set dx = New DirectX8

    'create the Direct3D object
    Set d3d = dx.Direct3DCreate()
    If d3d Is Nothing Then
        MsgBox "Error initializing Direct3D!"
        Shutdown
    End If

    'tell D3D to use the current color depth
    d3d.GetAdapterDisplayMode D3DADAPTER_DEFAULT, dispmode

    'set the display settings used to create the device
    Dim d3dpp As D3DPRESENT_PARAMETERS
    d3dpp.hDeviceWindow = hwnd
    d3dpp.BackBufferCount = 1
    d3dpp.BackBufferWidth = lWidth
    d3dpp.BackBufferHeight = lHeight
```

```
        d3dpp.SwapEffect = D3DSWAPEFFECT_COPY_VSYNC
        d3dpp.BackBufferFormat = dispmode.Format

        'set windowed or fullscreen mode
        If bFullscreen Then
            d3dpp.Windowed = 0
        Else
            d3dpp.Windowed = 1
        End If

        'chapter 9
        d3dpp.MultiSampleType = D3DMULTISAMPLE_NONE
        d3dpp.AutoDepthStencilFormat = D3DFMT_D32

        'create the D3D primary device
        Set d3ddev = d3d.CreateDevice( _
            D3DADAPTER_DEFAULT, _
            D3DDEVTYPE_HAL, _
            hwnd, _
            D3DCREATE_SOFTWARE_VERTEXPROCESSING, _
            d3dpp)

        If d3ddev Is Nothing Then
            MsgBox "Error creating the Direct3D device!"
            Shutdown
        End If

        Exit Sub
fatal_error:
        MsgBox "Critical error in Start_Direct3D!"
        Shutdown
End Sub

Private Function LoadSurface( _
        ByVal filename As String, _
        ByVal width As Long, _
        ByVal height As Long) _
        As Direct3DSurface8

        On Local Error GoTo fatal_error
        Dim surf As Direct3DSurface8
```

```
    'return error by default
    Set LoadSurface = Nothing

    'create the new surface
    Set surf = d3ddev.CreateImageSurface(width, height, dispmode.Format)
    If surf Is Nothing Then
        MsgBox "Error creating surface!"
        Exit Function
    End If

    'load surface from file
    d3dx.LoadSurfaceFromFile surf, ByVal 0, ByVal 0, filename, _
        ByVal 0, D3DX_DEFAULT, 0, ByVal 0

    If surf Is Nothing Then
        MsgBox "Error loading " & filename & "!"
        Exit Function
    End If

    'return the new surface
    Set LoadSurface = surf

fatal_error:
    Exit Function
End Function

Public Sub ScrollScreen()
    'update horizontal scrolling position and speed
    ScrollX = ScrollX + SpeedX
    If (ScrollX < 0) Then
        ScrollX = 0
        SpeedX = 0
    ElseIf ScrollX > GAMEWORLDWIDTH - SCREENWIDTH Then
        ScrollX = GAMEWORLDWIDTH - SCREENWIDTH
        SpeedX = 0
    End If

    'update vertical scrolling position and speed
    ScrollY = ScrollY + SpeedY
    If ScrollY < 0 Then
        ScrollY = 0
        SpeedY = 0
```

```
    ElseIf ScrollY > GAMEWORLDHEIGHT - SCREENHEIGHT Then
        ScrollY = GAMEWORLDHEIGHT - SCREENHEIGHT
        SpeedY = 0
    End If

    'set dimensions of the source image
    Dim r As DxVBLibA.RECT
    r.Left = ScrollX
    r.Top = ScrollY
    r.Right = ScrollX + SCREENWIDTH - 1
    r.Bottom = ScrollY + SCREENHEIGHT - 1

    'set the destination point
    Dim point As DxVBLibA.point
    point.X = 0
    point.Y = 0

    'draw the current game world view
    d3ddev.CopyRects gameworld, r, 1, backbuffer, point
End Sub

Private Sub Form_KeyDown(KeyCode As Integer, Shift As Integer)
    'hit ESC key to quit
    If KeyCode = 27 Then Shutdown
End Sub

Private Sub Form_MouseMove(Button As Integer, Shift As Integer, _
X As Single, Y As Single)

    'move mouse on left side to scroll left
    If X < SCREENWIDTH / 2 Then SpeedX = -STEP

    'move mouse on right side to scroll right
    If X > SCREENWIDTH / 2 Then SpeedX = STEP

    'move mouse on top half to scroll up
    If Y < SCREENHEIGHT / 2 Then SpeedY = -STEP

    'move mouse on bottom half to scroll down
    If Y > SCREENHEIGHT / 2 Then SpeedY = STEP

End Sub
```

```
Private Sub Form_QueryUnload(Cancel As Integer, UnloadMode As Integer)
    Shutdown
End Sub

Private Sub Shutdown()
    Set gameworld = Nothing
    Set d3ddev = Nothing
    Set d3d = Nothing
    Set dx = Nothing
    End
End Sub
```

Level Up

This chapter provided an introduction to scrolling using the simple technique of saving a large bitmap of the game world using Mappy's export features. The important concepts you learned in this chapter include the ability to draw a portion of the game world inside the visible part of the screen and the ability to manipulate the position of the game world's current view using player input. The next two chapters expand on this concept and teach you more advanced forms of scrolling.

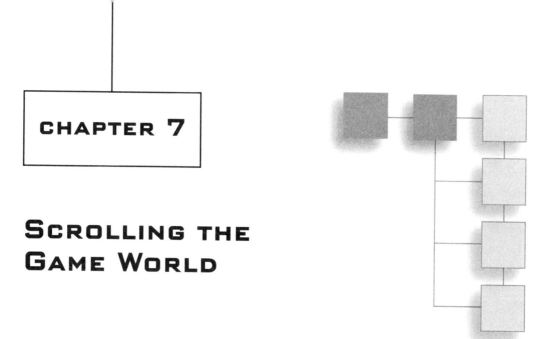

CHAPTER 7

SCROLLING THE GAME WORLD

This chapter focuses on creating a tile-based background that scrolls with a generated bitmap in memory. In the preceding chapter, which introduced you to scrolling, you learned how to export one large bitmap file from Mappy that could be directly used as the game world in memory. Your program's window draws a portion of this large bitmap image in memory, and that produces a scrolling effect. This chapter takes it to the next step by teaching you how to generate that game-world image at runtime using the source tiles and the map data exported by Mappy.

Here is a breakdown of the major topics in this chapter:

- Constructing the tiled image at runtime
- Creating a tile-based background
- Professional tile work
- Using the tile data

Constructing the Tiled Image at Runtime

The ScrollScreen program seemed to work just great, but that method of scrolling has a very serious limitation. When you create a game world, the whole point is to interact with that game world. A single, large bitmap used to render the game world prevents you from actually tracking where the player is located on the map, as well as what other objects are on the map. Of course, you could create a new array or some other method to keep track of the player, various enemies, and objects in the game world, but that requires a lot of unnecessary extra work. There's a better way to do it.

Creating a Tile-Based Background

You have seen what a simple scroller looks like, even though it relied on mouse movement to scroll. A high-speed scrolling arcade game automatically scrolls horizontally or vertically, displaying a ground-, air-, or space-based terrain below the player (usually represented by an airplane or spaceship). The point of such games is to keep the action moving so fast that the player doesn't have a chance to rest from one wave of enemies to the next.

Creating Backgrounds from Tiles

The real power of a scrolling background comes from a technique called tiling. *Tiling* is a process in which there really is no background, just an array of small images that make up the background as it is displayed. In other words, it is a virtual background and takes up very little memory compared to a full bitmapped background (such as the one in ScrollScreen). You are already familiar with how tiling works after learning about Mappy in the previous two chapters, but you are probably wondering: How can I load tiles and make a scrolling game world out of a Mappy level?

The TileScroll program that you write next uses tiles to fill the large background bitmap when the program starts. Other than that initial change, the program functions exactly like the ScrollScreen program. In this case, this program still needs a large bitmap image of the game world, but the difference this time around is that the game world bitmap is generated *on the fly* using map tile data from Mappy.

Use Mappy to Cut and Shape Your Tiles

As you may recall from the last two chapters, Mappy can rebuild a bitmap file containing tiles for you. It's therefore possible to import as many different tiles as you need and then not worry about those source tiles any longer, because Mappy just creates a new single bitmap containing all of the tiles in the map (when you use the Export option from the File menu). In the last program, ScrollScreen, the saved tile bitmap was not needed because all of the tiles were already saved in the large bitmap file created by Mappy.

Now, I realize you could easily just go into Mappy and save another large bitmap file every time you need to make a change to your game world map, but that is not the best way to do it. The best way is to save the tiles to a separate bitmap image and save the map data to a data file using those parts to build a game map in your program. The reason for this will be evident in the next chapter when you learn to render a truly *huge* scrolling game world on the screen that could never be contained in a large bitmap image.

caution

Be sure to use the exact dimensions of the Mappy-generated bitmap file or `LoadSurface` will error out.

For small maps it seems like a logical thing to do, but the fact is, game maps are never as small as the one you use in this chapter (as an example). Most levels in a scrolling arcade game (think of classic games like R-Type and the more recent Mars Matrix for Dreamcast) are quite large, comprised of thousands of tiles in one orientation or the other (usually just scrolling up and down—vertically—or left to right—horizontally). These types of games are called *shooters* for the most part, although the horizontally scrolling games are usually *platformers* (think about games like Super Mario World, which was called Super Mario Advance 2 on the Game Boy Advance). Not only does Super Mario World have large horizontally scrolling levels, but those levels have parallax layers that make the background in the distance scroll by more slowly than the layer that the player's character is walking on. These subjects are beyond the scope of this book, although it sure would be fun to work on a platform game like Super Mario World; just think how much work it would take to make a game like that, with hundreds of levels and an equal number of animated sprites.

Professional Tile Work

A single large bitmap is just not used; it's what you might call amateur work. But you have to start somewhere, which is why I'm taking you through this progression from amateur to professional scrolling techniques. The TileScroll program (which you will see later in this chapter) is a step in the right direction. Although this program does generate the game world on the fly, a large bitmap image representing the game world is in memory, which is not quite the ideal solution.

In the next chapter, you learn how to draw tiles on the screen on the fly. In the meantime, let's get to work on the problem at hand. You want to be able to scroll the game world on the screen. First, you need to figure out how to load the map data saved by Mappy into your Visual Basic program. You might recall that Mappy's export features are very versatile. When you have the map just the way you want it, you can bring up the Export dialog box from the File menu, as shown in Figure 7.1.

The options you are interested in are the following:

- Map array as comma values only (?.CSV)
- Current layer as big picture (?scrn.BMP)
- Graphics Blocks as picture (?.BMP)

You may ignore the rest of the options, as they are not needed. An interesting item of note here is the first option, Map Array (?.MAR). This item may be of interest to you later on, as you grow more proficient with your programming skills. This option exports the map tile data into a binary file that looks like an array of integers (each comprised of 2 bytes). These binary files are very small, with just 2 bytes per tile, about a thousand times smaller than a text file with the same data (separated by commas).

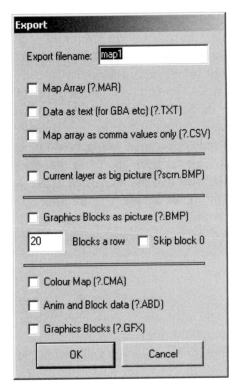

Figure 7.1 Mappy's Export dialog box has a lot of useful options.

As you learned in the previous chapter, you can use the second option, Current Layer as Big Picture, to generate one large bitmap image of the entire map. The other two options are for saving the tile images into a new bitmap file, as well as for saving the map data into a text file. You can choose all three options if you want, and Mappy obliges by creating all three files for you. For the TileScroll program, you need the CSV file and the tile images.

Using the Tile Data

Mappy exported a file called map1.CSV with the tile data inside. I would like you to first rename this file to map1.txt so it is easy to open with a simple text editor like Notepad. When you open the file, you see something like the image in Figure 7.2.

I showed you a similar file in the last chapter. Do you recall what settings you used to create this map file in Mappy? The dimensions are important because you must know how many tiles are in the data file. You can specify the number of columns and rows when you create a new map in Mappy, or you can view the properties of the current map in Mappy using the MapTools menu and selecting Map Properties. You should see the dialog box shown in Figure 7.3.

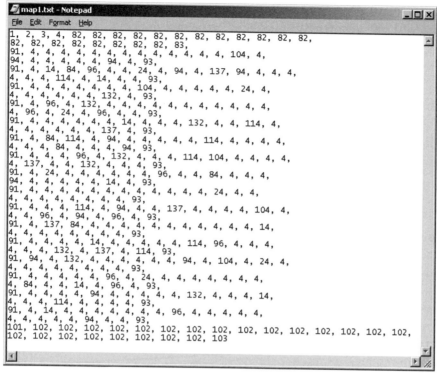

Figure 7.2 The basic tile data saved to a text file by Mappy.

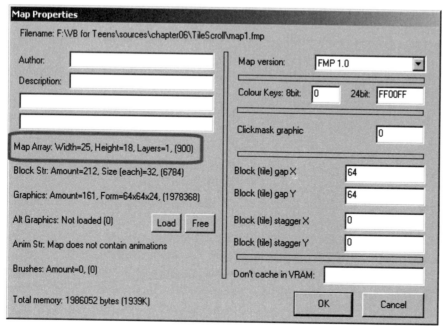

Figure 7.3 The Map Properties dialog box in Mappy.

This dialog box shows you a lot of information, but the part I want you to focus on is the Map Array values shown in Figure 7.3. Here, you can see that this map has a width of 25 and a height of 18. Therefore, you want to use those values in your program when you're ready to draw the tiles.

Formatting the Map Data

Now let's talk about actually getting the tile data into your Visual Basic program. You already know how to load a bitmap file, so reading the tile images is not a problem. The tile data stored in that text file, however, is a bit of a problem. You have two choices here:

- Read the data directly out of the file.
- Store the data into your program as a constant.

The first option can be accomplished using the file input/output routines built into Visual Basic, although I'd like to focus on the section option at this time. I go over the code that loads a map data file in the next chapter. You can copy the map data out of that map1.txt file (which you renamed from map1.CSV) right into your Visual Basic source code file and then convert it to a string. Does that sound strange? Well, I'll admit that is rather odd. It would be much nicer to store the data as an array, which is something you can do in more powerful languages like C. Visual Basic takes a different approach to most programming problems, though, so you have to use a string.

> **tip**
> _____
>
> In the next chapter you learn how to load a map file directly, along with the dimensions of the map, so manual work is reduced.

Here is how I converted the data in map1.txt to a string. Note the line continuation underscores, which keep it as one large string:

```
Const MAPWIDTH As Long = 25
Const MAPHEIGHT As Long = 18
Const RAWMAPDATA As String = _
"81,82,82,82,82,82,82,82,82,82,82,82,82,82,82,82,82,82,82,82,82,82,82," & _
"83,91,4,4,4,4,4,4,4,4,4,4,4,4,104,4,94,4,4,4,4,94,4,93,91,4,14," & _
"84,96,4,4,24,4,94,4,137,94,4,4,4,4,4,4,114,4,14,4,4,93,91,4,4,4,4,4," & _
"4,4,104,4,4,4,4,4,24,4,4,4,4,4,4,4,132,4,93,91,4,96,4,132,4,4,4,4,4," & _
"4,4,4,4,4,4,4,96,4,24,4,96,4,4,93,91,4,4,4,4,4,4,14,4,4,4,132,4,4," & _
"114,4,4,4,4,4,4,4,137,4,93,91,4,84,114,4,94,4,4,4,4,4,114,4,4,4,4,4," & _
"4,4,84,4,4,4,94,93,91,4,4,4,96,4,132,4,4,4,114,104,4,4,4,4,4,137,4,4," & _
"132,4,4,4,93,91,4,24,4,4,4,4,4,4,96,4,4,84,4,4,4,94,4,4,4,4,4,14,4," & _
"93,91,4,4,4,4,4,4,4,4,4,4,4,4,24,4,4,4,4,4,4,4,4,4,4,93,91,4,4,4,114," & _
```

```
"4,94,4,4,137,4,4,4,4,104,4,4,4,96,4,94,4,96,4,93,91,4,137,84,4,4,4,4," & _
"4,4,4,4,4,4,4,14,4,4,4,4,4,4,4,93,91,4,4,4,4,14,4,4,4,4,4,114,96,4," & _
"4,4,4,4,4,132,4,137,4,114,93,91,94,4,132,4,4,4,4,4,4,94,4,104,4,24,4," & _
"4,4,4,4,4,4,4,4,93,91,4,4,4,4,4,96,4,24,4,4,4,4,4,4,4,4,84,4,4,14,4," & _
"96,4,93,91,4,4,4,4,94,4,4,4,4,4,132,4,4,4,14,4,4,4,114,4,4,4,4,93,91," & _
"4,14,4,4,4,4,4,4,4,96,4,4,4,4,4,4,4,4,4,4,94,4,4,93,101,102,102,102," & _
"102,102,102,102,102,102,102,102,102,102,102,102,102,102,102,102,102," & _
"102,102,102,103"
```

tip

> If storing map data in the program appeals to you, then you may want to organize the levels for your game in module files (.BAS), with one map per file, for easy editing.

A Comment About Map Size

That might look like a lot of numbers, but it really is tiny compared to most game levels! In fact, if you can see this on a single screen or single page, then that's a good sign it's tiny by most standards. However, it works well for the purpose of teaching the subject of scrolling.

As you can see, I have declared two constants, MAPWIDTH and MAPHEIGHT, that define the size of this map. After that, I declared RAWMAPDATA as the name of the string constant, followed by 450 numbers representing the values in the 25×18 map.

This is *almost* good enough to use in a game, and it is certainly nice having the map data right here, where it is compiled into the EXE file. That is the best way to keep someone from tampering with your game levels! The only problem with it is when you make changes to a large game world in Mappy, it can be quite the chore to paste into your program again. All those quotation marks, ampersands, and underscore characters can be tedious to insert, but that's required to turn a map into a string like this.

Converting the Map Data to an Array

In fact, just go ahead and write a subroutine to convert the raw map data constant into an array right now, while I'm on the subject. I wrote a subroutine that parses this map data string into an array of integers that can be used to draw the tiles. This subroutine is called ConvertMapDataToArray.

Take a look at the first For loop, which uses len(RAWMAPDATA) to run through the entire map data constant string. Since this is a string of comma-separated values, the fastest way to parse it is one character at a time, checking for the commas between numbers. This subroutine checks each character in the RAWMAPDATA string for a comma and adds the character to a temporary string called value. When a comma is found, value is converted to an integer and stored inside the mapdata array. This is a simple, effective way to transform the map data into a format that Visual Basic can use (and in addition, the integer array is fast).

```
Public Sub ConvertMapDataToArray()
    Dim pos As Long
    Dim s As String
    Dim value As String
    Dim index As Long

    'convert the rawmapdata string to an array of integers
    For pos = 1 To Len(RAWMAPDATA)

        'get next character
        s = Mid$(RAWMAPDATA, pos, 1)

        'tiles are separated by commas
        If s = "," Then

            If Len(value) > 0 Then

                'store tile # in array
                mapdata(index) = CInt(value - 1)

                index = index + 1
            End If

            'get ready for next #
            value = ""
            s = ""

        Else
            value = value & s
        End If
    Next pos
End Sub
```

Drawing Tiles Onto the Game World

Thanks to the subroutine you just learned, you now have an array of integers representing the tile map. These tile values were originally stored in a Mappy file and have since been saved to a text file, copied into the program's source code file, and converted to an array. Whew! Let me spell it out more clearly:

1. Design map using Mappy.

2. Export map to a text file.

3. Copy the textual map data into source code file.

4. Format map data into a Visual Basic string constant.

5. Convert map data string into an integer array.

6. Use array to draw tiles on the screen.

That's a whole lot of data manipulation! I admit it sure would have been great if we could just load the native Mappy file directly, but that's not an option. Besides, if you had a subroutine that loaded an .FMP file directly, with tile images and everything in one fell swoop, then you wouldn't have to learn anything else about scrolling!

Building the World

The next step after converting the map data to an array is to create a new surface in memory and then draw the tiles onto that image that matches the original map that you designed in Mappy. The key in the following source code for BuildGameWorld is the two For loops, For Y and For X. The reason Y comes first is because the tile data is laid out with rows first, then columns, so you process it in Y-X order. Inside these two loops is a call to a subroutine called DrawTile, which I cover next.

```
Public Sub BuildGameWorld()
    Dim X As Long
    Dim Y As Long
    Dim cols As Long
    Dim rows As Long
    Dim tiles As Direct3DSurface8

    'load the bitmap file containing all the tiles
    Set tiles = LoadSurface(App.Path & "\map1.bmp", 1024, 640)

    'create the scrolling game world bitmap
    Set gameworld = d3ddev.CreateImageSurface( _
        GAMEWORLDWIDTH, GAMEWORLDHEIGHT, dispmode.Format)
    If gameworld Is Nothing Then
        MsgBox "Error creating working surface!"
        Shutdown
    End If
```

```
'fill the gameworld bitmap with tiles
For Y = 0 To 17
    For X = 0 To MAPWIDTH - 1
        DrawTile tiles, mapdata(Y * MAPWIDTH + X), 64, 64, 16, _
            gameworld, X * 64, Y * 64
    Next X
Next Y

'now the tiles bitmap is no longer needed
Set tiles = Nothing
End Sub
```

Stepping Stones of the World

The process of drawing tiles to fill the game world reminds me of laying down stepping stones, although tiling is admittedly a perfect analogy for what happens. Basically, tiles of a larger pattern are laid down from left to right, top to bottom, in that order. The first row is added, one tile at a time, all the way across; then the next row down is filled in from left to right, and so on until the entire map is filled.

The code to add each game world tile is similar to the code you saw in the previous chapter's ScrollWorld program, where CopyRects draws a portion of one surface onto another surface. The DrawTile subroutine looks very similar to the ScrollScreen subroutine in how it sets up the RECT and POINT structures (remember, VB uses the word Type to define a structure) for the call to CopyRects. Here is the code for this subroutine:

```
Private Sub DrawTile( _
    ByRef source As Direct3DSurface8, _
    ByVal tilenum As Long, _
    ByVal width As Long, _
    ByVal height As Long, _
    ByVal columns As Long, _
    ByVal dest As Direct3DSurface8, _
    ByVal destx As Long, _
    ByVal desty As Long)

    'create a RECT to describe the source image
    Dim r As DxVBLibA.RECT

    'set the upper left corner of the source image
    r.Left = (tilenum Mod columns) * width
    r.Top = (tilenum \ columns) * height
```

```
'set the bottom right corner of the source image
r.Right = r.Left + width
r.Bottom = r.Top + height

'create a POINT to define the destination
Dim point As DxVBLibA.point

'set the upper left corner of where to draw the image
point.X = destx
point.Y = desty

'draw the source bitmap tile image
d3ddev.CopyRects source, r, 1, dest, point

End Sub
```

Writing the TileScroll Program

The next step is to write the TileScroll program to demonstrate how to create a tile-based game world at runtime. The output of the program is shown in Figure 7.4.

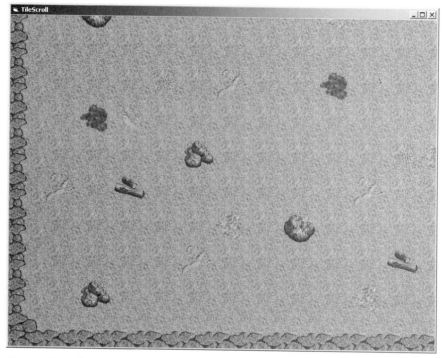

Figure 7.4 The TileScroll program demonstrates how to create a tiled game world at runtime.

You have already met most of the code used in this program, so I'd like you to create a new Visual Basic project, add the DirectX Type Library as usual, and then copy and paste the reusable subroutines into the source code file for the new Form1. Copy these subroutines from the ScrollScreen program (to cut down on typing, as these subroutines have not changed):

- ScrollScreen
- DrawTile
- InitDirect3D
- LoadSurface

I still show the code for these subroutines in the program listing for TileScroll, but want you to start thinking about code reuse. Wouldn't it be great if you could just store these oft-used subroutines inside a source code file and then reuse that source code file for each new game project? You can do that if you want, although I go over code reuse a little more in each new chapter. You can just add a new file to your Visual Basic project by opening the Project menu and selecting Add Module. You then paste whatever reusable subroutines you want into this new code module, which has a file extension of .BAS. *Module files* are just simple text files, and they help to clean up your projects, since the code in a form can become quite long in a typical game.

note

I realize that a "real" Visual Basic program should use classes and object-oriented programming, which is a "better" form of code reuse than pasting code into a source code module. That is an advanced feature, as far as I'm concerned, that requires a whole new thought process, which I'm not interested in discussing in this book. Classes are very powerful, have the ability to keep track of data, and provide their own subroutines and functions that use that data. There is no doubting that a class for Direct3D, for surfaces, and for a tile-based scroller would be very helpful. But before you are able to compete in a marathon, you have to learn how to walk.

Reusing Code

In addition to those reusable subroutines from the ScrollScreen program, incorporate the RAWMAPDATA constants listed earlier, as well as the subroutines ConvertMapDataToArray, BuildGameWorld, and DrawTile, which I have already covered. Although I am including the rest of the entire source code listing for the TileScroll program here, I want you to get used to reusing code, so in future chapters I might ask you to paste code into the program that you've already seen. For now, though, I just list the entire program since you're still learning a lot of new concepts. In the next chapter, I have you create a secondary Module file (with a .BAS extension) for these subroutines.

I want to get to the point where you are so familiar with these common routines that I no longer need to list them in each chapter, and can then focus on just the subjects at hand (which is possible when you gain a certain mastery of the subjects).

TileScroll Source Code

This program uses the same map1.FMP file that I created in Mappy in the previous chapter. Incidentally, I would like for you to create your own maps in Mappy and use them in these programs, so you really get a good grasp of how the whole process works. If you only use *my* map files, then you aren't gaining as much experience with the tool as you should. The same map1.BMP file also contains the exported tile images, shown in Figure 7.4; I explained how to use Mappy's export features in the previous chapter.

```
'-----------------------------------------------------------
' Visual Basic Game Programming for Teens
' Chapter 6 - TileScroll program
'-----------------------------------------------------------

Private Declare Function GetTickCount Lib "kernel32" () As Long

Option Explicit
Option Base 0

Const MAPWIDTH As Long = 25
Const MAPHEIGHT As Long = 18
*** insert RAWMAPDATA lines here ***

'customize the program here
Const SCREENWIDTH As Long = 800
Const SCREENHEIGHT As Long = 600
Const FULLSCREEN As Boolean = False
Const GAMEWORLDWIDTH As Long = 1600
Const GAMEWORLDHEIGHT As Long = 1152
Const TILEWIDTH As Long = 64
Const TILEHEIGHT As Long = 64

'the DirectX objects
Dim dx As DirectX8
Dim d3d As Direct3D8
Dim d3dx As New D3DX8
Dim dispmode As D3DDISPLAYMODE
Dim d3dpp As D3DPRESENT_PARAMETERS
Dim d3ddev As Direct3DDevice8
```

```
'some surfaces
Dim backbuffer As Direct3DSurface8
Dim gameworld As Direct3DSurface8

'map data
Dim mapdata(MAPWIDTH * MAPHEIGHT) As Integer

'scrolling values
Const STEP As Long = 8
Dim ScrollX As Long
Dim ScrollY As Long
Dim SpeedX As Integer
Dim SpeedY As Integer

Private Sub Form_Load()
    'set up the main form
    Form1.Caption = "DrawTile"
    Form1.ScaleMode = 3
    Form1.width = Screen.TwipsPerPixelX * (SCREENWIDTH + 12)
    Form1.height = Screen.TwipsPerPixelY * (SCREENHEIGHT + 30)
    Form1.Show

    'initialize Direct3D
    InitDirect3D Me.hwnd, SCREENWIDTH, SCREENHEIGHT, FULLSCREEN

    'get reference to the back buffer
    Set backbuffer = d3ddev.GetBackBuffer(0, D3DBACKBUFFER_TYPE_MONO)

    'create gameworld map in memory using tiles
    ConvertMapDataToArray
    BuildGameWorld

    'this helps to keep a steady framerate
    Dim start As Long
    start = GetTickCount()

    'main loop
    Do While (True)
        'update the scrolling viewport
        ScrollScreen
```

```
        'set the screen refresh to about 40 fps
        If GetTickCount - start > 25 Then
            d3ddev.Present ByVal 0, ByVal 0, 0, ByVal 0
            start = GetTickCount
            DoEvents
        End If
    Loop

End Sub


*** insert ConvertMapDataToArray here ***


*** insert BuildGameWorld here ***


*** insert DrawTile here ***

Public Sub ScrollScreen()
    'update horizontal scrolling position and speed
    ScrollX = ScrollX + SpeedX
    If (ScrollX < 0) Then
        ScrollX = 0
        SpeedX = 0
    ElseIf ScrollX > GAMEWORLDWIDTH - SCREENWIDTH Then
        ScrollX = GAMEWORLDWIDTH - SCREENWIDTH
        SpeedX = 0
    End If


    'update vertical scrolling position and speed
    ScrollY = ScrollY + SpeedY
    If ScrollY < 0 Then
        ScrollY = 0
        SpeedY = 0
    ElseIf ScrollY > GAMEWORLDHEIGHT - SCREENHEIGHT Then
        ScrollY = GAMEWORLDHEIGHT - SCREENHEIGHT
        SpeedY = 0
    End If


    'set dimensions of the source image
    Dim r As DxVBLibA.RECT
    r.Left = ScrollX
    r.Top = ScrollY
    r.Right = ScrollX + SCREENWIDTH
    r.Bottom = ScrollY + SCREENHEIGHT
```

```
        'set the destination point
        Dim point As DxVBLibA.point
        point.X = 0
        point.Y = 0

        'draw the current game world view
        d3ddev.CopyRects gameworld, r, 1, backbuffer, point

End Sub

Public Sub InitDirect3D( _
    ByVal hwnd As Long, _
    ByVal lWidth As Long, _
    ByVal lHeight As Long, _
    ByVal bFullscreen As Boolean)

    'catch any errors here
    On Local Error GoTo fatal_error

    'create the DirectX object
    Set dx = New DirectX8

    'create the Direct3D object
    Set d3d = dx.Direct3DCreate()
    If d3d Is Nothing Then
        MsgBox "Error initializing Direct3D!"
        Shutdown
    End If

    'tell D3D to use the current color depth
    d3d.GetAdapterDisplayMode D3DADAPTER_DEFAULT, dispmode

    'set the display settings used to create the device
    Dim d3dpp As D3DPRESENT_PARAMETERS
    d3dpp.hDeviceWindow = hwnd
    d3dpp.BackBufferCount = 1
    d3dpp.BackBufferWidth = lWidth
    d3dpp.BackBufferHeight = lHeight
    d3dpp.SwapEffect = D3DSWAPEFFECT_COPY_VSYNC
    d3dpp.BackBufferFormat = dispmode.Format
```

```vb
    'set windowed or fullscreen mode
    If bFullscreen Then
        d3dpp.Windowed = 0
    Else
        d3dpp.Windowed = 1
    End If

    'chapter 9
    d3dpp.MultiSampleType = D3DMULTISAMPLE_NONE
    d3dpp.AutoDepthStencilFormat = D3DFMT_D32

    'create the D3D primary device
    Set d3ddev = d3d.CreateDevice( _
        D3DADAPTER_DEFAULT, _
        D3DDEVTYPE_HAL, _
        hwnd, _
        D3DCREATE_SOFTWARE_VERTEXPROCESSING, _
        d3dpp)

    If d3ddev Is Nothing Then
        MsgBox "Error creating the Direct3D device!"
        Shutdown
    End If

    Exit Sub
fatal_error:
    MsgBox "Critical error in Start_Direct3D!"
    Shutdown
End Sub

Private Function LoadSurface( _
    ByVal filename As String, _
    ByVal width As Long, _
    ByVal height As Long) _
    As Direct3DSurface8

    On Local Error GoTo fatal_error
    Dim surf As Direct3DSurface8

    'return error by default
    Set LoadSurface = Nothing
```

```
    'create the new surface
    Set surf = d3ddev.CreateImageSurface(width, height, dispmode.Format)
    If surf Is Nothing Then
        MsgBox "Error creating surface!"
        Exit Function
    End If

    'load surface from file
    d3dx.LoadSurfaceFromFile surf, ByVal 0, ByVal 0, filename, _
        ByVal 0, D3DX_DEFAULT, 0, ByVal 0

    If surf Is Nothing Then
        MsgBox "Error loading " & filename & "!"
        Exit Function
    End If

    'return the new surface
    Set LoadSurface = surf

fatal_error:
    Exit Function
End Function

Private Sub Form_MouseMove(Button As Integer, Shift As Integer, _
X As Single, Y As Single)

    'move mouse on left side to scroll left
    If X < SCREENWIDTH / 2 Then SpeedX = -STEP

    'move mouse on right side to scroll right
    If X > SCREENWIDTH / 2 Then SpeedX = STEP

    'move mouse on top half to scroll up
    If Y < SCREENHEIGHT / 2 Then SpeedY = -STEP

    'move mouse on bottom half to scroll down
    If Y > SCREENHEIGHT / 2 Then SpeedY = STEP

End Sub

Private Sub Form_KeyDown(KeyCode As Integer, Shift As Integer)
    If KeyCode = 27 Then Shutdown
End Sub
```

```
Private Sub Form_QueryUnload(Cancel As Integer, UnloadMode As Integer)
    Shutdown
End Sub

Private Sub Shutdown()
    Set gameworld = Nothing
    Set d3ddev = Nothing
    Set d3d = Nothing
    Set dx = Nothing
    End
End Sub
```

Level Up

This chapter pushed the envelope of tile-based scrolling even further with a discussion of using map data and tiles to construct the game world on the fly and then draw it on the screen, with full scrolling capability. This type of scrolling is much more powerful than the method used in Chapter 6, "The Basics of Tile-Based Scrolling," where a single bitmap file is loaded (although there are still improvements to be made). Although you can create entire games based on just the knowledge you have gained so far, I want to take you to the next level by explaining how to render tiles individually on the screen to create a scroller without a secondary surface in memory, which you learn how to do in the next chapter.

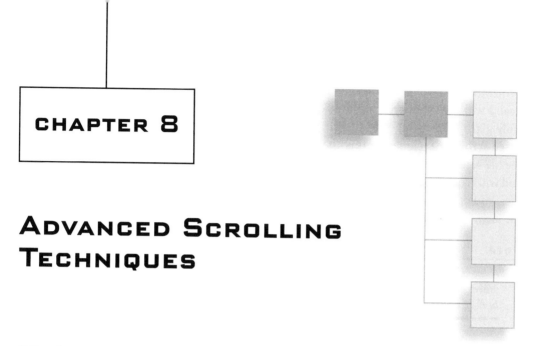

CHAPTER 8

ADVANCED SCROLLING TECHNIQUES

This chapter is the last in a series on tile-based scrolling. In the previous two chapters you learned how to perform scrolling by drawing a portion of a larger surface in memory to the screen, first by loading a single large bitmap file to be scrolled, and then by generating a similarly large surface at runtime and filling it with the appropriate tiles. Neither of these methods are suitable for game levels of any sufficient size unless the game reuses the same surface and loads multiple levels into the surface based on the player's movements in the game world (which is still an impractical solution). A far better method of implementing scrolling is drawing the individual tiles to the screen at runtime without using a large surface in memory at all. By using a small surface about the same size as the screen, you can draw tiles to the surface based on the current scroll position, and then draw that "triple buffer" to the screen to produce a scrolling game world. This chapter builds a tile scrolling engine based on this concept and is the foundation for the Celtic Crusader game described back in Chapter 3, "Designing the Game."

Here is a breakdown of the major topics in this chapter:

- Direct partial-tile scrolling
- Loading an exported Mappy file
- Aligning tiles to the scroll buffer
- The ScrollWorld source code

Direct Partial-Tile Scrolling

The problem with scrolling a large game world is that too much memory is required to create a surface in memory sufficient to hold a large enough map for the game (even if you break the map into sections). The preceding two chapters used a method of creating, in memory, a large surface image that was used as a source for scrolling, which is not practical. I will now show you a more advanced method of tile-based scrolling that supports truly giant maps using very little memory. In fact, all the memory required for the tile-based scroller developed in this chapter is a bitmap for the tiles and an array with all of the tile values. A map comprised of several million tiles can be rendered by this tile engine and will require only a few megabytes to do so. Although Mappy is limited to about 30,000 tiles, you can certainly load several map files and attach them in memory using one large tile array (comprised of simple integers).

note

A *triple buffer*—used in this chapter's ScrollScreen program—is the surface upon which tiles are drawn. The triple buffer is then copied to the *back buffer* (also known as the *double* or *second buffer*), which is actually drawn to the screen with the Present method of Direct3DDevice8.

The key to implementing a direct partial-tile scrolling engine is the use of a third buffer in memory (so called because the screen and back buffers are the first two), upon which the tiles are drawn based on the current scroll position. The full tiles can be drawn easily enough, and you have seen how to do so in the previous chapter with the TileScroll program, which included a DrawTile subroutine that used CopyRects (with which you should be familiar at this point).

The word *direct* in the title refers to the way the tile engine draws directly what is needed at that particular point in the game world, while *partial-tile* refers to the way it draws full tiles and partial tiles to fill the borders around the current scroll position. If you think about it, the tiles are 64 × 64 pixels in size (at least, in my examples they are; you may use any tile size you wish), so without the partial-tile capability, drawing tiles directly to the screen one portion at a time results in very jumpy scrolling, where the screen is only updated whenever complete tiles can be drawn.

Contrast this with the simplicity of the scrollers in Chapters 6 and 7. They simply blasted a portion of the scroller source image to the screen. Now you have no such luxury because the tiles have to be redrawn every time the screen is updated (with the obvious benefits of nearly unlimited map sizes and a small memory footprint). You may recall that two variables were used to keep track of the current scroll position: ScrollX and ScrollY. When drawing tiles directly, these variables give a precise position (as an X-Y pair) at which the tiles should start drawing in a left-to-right, up-to-down direction. So, if the current position is at (500,500), what does this mean, exactly? It means that the tiles specified in the map should be drawn at the upper-left corner of the screen, but that the drawn should be *from* the 500 × 500 point in the game world. Try to keep this concept in mind when you are working on scrolling, because the screen position is always the same: 0 × 0. While the scroll position changes all the time, the destination location on the screen (0 × 0) never changes.

note

You learn how to load the map file directly into the map data array later in this chapter, in the section titled "Loading an Exported Mappy File."

Now, to make this subject easier to understand, I'm going to use the same map file that I have used in the last two chapters, shown in Figure 8.1. In case I have neglected to mention this so far, the rock border around the map is helpful when you are working on the scrolling code, because it shows clearly where you are currently at in the map and provides a nice border so you can make sure the scroller is working properly. (In other words, it should stop scrolling when it reaches the edge, but should also not leave out any tiles.)

Now let's assume that you're using a screen resolution of 800 × 600, because this is a good resolution to use; it's relatively small so the screen updates quickly, but it is large enough to display a lot of details on the screen without crowding. (640 × 480 is just too small!)

You are already familiar with the variables used to track the scroll position, as well as the map data array, so I can talk about these variables without any more explanation. Something new to this chapter is the concept of the partial tile. In fact, there is a simple calculation that gives you the tile number as well as the partial tile values relatively easily. Are

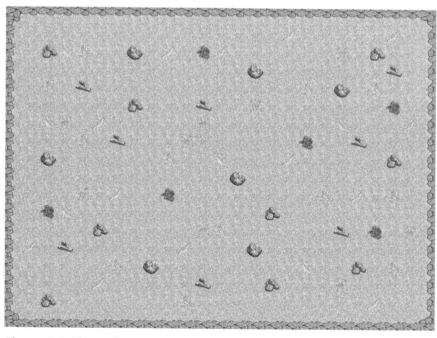

Figure 8.1 The small game world used as an example map file.

you familiar with *modulus*? This is a mathematical operation that produces the *remainder* of a division operation. Let me give you a simple example:

10/5 = 2

This is simple enough to understand, right? What happens when you are using numbers that are not evenly divisible?

10/3 = 3.33333333

This is a problem, because the remainder is not an even number, and we're talking about pixels here. You can't deal with parts of a pixel! However, you can work with parts of a tile, because tiles are made up of many pixels. Thinking in terms of complete tiles here, let's take a look at that division again:

10/3 = 3, with a remainder of 0.33333333

Let me now use numbers more relevant to the problem at hand:

800/64 = 12.5

This represents a calculation that returns the number of tiles that fit on a screen with a width of 800 pixels (assuming the tiles are 64 pixels wide). What does 12.5 tiles mean when you are writing a scroller? The .5 represents a *part* of a tile that must be drawn; hence, I call it *partial-tile scrolling*.

Here is where it gets really interesting—at least, I think so! After you have drawn 12 tiles across the screen, and you want to fill in the remaining .5 of a tile, you can calculate the size of the tile like so:

64 × 0.5 = 32

That is, 32 pixels of the partial tile must be drawn to handle the scrolling edge that was not lined up with a tile edge on the map. Rather than keeping track of the remainder at all, there is a simpler way to calculate the portion of the tile that must be drawn, in the measurement of pixels:

800 Mod 64 = 32

note

The *modulus* operator ("Mod" in VB) is similar to operators like multiply, divide, add, and subtract, but it simply returns the remainder of a division, which works great for our purposes here.

Try not to think of scrolling in screen terms, because the whole discussion revolves around the tile map in memory (the tile data itself). The tile data is expanded to full tiles when drawn to the screen, but until that happens, these tiles might be thought of as a huge virtual game world from which the scrolling window is drawn. Figure 8.2 shows the game world with the scroll window superimposed, so you can see how the screen represents a portion of the game world. While viewing this figure, imagine there is no image contain-

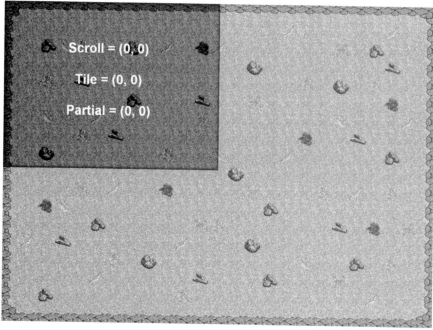

Figure 8.2 Direct partial-tile scrolling generates the scrolled window at runtime using the map data.

ing this game world map, just a virtual array of tile numbers. Those tiles are drawn *just* to the screen, based on what is visible in the darkened part of the figure.

Try another problem so you get the hang of calculating partial tiles before I get into the source code for this chapter. Suppose the scroll position is at (700,0) on the map. Which would be the starting tile, and what is the value of the partial tile (in pixels)? To calculate first the tile position in the map data array, just drop the decimal part, which represents the remainder:

> 700/64 = 10.9375 (10 tiles)

Next, you *do* want to keep the remainder, and actually drop the tile position itself, because now you're interested in pixels.

> 700 Mod 64 = 60

To verify that this calculation is correct, you can do the following:

> 64 × 0.9375 = 60

The modulus operator greatly helps with this calculation by skipping that middle step. It simply provides the remainder value directly, giving the exact number of pixels that must be drawn from the partial tile to fill in the top and left edges of the screen. I have shown the calculation in Figure 8.3.

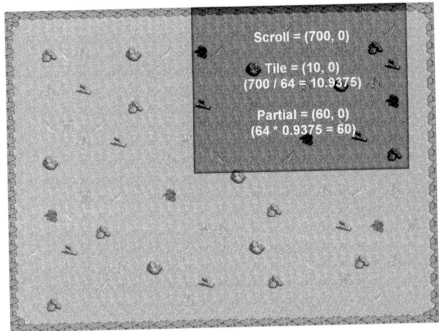

Figure 8.3 An example of how the partial tile calculation is performed at position (700,0).

Ready for another try at it? This time, calculate the tile numbers and partial-tile values for both the X and Y position of the scroll window at (372, 489). Figure 8.4 shows the answer graphically.

First the X value:

372/64 = 5.8125 (tile X = 5)

64 × 0.8125 = 52 (pixels)

Now for the Y value:

489/64 = 7.640625 (tile Y = 7)

64 × 0.640625 = 41 (pixels)

Coding the Partial-Tile Scrolling Subroutine

Are you ready to put this algorithm into code and see how it works? The first subroutine in this brave new world is called to update the scroll position due to user input:

```
Public Sub UpdateScrollPosition()
    'update horizontal scrolling position and speed
    ScrollX = ScrollX + SpeedX
```

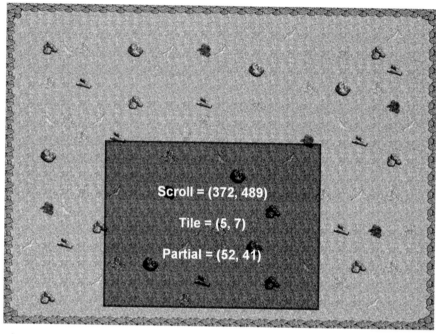

Figure 8.4 The partial tile calculation makes it possible to perform true tile-based scrolling.

```
    If (ScrollX < 0) Then
        ScrollX = 0
        SpeedX = 0
    ElseIf ScrollX > GAMEWORLDWIDTH - WINDOWWIDTH Then
        ScrollX = GAMEWORLDWIDTH - WINDOWWIDTH
        SpeedX = 0
    End If

    'update vertical scrolling position and speed
    ScrollY = ScrollY + SpeedY
    If ScrollY < 0 Then
        ScrollY = 0
        SpeedY = 0
    ElseIf ScrollY > GAMEWORLDHEIGHT - WINDOWHEIGHT Then
        ScrollY = GAMEWORLDHEIGHT - WINDOWHEIGHT
        SpeedY = 0
    End If
End Sub
```

Filling the Screen with Tiles

The DrawTiles subroutine copies tiles from the tile palette image (think of a painter's paint palette as the source of color in this analogy) onto the scroll buffer, a surface image that is just slightly larger than the screen resolution. It does this to take into account the tile overlap that may occur at some resolutions.

```
Public Sub DrawTiles()
    Dim tilex As Integer
    Dim tiley As Integer
    Dim columns As Integer
    Dim rows As Integer
    Dim X As Integer
    Dim Y As Integer
    Dim tilenum As Integer

    'calculate starting tile position
    'integer division drops the remainder
    tilex = ScrollX \ TILEWIDTH
    tiley = ScrollY \ TILEHEIGHT

    'calculate the number of columns and rows
    'integer division drops the remainder
    columns = WINDOWWIDTH \ TILEWIDTH
    rows = WINDOWHEIGHT \ TILEHEIGHT

    'draw tiles onto the scroll buffer surface
    For Y = 0 To rows
        For X = 0 To columns

            '*** This condition shouldn't be necessary. I will try to
            '*** resolve this problem and make the change during AR.
            If tiley + Y = mapheight Then tiley = tiley - 1

            tilenum = mapdata((tiley + Y) * mapwidth + (tilex + X))
            DrawTile tiles, tilenum, TILEWIDTH, TILEHEIGHT, 16, scrollbuffer, _
                X * TILEWIDTH, Y * TILEHEIGHT
        Next X
    Next Y
End Sub
```

For the sake of consistency, let me show you the DrawTile subroutine here because it is called by the preceding subroutine to draw each tile. There is an interesting way to optimize this code that you may consider down the road when you are working on your own complete game. The CopyRects function will draw as many images as you specify in the rectangle and point arrays. While the DrawTiles subroutine calls DrawTile for every single tile, a good optimization would be to utilize this advanced capability in CopyRects to draw all of the tiles with a single call. I recommend you only keep this in mind for later, as there is no point thinking about optimization this early.

```
Public Sub DrawTile( _
    ByRef source As Direct3DSurface8, _
    ByVal tilenum As Long, _
    ByVal width As Long, _
    ByVal height As Long, _
    ByVal columns As Long, _
    ByVal dest As Direct3DSurface8, _
    ByVal destx As Long, _
    ByVal desty As Long)

    'create a RECT to describe the source image
    Dim r As DxVBLibA.RECT

    'set the upper left corner of the source image
    r.Left = (tilenum Mod columns) * width
    r.Top = (tilenum \ columns) * height

    'set the bottom right corner of the source image
    r.Right = r.Left + width
    r.Bottom = r.Top + height

    'create a POINT to define the destination
    Dim point As DxVBLibA.point

    'set the upper left corner of where to draw the image
    point.X = destx
    point.Y = desty

    'draw the source bitmap tile image
    d3ddev.CopyRects source, r, 1, dest, point

End Sub
```

Drawing the Scroll Window

After you have filled the scroll buffer with tiles for the current scroll position within the game world, the next thing you must do is actually draw the scroll buffer to the screen.

This is where things get a little interesting. The scroll buffer is filled only with complete tiles, but it is from here that the partial tiles are taken into account. This is interesting because the whole tiles were drawn onto the scroll buffer, but the partial tiles are handled when drawing the scroll buffer to the screen. The `partialx` and `partialy` variables are given the result of the modulus calculation, and these values are then used as the upper-left corner of the scroll buffer that is copied to the screen.

I don't usually like to use global variables in a subroutine, because good coding practice produces subroutines that are independent and reusable from one project to the next. The `DrawTile` subroutine is much more independent than `DrawScrollWindow`, but it also uses the global mapdata array. In the final analysis, some of this can't be helped if you want the game to run at a fast frame rate, because passing variables to subroutines is a very time-consuming process, and you want the game to run as fast as possible.

Remember, the scrolling window is just the beginning. The rest of the game still has to be developed, and that includes a lot of animated sprites for the player's character, non-player characters (NPCs), plus buildings, animals, and any other objects that appear in the game. The bottom line is that the scroller needs to be as efficient as possible. (Yes, even with today's fast PCs, the scroller needs to be fast—never use the argument that PCs are fast to excuse poorly written code!)

Therefore, the `DrawScrollWindow` subroutine uses the global variables for the map data, tile source bitmap, the scroll buffer, and the back buffer. To pass these values to the subroutine every time consumes too many processor cycles, slowing down the game.

```
Public Sub DrawScrollWindow()
    Dim r As DxVBLibA.RECT
    Dim point As DxVBLibA.point
    Dim partialx As Integer
    Dim partialy As Integer

    'calculate the partial sub-tile lines to draw
    partialx = ScrollX Mod TILEWIDTH
    partialy = ScrollY Mod TILEHEIGHT

    'set dimensions of the source image
    r.Left = partialx
    r.Top = partialy
    r.Right = partialx + WINDOWWIDTH
    r.Bottom = partialy + WINDOWHEIGHT

    'set the destination point
    point.X = 0
    point.Y = 0
```

```
     'draw the scroll window
     d3ddev.CopyRects scrollbuffer, r, 1, backbuffer, point
End Sub
```

Loading an Exported Mappy File

In the last chapter you learned a trick for importing Mappy data files into a Visual Basic program. That trick was to paste the map data into a Visual Basic source code file and then convert it to one big string constant. You then learned how to parse the string and convert the comma-separated map data values into an integer array.

You can still use that method if you wish, although it is much more convenient to let the program load a map file directly from disk rather than going through all the trouble of formatting and stuffing the data into a string constant in the source code file.

The code that loads a text file exported by Mappy is fairly simple because it mimics the process used in the previous chapter, which converts a large string into an integer array. The only difference is that this time the data values are read from a text file; otherwise the code is similar to the parsing code from the previous chapter. In fact, you may recognize most of the code in LoadMap because the parsing code is the same.

There is just one thing that you *must* do first! You have to edit the text file and insert two values at the very beginning of the file, specifying the width and height of the map, in number of tiles. Figure 8.5 shows an example file exported from Mappy, and I have added two comma-separated values to the very beginning of the file: 25,18, (be sure to include the trailing comma as well). This text is picked up by the LoadMap subroutine when it opens the file, so that it can automatically read the size of the map instead of you having to specify the size in source code. The code that reads these two values is shown here:

tip

In Chapter 12, "Walking Around in the Game World," I will show you how to load a binary map file that loads at least 10 times faster than the text file used in this chapter. But it's best to take this process one step at a time, as it is natural to start with a text format and then graduate up to the faster binary format as you come to learn how tiling works.

```
Input #num, mapwidth, mapheight
```

Here is the complete source code for the LoadMap subroutine (which loads a text file filled with comma-separated tile values):

```
Public Sub LoadMap(ByVal filename As String)
    Dim num As Integer
    Dim line As String
    Dim buffer As String
```

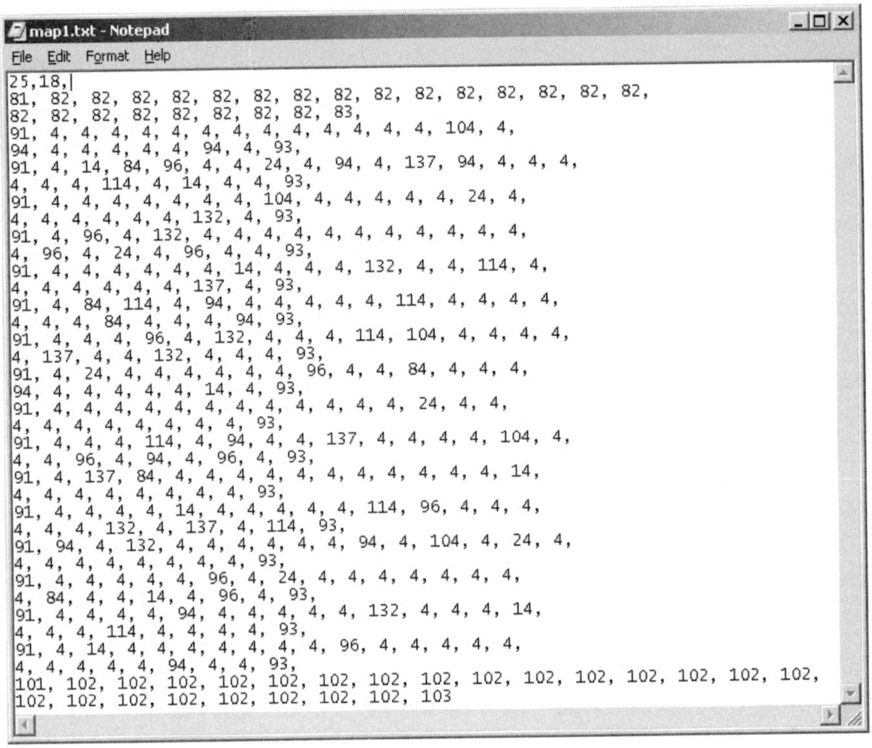
map1.txt - Notepad
File Edit Format Help
25,18,
81, 82, 82, 82, 82, 82, 82, 82, 82, 82, 82, 82, 82, 82, 82, 82,
82, 82, 82, 82, 82, 82, 82, 82, 83,
91, 4, 4, 4, 4, 4, 4, 4, 4, 4, 4, 4, 4, 4, 104, 4,
94, 4, 4, 4, 4, 4, 94, 4, 93,
91, 4, 14, 84, 96, 4, 4, 24, 4, 94, 4, 137, 94, 4, 4, 4,
4, 4, 4, 114, 4, 14, 4, 4, 93,
91, 4, 4, 4, 4, 4, 4, 4, 104, 4, 4, 4, 4, 4, 24, 4,
4, 4, 4, 4, 4, 4, 132, 4, 93,
91, 4, 96, 4, 132, 4, 4, 4, 4, 4, 4, 4, 4, 4, 4, 4,
4, 96, 4, 24, 4, 96, 4, 4, 93,
91, 4, 4, 4, 4, 4, 4, 14, 4, 4, 4, 132, 4, 4, 114, 4,
4, 4, 4, 4, 4, 4, 137, 4, 93,
91, 4, 84, 114, 4, 94, 4, 4, 4, 4, 4, 114, 4, 4, 4, 4,
4, 4, 4, 84, 4, 4, 4, 94, 93,
91, 4, 4, 4, 96, 4, 132, 4, 4, 4, 114, 104, 4, 4, 4, 4,
4, 137, 4, 4, 132, 4, 4, 4, 93,
91, 4, 24, 4, 4, 4, 4, 4, 4, 96, 4, 4, 84, 4, 4, 4,
94, 4, 4, 4, 4, 4, 14, 4, 93,
91, 4, 4, 4, 4, 4, 4, 4, 4, 4, 4, 4, 4, 24, 4, 4,
4, 4, 4, 4, 4, 4, 4, 4, 93,
91, 4, 4, 4, 114, 4, 94, 4, 4, 137, 4, 4, 4, 4, 104, 4,
4, 4, 96, 4, 94, 4, 96, 4, 93,
91, 4, 137, 84, 4, 4, 4, 4, 4, 4, 4, 4, 4, 4, 4, 14,
4, 4, 4, 4, 4, 4, 4, 4, 93,
91, 4, 4, 4, 4, 14, 4, 4, 4, 4, 4, 114, 96, 4, 4, 4,
4, 4, 4, 132, 4, 137, 4, 114, 93,
91, 94, 4, 132, 4, 4, 4, 4, 4, 4, 94, 4, 104, 4, 24, 4,
4, 4, 4, 4, 4, 4, 4, 4, 93,
91, 4, 4, 4, 4, 4, 96, 4, 24, 4, 4, 4, 4, 4, 4, 4,
4, 84, 4, 4, 14, 4, 96, 4, 93,
91, 4, 4, 4, 4, 94, 4, 4, 4, 4, 4, 132, 4, 4, 4, 14,
4, 4, 4, 114, 4, 4, 4, 4, 93,
91, 4, 14, 4, 4, 4, 4, 4, 4, 4, 96, 4, 4, 4, 4, 4,
4, 4, 4, 4, 4, 94, 4, 4, 93,
101, 102, 102, 102, 102, 102, 102, 102, 102, 102, 102, 102, 102, 102, 102, 102,
102, 102, 102, 102, 102, 102, 102, 102, 103

Figure 8.5 Saving the new Visual Basic source code (module) file.

```
Dim s As String
Dim value As String
Dim index As Long
Dim pos As Long
Dim buflen As Long

'open the map file
num = FreeFile()
Open filename For Input As num

'read the width and height
Input #num, mapwidth, mapheight

'read the map data
While Not EOF(num)
    Line Input #num, line
    buffer = buffer & line
Wend
```

```
    'close the file
    Close num

    'prepare the array for the map data
    ReDim mapdata(mapwidth * mapheight)
    index = 0
    buflen = Len(buffer)

    'convert the text data to an array
    For pos = 1 To buflen

        'get next character
        s = Mid$(buffer, pos, 1)

        'tiles are separated by commas
        If s = "," Then
            If Len(value) > 0 Then

                'store tile # in array
                mapdata(index) = CInt(value - 1)
                index = index + 1
            End If

            'get ready for next #
            value = ""
            s = ""
        Else
            value = value & s
        End If
    Next pos

    'save last item to array
    mapdata(index) = CInt(value - 1)
End Sub
```

The ScrollWorld Program

Let's put all this code together into a complete program to see how this scrolling technique works in the real world. Create a new project called "ScrollWorld" and add the "DirectX 8 for Visual Basic Type Library" reference to the project using the Project, References menu option. Next, I'd like to do something a little differently in this program from what you have done in previous chapters.

Aligning Tiles to the Scroll Buffer

There is one factor that you must take into consideration while designing the screen layout of your game with a scrolling window. The size of the scrolling window must be evenly divisible by the size of the tiles, or you end up with a *floating overlap* at the uneven edge. This is an issue that I considered solving in the scrolling code itself. I decided that it would require too much extra logic to fix up the right and bottom edges of the scrolling window when it is not evenly divisible by the tile width and height. The scroller works with tiles other than 64 × 64; the important thing is that the widths and heights are evenly divisible.

If using a screen resolution of 640 × 480 with 64 × 64 tiles, your width is fine, but height is a problem. Cut off the bottom of the scroll window at 448 (which is 7 tiles high), leaving the remaining 32 pixels unused at the bottom. This shouldn't be a problem because you can use that screen real estate for things like an in-game menu system, player status information, or perhaps in-game dialog. (Don't confuse this with the discussion earlier about partial tiles, because the partial tile drawing is different than the overall alignment of tiles on the scroll buffer surface.) Figure 8.6 illustrates how you could position the scroll window, leaving a small portion at the bottom of the screen, which might be used for other things.

I recommend limiting the scrolling window to a portion of the screen anyway, as it makes more sense than displaying game information over the top of the scrolling window. This

Figure 8.6 The scrolling window should be evenly divisible by the tile size.

holds true unless you are doing something cool, like drawing transparent windows over the top of the background (which is possible using Direct3D textures and is discussed in the next chapter).

Figure 8.7 shows the ScrollWorld program running at 800 × 600, with some blank space showing at the right and bottom edges of the scroll window. This is intentional, keeping the scroller code as efficient as possible (without too many conditions placed upon it). By simply making the scroll window evenly divisible by the tiles, there is no special-case code required to keep the scrolling tiles in view beyond the scroll window.

The next screenshot of ScrollWorld, in Figure 8.8, shows the program running at a resolution of 640 × 480. As you can see, the screen was evenly divisible with the 64 × 64 tiles, so the right edge is flush with the screen, while the bottom edge (in which 480 is not evenly divisible by 64) leaves a portion of the screen unused.

Finally, the screenshot in Figure 8.9 shows the program running at 1024 × 768, with an even distribution of tiles from left to right and top to bottom, completely filling in the screen. Although this particular resolution does work well with this tile size, that shouldn't be your goal with a scrolling game; a portion of the screen is used for other aspects of the game, anyway (such as status information or the score). Once you have the main screen

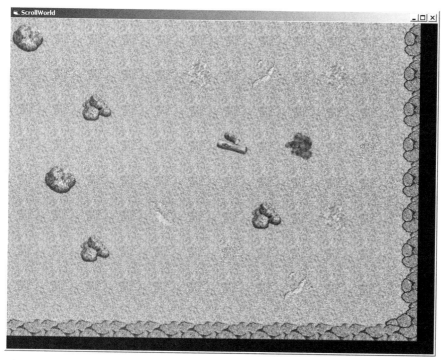

Figure 8.7 The ScrollWindow program cannot uniformly fill the 800 × 600 screen.

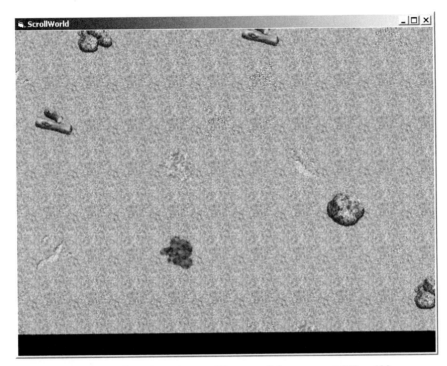

Figure 8.8 The ScrollWindow program fills most of the screen at 640 × 480.

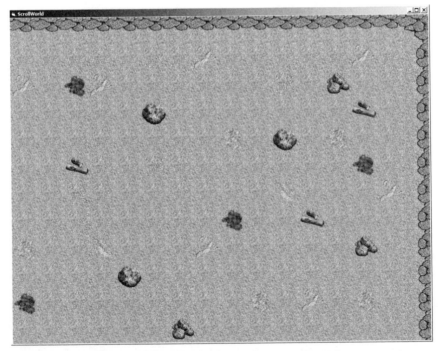

Figure 8.9 At 1024 × 768, the scroller fills the entire screen evenly.

designed for your game, you have a better idea about how large of a scroll window you need.

The ScrollWorld Source Code

At this point, it is becoming somewhat tedious to type in the common reusable code from one project to the next, so I'd like to show you how to add another source code file to your project for those reused subroutines. Not only does this make the code more reusable, but it also organizes your game's source code. There will be four files in the project overall by the time you're done putting it together:

- Form1.frm
- Globals.bas
- Direct3D.bas
- TileScroller.bas

Adding the Globals.bas File

First of all, I need to explain a little bit about how Visual Basic projects work. You can share a constant, variable, or subroutine with the source code files in your project as long as those sharable items are located inside a *Module file*. You can't share items in a Form, because forms are treated like classes (or objects), which can't share code. Therefore, anything you want to make reusable has to be stored in a .BAS module file.

Let's start with the most obvious code that should be shared with the entire project: the constants.

1. Add a new file to the project by opening the Project menu and selecting Add Module.

   You see a blank source code window with a new file added to your project. The new file is called Module1.

2. Looking over at the Properties window (press F4 if it is not visible), change the name of Module1 using the Properties window.

3. Change the name of the file to Globals and click Save from the File menu.

   You see the dialog box shown in Figure 8.10, with the option to change the filename.

4. Go ahead and accept the filename Globals.BAS.

5. Save the file.

As is always the case when restructuring and organizing a project, extra work up front results in more code listings than you may be used to. The real benefit is this: After you have put together this project, you can just copy these source code files to your new Visual

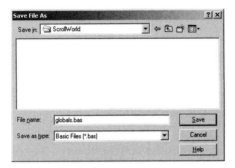

Figure 8.10 Saving the new Visual Basic source code (module) file.

Basic games in the future and reuse the files, without having to type or even copy-paste any of the code again. It is all available for immediate use in these files. Incidentally, after you have created a sharable Visual Basic module (.BAS) file, you can add it to a new project by selecting Project, Add File.

Now type the following code into Globals.BAS:

```
'-------------------------------------------------------
' Visual Basic Game Programming for Teens
' Globals File
'-------------------------------------------------------

Option Explicit
Option Base 0

'Windows API functions
Public Declare Function GetTickCount Lib "kernel32" () As Long

'colors
Public Const C_BLACK As Long = &H0

'customize the program here
Public Const FULLSCREEN As Boolean = False
Public Const SCREENWIDTH As Long = 800
Public Const SCREENHEIGHT As Long = 600
Public Const STEP As Integer = 8

'game world size
Public Const GAMEWORLDWIDTH As Long = 1600
Public Const GAMEWORLDHEIGHT As Long = 1152
```

```
'tile size
Public Const TILEWIDTH As Integer = 64
Public Const TILEHEIGHT As Integer = 64

'scrolling window size
Public Const WINDOWWIDTH As Integer = (SCREENWIDTH \ TILEWIDTH) * TILEWIDTH
Public Const WINDOWHEIGHT As Integer = (SCREENHEIGHT \ TILEHEIGHT) * TILEHEIGHT

'scroll buffer size
Public Const SCROLLBUFFERWIDTH As Integer = SCREENWIDTH + TILEWIDTH
Public Const SCROLLBUFFERHEIGHT As Integer = SCREENHEIGHT + TILEHEIGHT
```

I thought about putting these constants into their respective module files to make it even more organized and reusable, because these constants are required by the Direct3D.BAS and TileScroller.BAS files (which you add to the project next). In the end, I realized it is more convenient to have these constants all available in a single file, where you can easily change how the program runs without having to open up several files to make changes to the globals.

Adding the Direct3D.bas File

Next, I show you how to move the common Direct3D code into a Visual Basic module file to get it out of your main code listing in Form1.

1. In Visual Basic, open the Project menu and select the Add Module option.
2. After the new module file has been added to your project, rename it to Direct3D using the Properties window.
3. Save the file as Direct3D.BAS.
4. Move the common Direct3D variables over to the Direct3D.BAS file, because they never change.

    This really cleans up the Form1 code and makes it easier to work on the core game without the huge list of variables at the top. Note that I have changed the Dim statements to Public to make the variables visible to the whole project.

```
'the DirectX objects
Public dx As DirectX8
Public d3d As Direct3D8
Public d3dx As New D3DX8
Public dispmode As D3DDISPLAYMODE
Public d3dpp As D3DPRESENT_PARAMETERS
Public d3ddev As Direct3DDevice8
Public backbuffer As Direct3DSurface8
```

Next, I'd like you to paste the following subroutines into Direct3D.BAS. You can find these subroutines listed in Chapter 7, "Scrolling the Game World." Make sure the subroutine declaration line uses the `Public` scope instead of `Private` scope, because `Public` makes the subroutines visible to the rest of the code in your project, while `Private` subroutines are only visible within the current file. When you paste the code and your program fails to run with an error message, it is probably due to a subroutine or variable that was moved to a module file without the use of `Public` scope. So, make sure your subroutines all start with the keyword `Public` instead of `Dim` and you should have no problems.

After you have typed in this code, the Direct3D.BAS file should have the variable declarations shown here, as well as the full code listing for the following subroutines: `Shutdown`, `InitDirect3D`, and `LoadSurface`. You can find these subroutines in the previous chapter, so I won't list the full source code for them here.

- `Shutdown`
- `InitDirect3D`
- `LoadSurface`

Adding the TileScroller.bas File

Next, add another Module file called TileScroller.bas to your project. This file hides away all of the tile scrolling code developed thus far, which also greatly reduces the amount of code in the main source code file (in `Form1`). Anything that is related to the tile-scrolling subroutines, including the scroller variables, should be put inside TileScroller.bas for safe-keeping (as well as for reusability).

Just be sure to change the `Private` scope of each subroutine to `Public`, and be sure to change `Dim` for each variable to `Public` (because `Dim` is the same as `Private`). By giving public scope to your subroutines and variables, the source code in other files in your project can see them. Just be sure not to put anything in these support files that you plan to change frequently, because it is best to keep oft-changed code inside your main source code file. (Note that parameters and return values, if any, are not shown in this list.)

First, here are the variables that have to be moved to TileScroller.BAS. Note that I have changed them all to `Public` scope. Type these lines into the top of the TileScroller.BAS, above the subroutines:

```
'tile scroller surfaces
Public scrollbuffer As Direct3DSurface8
Public tiles As Direct3DSurface8

'map data
Public mapdata() As Integer
Public mapwidth As Long
Public mapheight As Long
```

```
'scrolling values
Public ScrollX As Long
Public ScrollY As Long
Public SpeedX As Integer
Public SpeedY As Integer
```

Here are the subroutines that you should paste or type into TileScroller.BAS. Since I listed the source code for these subroutines earlier in this chapter, I won't list them again here. Refer to their listings and type the code into TileScroller.BAS.

- UpdateScrollPosition
- DrawTiles
- DrawScrollWindow
- DrawTile
- LoadMap

The Main Source Code for ScrollWorld

Now that you have created Globals.BAS, Direct3D.BAS, and TileScroller.BAS, your project is much easier to modify—especially since the Form1 source code is so much shorter. In fact, with the support code moved out of Form1, the source code for ScrollWorld is really short!

```
'-------------------------------------------------------
' Visual Basic Game Programming for Teens
' Chapter 8 - ScrollWorld program
'
' Requires: Globals.bas, Direct3D.bas, TileScroller.bas
'-------------------------------------------------------

Option Explicit
Option Base 0

Private Sub Form_Load()
    'set up the main form
    Form1.Caption = "ScrollWorld"
    Form1.ScaleMode = 3
    Form1.width = Screen.TwipsPerPixelX * (SCREENWIDTH + 12)
    Form1.height = Screen.TwipsPerPixelY * (SCREENHEIGHT + 30)
    Form1.Show

    'initialize Direct3D
    InitDirect3D Me.hwnd, SCREENWIDTH, SCREENHEIGHT, FULLSCREEN
```

```
'get reference to the back buffer
Set backbuffer = d3ddev.GetBackBuffer(0, D3DBACKBUFFER_TYPE_MONO)

'load the bitmap file
Set tiles = LoadSurface(App.Path & "\map1.bmp", 1024, 640)

'load the map data from the Mappy export file
LoadMap App.Path & "\map1.txt"

'create the small scroll buffer surface
Set scrollbuffer = d3ddev.CreateImageSurface( _
    SCROLLBUFFERWIDTH, _
    SCROLLBUFFERHEIGHT, _
    dispmode.Format)

'this helps to keep a steady framerate
Dim start As Long
start = GetTickCount()

'clear the screen to black
d3ddev.Clear 0, ByVal 0, D3DCLEAR_TARGET, C_BLACK, 1, 0

'main loop
Do While (True)
    'update the scroll position
    UpdateScrollPosition

    'draw tiles onto the scroll buffer
    DrawTiles

    'draw the scroll window onto the screen
    DrawScrollWindow

    'set the screen refresh to about 40 fps
    If GetTickCount - start > 25 Then
        d3ddev.Present ByVal 0, ByVal 0, 0, ByVal 0
        start = GetTickCount
        DoEvents
    End If
Loop
End Sub
```

```
Private Sub Form_MouseMove(Button As Integer, Shift As Integer, _
    X As Single, Y As Single)

    'move mouse on left side to scroll left
    If X < SCREENWIDTH / 2 Then SpeedX = -STEP

    'move mouse on right side to scroll right
    If X > SCREENWIDTH / 2 Then SpeedX = STEP

    'move mouse on top half to scroll up
    If Y < SCREENHEIGHT / 2 Then SpeedY = -STEP

    'move mouse on bottom half to scroll down
    If Y > SCREENHEIGHT / 2 Then SpeedY = STEP
End Sub

Private Sub Form_KeyDown(KeyCode As Integer, Shift As Integer)
    If KeyCode = 27 Then Shutdown
End Sub

Private Sub Form_QueryUnload(Cancel As Integer, UnloadMode As Integer)
    Shutdown
End Sub
```

Level Up

This chapter has really knocked out the subject of tile-based scrolling by providing the code you need to present the game world to the player in the Celtic Crusader game. You continue to learn the things needed to get this game functional in the chapters to come, but have learned the most important techniques needed to make the game a reality. The ability to scroll a game world of any size was the primary goal of the book thus far, because Celtic Crusader has a very large game world. This chapter (which built on the previous two chapters) has fulfilled that requirement. You may now move on to the coming chapters to learn about sprites and animation, which is the next core technique covered in this book.

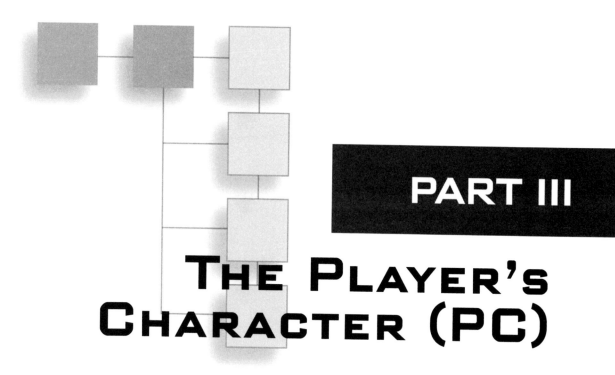

PART III

THE PLAYER'S CHARACTER (PC)

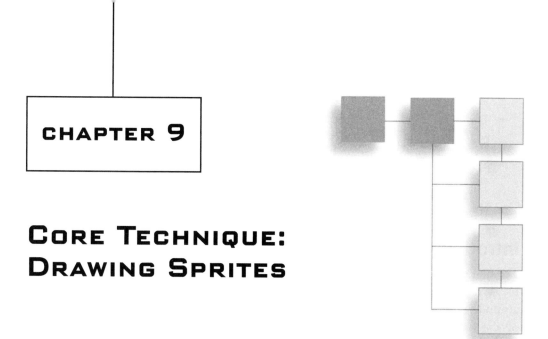

CHAPTER 9

CORE TECHNIQUE: DRAWING SPRITES

The last few chapters on building a tile-based scroller sure have been rewarding— at least from the point of view of having built a complete scroller. Although the discussion has been somewhat terse, it is my hope that you have managed to grasp the subject with enough understanding to create your own scrolling games. In fact, with the tools now available, you can create a scrolling game of your own, although you need to learn about sprites first. You might want to hold off until you've finished at least this chapter!

This chapter and Chapter 10, "Core Technique: Animating Sprites," both focus on the next critical component of any 2D game: how to draw transparent sprites and animate them on the screen. This is a fascinating chapter because the subject is a lot of fun to learn about, especially when you see how quickly you have a terrific-looking transparent character up on the screen. Within just the next few chapters you move an animated Hero character around within the game world of Celtic Crusader (which was introduced in Chapter 3, "Designing the Game"). When you see your first transparent sprite up on the screen, it is usually a wonderful and exciting first step, especially if you have never worked on a game of your own before. Let me tell you, I get the same rush whenever I write a basic sprite handler (as you do in this chapter) and see a sprite appear on the screen for the first time. It never gets old!

So, get ready to dive right in to the discussion of sprites. This chapter moves along at a pretty good clip, so you don't want to skip a single paragraph or you might miss some important detail. However, I believe you can grasp the basics quickly and blast sprites all over the screen in a very short time! Here is what you find in this chapter:

- Introduction to sprites
- Loading a texture

- Using the D3DXSprite class
- The sprite handler structure
- Rendering in 2D
- Sprite position, scaling, and rotation
- The SpriteTest program
- Having some fun with sprites

Introduction to Sprites

The first question that often arises when the discussion of sprites comes up is the veritable "What is a sprite?" To answer this question simply, a *sprite* is a small object that moves around on the screen. But the term *sprite* has been used to describe just about any object on the screen that is drawn transparently. You might have trees or rocks or buildings in your game that don't move at all, but because those objects are loaded from a bitmap file when the game starts running, and drawn in the game separately from the background, it is reasonable to call them sprites. Just note that in the old days, sprites were originally just the things moving around on the screen.

There are two basic types of sprites. One type of sprite is the "normal" sprite that I just described, which I refer to as a *dynamic sprite*. The other type of sprite might be called a *static sprite* and is the sort that doesn't move around on the screen. A static sprite is used for scenery or objects that the player uses (such as items that might be picked up in the game world).

Nevertheless, I'm just going to define any graphic image that is loaded and drawn separately from the background as a sprite. So, I might have a whole house, which normally would be considered part of the background, as a sprite. I use that concept in the sample program later in this chapter.

Doing Sprites with Direct3D?

One of the problems that may confuse someone new to DirectX is just how to handle sprites when there is only one way to do graphics: using Direct3D. Direct3D is a high-performance 3D rendering library that powers most of the games created today for the Windows platform. But how suited is Direct3D for handling 2D sprites? You learned in previous chapters that Direct3D lets you use surfaces to draw tiles on the screen, and thus create a tile-based scrolling game world. But what about drawing sprites, which must be transparent?

Figure 9.1 shows an example sprite of an Orc warrior. The sprite is really just the detailed pixels that you see at the center of the image, showing the Orc warrior holding a mace and shield. The sprite itself only takes up about half of the actual size of the sprite because the

Transparent Pixels

Sprite Boundary

Figure 9.1 The sprite boundary is a rectangle that encloses the sprite with transparent pixels.

computer only sees sprites in the shape of a rectangle. It is physically impossible to even store a sprite without the rectangular boundary because bitmap images are themselves rectangular. The real question here is not how to draw a sprite; you have already seen how to draw tiles from one surface to another. The real problem with a sprite is what to do about all the transparent pixels that should *not* be shown when the image is displayed on the screen (or rather, on the back buffer surface).

The amateur game programmer will write the code to draw a sprite using two loops that go through each pixel of the sprite's bitmap image, drawing only the solid pixels. Here is the pseudocode for how one might do this:

```
For Y = 1 To Sprite_Height
  For X = 1 to Sprite_Width
    If Pixel At X,Y Is Solid Then
      Draw Pixel At X,Y
    End If
  Next X
Next Y
```

This pseudocode algorithm goes through each pixel of the sprite image, checking for solid pixels, which are then drawn while transparent pixels are ignored. This draws a transparent sprite, but runs so slowly that the game probably won't be playable (even on a top-of-the-line PC).

And yet, this is the *only* way to draw a transparent sprite! That's right, I did not misspeak. That is the only way. By one method or another, some process must check the pixels that are solid and render them. The key here is understanding how Direct3D works, because this very critical and time-consuming algorithm is quite old and has been built into the silicon of video cards for many years now. The process of copying a transparent image from one surface to another has been provided by video cards since Windows 3.11 first started supporting the concept of a video accelerator. The process is called *bit block transfer* or just *blit* for short. Since this important process is handled by an extremely optimized and custom video chip, you don't need to worry about writing your own *blitter* for a game any longer. (Even the Nintendo Game Boy Advance has a hardware blitter!)

How Does Direct3D Draw Sprites?

Direct3D doesn't use the term *blit* to describe the process of drawing a texture onto a polygon or a surface, because that does not use a bit-block transfer. Rather it uses an algorithm called *texturing*, from which we get the name for textures. The video card uses a process called *alpha blending* to draw textures with a translucent effect (which means you can see through it like a window). Fifty-percent translucency means that half of the light rays are blocked by the texture, and you can only see about half of the image. Zero-percent translucency is called *opacity*, meaning that *none* of the image is visible (it is completely blacked out), and in 3D terms this means that no light passes through an opaque texture. The opposite is 100-percent translucency, which lets *all* light to pass through, which means that the texture is *transparent*. Figure 9.2 illustrates the difference between a fully opaque sprite and a transparent sprite. (Notice how the shadow is also visible on the background.)

Therefore, when an image needs to be drawn with transparency in Direct3D, a texture is used where a certain pixel color on the texture image is considered the "transparent" color, and the process of alpha blending causes that particular pixel color to be completely blended with the background. At the same time, no other pixels in the texture are affected by this alpha blending, and the result is a transparent sprite. In addition to transparency support, you can also draw a Direct3D texture with a global translucency effect so that the solid pixels become translucent. This is a very cool effect that you might use, for example, for a ghost or wraith creature in your game.

Figure 9.2 The sprite on the right is drawn without the transparent pixels.

Creating Direct3D Sprites

The key to drawing transparent sprites with Direct3D, as you might have guessed at this point, is through the use of a texture. Now, if you are at all familiar with 3D graphics, then I'm sure you have heard the word *texture* used many times before. It is second only in popularity to the ubiquitous polygon in 3D lore. Textures are used to paint the surface of a polygon in 3D space. If you have ever painted before, then you may think of how a wall feels after a fresh coat of paint has dried on it, and you probably remember how the wall's texture feels beneath your fingers. The texture of paint also affects how the surface looks and feels when it is cured.

But in the 3D realm, *texture* is a misused term that describes the application of a bitmap to a polygon. In effect, a texture in the context of 3D graphics is nothing more than a bitmap image; on the other hand, the word *texture* brings up quite a different meaning when you ponder it outside the context of computer graphics. So, it's more of a term that describes *how* an image is applied to a polygon rather than *what* that image is. Textures are *textured*; bitmaps are *blitted*. This is why you can't use a `Direct3DSurface8` object to draw a sprite—this object does not support transparency. Instead, you have to use a `Direct3DTexture8` object.

A Direct3D texture is similar to a Direct3D surface. While a surface represents the image that is visible on the screen (and is only addressed in 2D terms), a texture exists in 3D when it is applied to a polygon; otherwise, the texture is just a bitmap in memory. You can load a bitmap file from disk and store it inside a Direct3D surface, as you have seen over the last several chapters. As a matter of fact, a very similar process loads a bitmap file and stores it inside a Direct3D texture.

Loading a Texture

The key to loading a bitmap file into a surface revolved around a subroutine in D3DX. (Remember, that is the Direct3D extension, a set of subroutines and classes that help Direct3D.) That subroutine (or rather, method as it is more properly called) is LoadSurfaceFromFile, and it quite literally fills the surface with the bitmap image loaded from the specified bitmap file in one fell swoop. You may also recall that the LoadSurface subroutine—which you were introduced to back in Chapter 4, "Core Technique: Drawing Bitmaps"—had to create the surface in memory first, before loading the bitmap image.

Textures are just about equal to surfaces in complexity, which means you should have no problem understanding how to use them once you have a chance to play around with some code to see how textures work. The D3DX object is also used to load a texture from a bitmap file, and this time the function's name is CreateTextureFromFileEx.

note

I have not fully explained the word *function* in this text. A *function* in Visual Basic is a subroutine (Sub) that returns a value, while a Sub does not return a value.

There is a bit of inconsistency with Direct3D textures. In contrast to surfaces, a texture need not be created in memory prior to calling CreateTextureFromFileEx. As the name implies, the texture is created in memory and the contents of the bitmap file are loaded, after which the texture may be used to paint a polygon or—in the interest of 2D games— a texture can be used to draw a transparent sprite, with some of the benefits of a 3D system. Direct3D textures can be scaled or *translated* (which means moved in 3D), as well as rotated. Although rotation is an interesting effect, it is seldom used in 2D games with professional artwork. The translation part of a 3D object allows that object to move around in the 3D world. In the context of a 2D sprite, this aspect of the sprite's textured nature gives it the ability to move around on the surface where it is drawn (more on that shortly). The ability to change the scale (or rather, *resolution*) of a texture also makes it possible to change the scale of a sprite as it is drawn.

There are a lot of options for CreateTextureFromFileEx because this function is a Direct3D powerhouse that handles almost all texture loading. There are parameters that you always set to a default value, and therefore I do not go into detail about what each parameter does. The important thing is that you pass the name of the bitmap file to this function and it returns a texture to you, which you can then use to draw transparent sprites. In order to make it easier to use, I wrote a function of my own in Visual Basic that calls `CreateTextureFromFileEx` with just the right parameters needed to get the job done. All you have to do is give it the name of your primary Direct3D device and the filename. After that this function returns the `Direct3DTexture8` object to you.

```
Public Function LoadTexture( _
    ByRef dev As Direct3DDevice8, _
    ByVal filename As String) _
    As Direct3DTexture8

    On Local Error GoTo error1

    Dim d3dx As New D3DX8
    Dim tex As Direct3DTexture8

    'load the source bitmap file into a texture
    Set tex = d3dx.CreateTextureFromFileEx( _
        dev, _
        filename, _
        D3DX_DEFAULT, _
        D3DX_DEFAULT, _
        1, 0, _
        D3DFMT_UNKNOWN, _
        D3DPOOL_MANAGED, _
        D3DX_FILTER_NONE, _
        D3DX_FILTER_NONE, _
        &HFF00FF, _
        ByVal 0, ByVal 0)

    If tex Is Nothing Then
        MsgBox "Error loading " & filename, vbOKOnly, "Error"
        Set LoadTexture = Nothing
    Else
        Set LoadTexture = tex
    End If

    Exit Function

error1:
    MsgBox "Error loading " & filename, vbOKOnly, "Error"
    Set LoadTexture = Nothing
End Function
```

Using the D3DXSprite Class

Direct3D includes a helper class called D3DX that I have only touched upon in this book. I have been using the parts of D3DX that have been useful but largely ignoring the rest of the features it provides you. Now I introduce you to another feature of D3DX that will now become extremely useful. There is a class provided by D3DX called D3DXSprite, which makes it much easier to work with Direct3D textures for drawing 2D images (such as sprites).

The first step to using D3DXSprite is to create a D3DXSprite object variable like this:

```
Dim spriteObject As D3DXSprite
```

The next step is to initialize the sprite using the CreateSprite function:

```
Dim d3dx As New D3DX
Set spriteObject = d3dx.CreateSprite(d3ddev)
```

Of course, normally, you have initialized the d3dx variable in advance, because it is used all over the place in a Direct3D game and is often just declared as a global variable. As you may recall, d3dx was put into the Direct3D.bas file in the previous chapter. As long as you include the Direct3D.BAS file in your Visual Basic project and have previously called InitDirect3D in your program, then you can just assume that d3dx is available.

D3DXSprite has a function called Draw that you can use to draw a sprite. I show you how to use this function shortly, but first I need to explain how to set up a sprite before it can be used.

The Sprite Handler Structure

There are a lot of properties that you have to keep track of when drawing sprites on the screen. If you think about if for a moment, you may wonder how you keep track of where each sprite is located on the screen and how you move it around. As an example, suppose you have a Hero character that is moved around using the keyboard arrow keys or perhaps a joystick. How do you take a texture full of sprites and turn that into something that moves around on the screen?

This discussion revolves around a subject called *logistics*, which is the organization of a complex task or the management of things being moved, and is often used to describe how military units are deployed. Dealing with sprites requires that you take care of all the logistics yourself! You might be able to imagine using simple variables like X and Y to track the sprite's location on the screen. What about the sprite's image size (required for the Draw function), and its speed, direction, and (as you learn about in the next chapter) animation variables? All of this data has to be handled, and that's just for one sprite.

A well-written game handles the logistics of sprite movement well, using what you might call a sprite handler. The *sprite handler* is like a colonel in the military who takes orders by the high-ranking general and carries out those orders to the lower-ranking officers who are in charge of the soldiers. *You* are the general, and you need a colonel to handle the logistics of sprite management, so that you can focus on the more important things (like winning the war). A sprite handler is simpler than you might imagine, because it is just made up of a structure and a couple of subroutines that work with the structure.

A *structure* is like a custom data type that you can create yourself, consisting of other minor data types (like Integer, Long, String, and so on). Visual Basic uses the Type keyword to define a structure (which is called struct in the C language). A custom data type in Visual Basic for handling sprites might look something like this:

```
'sprite properties
Public Type TSPRITE
    spriteObject As D3DXSprite
    x As Long
    y As Long
    width As Long
    height As Long
    FramesPerRow As Long
    StartFrame As Long
    FrameCount As Long
    CurrentFrame As Long
    Animating As Boolean
    AnimSeq As Long
    AnimDelay As Long
    AnimCount As Long
    SpeedX As Long
    SpeedY As Long
    DirX As Long
    DirY As Long
    ScaleFactor As Single
End Type
```

I have all kinds of interesting data in the TSPRITE structure, some of which you might not understand at first glance. Some of the variables in TSPRITE aren't even used until the next chapter, because they deal with animation. I wanted to just give you the whole structure here and now so you gain some familiarity with it throughout this chapter, in preparation for animation.

Obviously, the most important variables in TSPRITE are x, y, width, and height. You can get away without any of the other variables and successfully draw sprites on the screen. Just get to know all these variables here and now; you use them a lot in the coming chapters! First, set all the variables in TSPRITE to their preferred default values, so that if you don't set the values yourself in code, the sprite still works (without causing some sort of automation error in Direct3D—something that you see often while working on a Direct3D game).

Initializing a Sprite

The InitSprite subroutine sets the default values for a sprite that you pass to the subroutine as a variable. Remember that a variable declared with ByRef is just a reference to the real variable, so any changes you make to a ByRef variable are made directly to that original variable. In contrast, any parameters that are declared using ByVal are just copied to your subroutine, and any changes you make are discarded when the subroutine is done.

```
Public Sub InitSprite( _
    ByRef dev As Direct3DDevice8, _
    ByRef spr As TSPRITE)

    'create sprite handler object
    Set spr.spriteObject = d3dx.CreateSprite(dev)

    'set initial values for the sprite
    spr.CurrentFrame = 0
    spr.FramesPerRow = 1
    spr.FrameCount = 1
    spr.AnimCount = 0
    spr.AnimDelay = 0
    spr.ScaleFactor = 1
    spr.x = 0
    spr.y = 0
    spr.width = 0
    spr.height = 0
    spr.SpeedX = 0
    spr.SpeedY = 0
    spr.DirX = 0
    spr.DirY = 0
End Sub
```

note

If any of this code is confusing to you, try not to worry too much at this point. You gain familiarity with TSPRITE and these associated subroutines by using them. I'm a big fan of the "learn through practice" method of teaching. I never explain everything with absolutely every detail spelled out, because nothing beats experience. You just can't learn to write a game solely from a book; you have to write some code yourself.

Well, then, you are probably wondering how you would use TSPRITE and InitSprite in a real game. First, you have to create your own sprite variable:

```
Dim sprite As TSPRITE
```

After you have a sprite variable, then you initialize it:

```
InitSprite d3ddev, sprite
```

Initializing the sprite is only the first step. You also have to set the sprite's position and size (in width and height), in order to draw the sprite properly. You can change the variables of a Type by referencing them with the dot (.) operator, which is the standard way of accessing items inside a Type (which is a user-defined structure that you can use to create your own data types, such as TSPRITE). InitSprite just sets the default values for the sprite so it won't behave oddly when displayed on the screen, but you still have to set the basic properties for the sprite yourself:

```
sprite.x = 200
sprite.y = 200
sprite.width = 64
sprite.height = 64
sprite.ScaleFactor = 1
```

After that, the sprite is ready to be used. Of course, you also have to load the sprite images from a bitmap file into a texture. For the sake of clarity, let me show you that code now:

```
Dim texture As Direct3DTexture8
Set texture = LoadTexture(d3ddev, App.Path & "\sprite.bmp")
```

With these tools at your disposal, you are ready to draw a sprite. The bitmap file containing the sprite's image usually holds a lot of images (similar to a bitmap containing tiles for the scroller), because most sprites are animated. Since I'm not covering animation until the next chapter, I just load a simple bitmap file with a single sprite image on it.

Drawing Direct3D Sprites

Do you remember how you were able to draw a portion of an image in order to create a scrolling game world in the previous chapter? That code uses the division and modulus operators to grab a certain tile out of the source image and draw it on the screen in a certain place to build the world, so to speak. The process is basically the same for drawing sprites, except that you work with a texture instead of a surface.

Rendering in 2D

You have access to a lot of great features when using a texture to render a 2D sprite on the screen. Those features include the ability to dynamically change the scale (or size) of a sprite while the game is running (and this is probably the most interesting effect). You can also rotate the sprite; while this is a compelling feature, I have chosen to ignore it because there's no reason to rotate sprites in a role-playing game, although you might find this useful in a space-based shooter or other type of arcade game.

note

I used sprite rotation to draw the tanks in my game Tank War in *Game Programming All In One, 2nd Edition*. Since each tank had 8 frames of animation and used 8 directions for movement, that would have required 64 images for each tank. By using sprite rotation, the game only needed the first 8 tank images and the rest were handled at runtime! So, I'm not discounting the value of rotation and freely encourage you to use rotation if you wish. The SpriteDraw subroutine that I cover shortly has support for rotation.

The Draw function that is provided by D3DX requires that you set up a rectangle specifying the source image on the texture drawn to the screen. That source rectangle is just a typical RECT, which you first saw back in Chapter 4.

Sprite Position, Scaling, and Rotation

Another aspect of Draw that you must take care of in advance is the initialization of three vectors. Now, I need to explain vectors because it's a new term. A *vector* is a position in 3D space with an X, Y, and Z value that defines where the vector is located relative to the origin. The origin in a 3D scene is the (0,0,0) point, and all rendering is relative to this position. Therefore, a vector with the values (1,1,1) is offset from the origin by a value of 1 for X, Y, and Z. These points are what you would call *3D vectors*, and Direct3D defines them with D3DVECTOR3. I'm not about to get into 3D graphics terminology in this book, aside from the discussion of textures and vectors. Direct3D also defines a 2D vector called D3DVECTOR2 that I use instead. The D3DVECTOR2 is similar to a POINT in that they both contain an X and Y variable, but vector uses floating-point numbers with a decimal, while POINT just has integers.

You must set up three vectors needed by the D3DX.Draw function. The first is a vector describing the position of the sprite on the screen. The second vector specifies the scale factor of the sprite. It is true that you can scale the width and height differently to produce a stretched sprite, but I am just using a single scale variable that sets both values equally for a properly scaled image. The third vector specifies the rotation of the sprite. As I mentioned already, I'm not particularly interested in rotation due to the type of game being developed in this book, but the feature is definitely available if you wish to use it.

The Reusable SpriteDraw Subroutine

That's about all there is to drawing a D3DXSprite. How about a subroutine that puts it all together in one place, taking care of everything automatically? The SpriteDraw subroutine follows:

```
Public Sub SpriteDraw( _
    ByRef tex As Direct3DTexture8, _
    ByRef spr As TSPRITE, _
    ByVal alpha as Long)

    'set the sprite's position
    Dim vecPos As D3DVECTOR2
    vecPos.x = spr.x
    vecPos.y = spr.y

    'set the sprite's scale factor
    Dim vecScale As D3DVECTOR2
    vecScale.x = spr.ScaleFactor
    vecScale.y = spr.ScaleFactor

    'set the sprite's rotation value (not used)
    Dim vecRot As D3DVECTOR2
    vecRot.x = 0
    vecRot.y = 0

    'start drawing
    spr.spriteObject.Begin

    'set the source rect
    Dim r As DxVBLibA.RECT
    r.Left = (spr.CurrentFrame Mod spr.FramesPerRow) * spr.width
    r.Top = (spr.CurrentFrame \ spr.FramesPerRow) * spr.height
    r.Right = r.Left + spr.width
    r.Bottom = r.Top + spr.height

    'draw the sprite
    spr.spriteObject.Draw tex, r, vecScale, vecRot, 0, vecPos, alpha

    'stop drawing
    spr.spriteObject.End
End Sub
```

The SpriteTest Program

Are you feeling pretty confident about how to draw sprites with Direct3D at this point? If not, then you gain a better understanding of the subject after writing the SpriteTest program that follows. This program draws a simple bitmap image to represent the background. Although the background looks like a tile-based scroller, it is really just a 640 × 480 copy of the exported tile map generated by Mappy in the previous chapter. There is no scrolling this time, although Figure 9.3 would indicate otherwise.

To represent a sprite that looks really great on the screen and also demonstrates transparency, I borrowed an image of a two-story house from Reiner's Tilesets (http://www.reinerstileset.de) for this example program. I like to think of this building as a tavern, so I have called the file tavern.bmp and show it in Figure 9.4. Note that this building includes a shadow, which looks absolutely great when it is drawn on a background with ground terrain.

The SpriteTest program, shown in Figure 9.5, loads the image of this tavern sprite and draws it transparently over the background surface image.

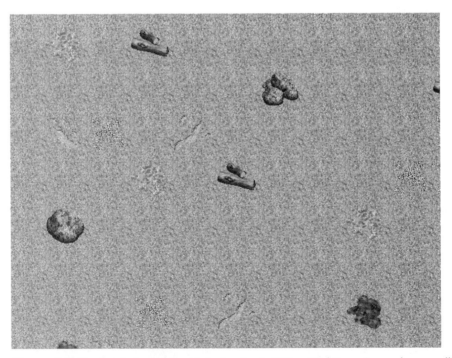

Figure 9.3 The terrain background is just a simple 640 × 480 bitmap image (non-scrolling).

Figure 9.4 The tavern sprite is a beautifully rendered 3D model from Reiner's Tilesets.

Creating the Project

Create the SpriteTest project:

1. Open Visual Basic and create a new project.

   If necessary, open the File menu and select New Project.

2. Add a reference to DirectX 8 for Visual Basic Type Library using the Project, References menu option.

3. Save the project, giving it the name SpriteTest.

   Don't skip the following important step!

Figure 9.5 The DrawSprite program demonstrates how to draw a transparent sprite using Direct3D surfaces and textures.

4. You have to copy the Direct3D.bas file from the previous chapter into the folder where you have saved this new project.

   The Direct3D.bas file was included in the ScrollWorld project in the previous chapter, so you can copy the file from that folder to where your new project is located.

5. Add the file to your project by opening the Project menu and selecting Add File.

   This lets you add an existing file to the project.

Adding the Sprite.bas File

I want the sprite code developed in this chapter to be reusable so you can use it in your own game projects. It also is used in the remaining chapters of this book (so the code doesn't have to be listed again). Create the new project now and add this sprite source file to the project:

1. Open Visual Basic and create a new project.

2. Add a reference to DirectX 8 for Visual Basic Type Library using the Project, References menu option.

3. After you have a new project waiting, open the Project menu again and select Add Module.

This module is named Sprite.bas and contains the source code for the sprite handler developed in this chapter. Here are the first few lines of code for Sprite.bas. Note that I have inserted comments specifying that you should type in the subroutines already covered earlier in this chapter (so I won't have to list them again).

```
'----------------------------------------------------------
' Visual Basic Game Programming for Teens
' Sprite Support File
'----------------------------------------------------------

Option Explicit
Option Base 0


'sprite properties
Public Type TSPRITE
    spriteObject As D3DXSprite
    x As Long
    y As Long
    width As Long
    height As Long
    FramesPerRow As Long
    StartFrame As Long
    FrameCount As Long
    CurrentFrame As Long
    Animating As Boolean
    AnimSeq As Long
    AnimDelay As Long
    AnimCount As Long
    SpeedX As Long
    SpeedY As Long
    DirX As Long
    DirY As Long
    ScaleFactor As Single
End Type


*** Public Function LoadTexture ***

*** Public Sub InitSprite ***

*** Public Sub DrawSprite ***
```

Be sure to type the code for LoadTexture, InitSprite, and DrawSprite into the Sprite.bas file as specified and save the file. You can begin working on the main source code for the SpriteTest program.

The SpriteTest Source Code

Your project is now loaded with useful support subroutines, so the next step is to write the main source code for the SpriteTest program. The source code here creates the variable for the terrain background surface, as well as for the sprite texture and sprite structure.

Since the previous chapters just deal with tiles, I needed to write a new subroutine that draws an entire surface to the screen.

caution

Be careful not to use an image that is larger than the screen for the background in this program, or DirectX will kill your program with an "Automation error" message.

```
'------------------------------------------------------------
' Visual Basic Game Programming With DirectX
' SpriteTest Source Code File
'------------------------------------------------------------

Option Explicit
Option Base 0

'Windows API functions and structures
Private Declare Function GetTickCount Lib "kernel32" () As Long

'program constants
Const SCREENWIDTH As Long = 640
Const SCREENHEIGHT As Long = 480
Const FULLSCREEN As Boolean = False

Dim tavernSprite As TSPRITE
Dim tavernImage As Direct3DTexture8

Dim terrain As Direct3DSurface8
Dim backbuffer As Direct3DSurface8

Private Sub Form_Load()
    Static lStartTime As Long
    Static lCounter As Long
    Static lNewTime As Long
```

```
'set up the main form
Form1.Caption = "DrawSprite"
Form1.KeyPreview = True
Form1.ScaleMode = 3
Form1.width = Screen.TwipsPerPixelX * (SCREENWIDTH + 12)
Form1.height = Screen.TwipsPerPixelY * (SCREENHEIGHT + 30)
Form1.Show

'initialize Direct3D
InitDirect3D Me.hwnd, SCREENWIDTH, SCREENHEIGHT, FULLSCREEN

Set backbuffer = d3ddev.GetBackBuffer(0, D3DBACKBUFFER_TYPE_MONO)

Set terrain = LoadSurface(App.Path & "\terrain.bmp", 640, 480)
If terrain Is Nothing Then
    MsgBox "Error loading bitmap"
    Shutdown
End If

Set tavernImage = LoadTexture(d3ddev, App.Path & "\tavern.bmp")
InitSprite d3ddev, tavernSprite
With tavernSprite
    .width = 220
    .height = 224
    .ScaleFactor = 1
    .x = 200
    .y = 100
End With

Dim start As Long
start = GetTickCount()

'start main game loop
Do While True

    If GetTickCount - start > 25 Then
        'draw the background image
        DrawSurface terrain, 0, 0

        'start rendering
        d3ddev.BeginScene
```

```
                    'draw the sprite
                    spritedraw tavernImage, tavernSprite

                    'stop rendering
                    d3ddev.EndScene

                    'draw the back buffer to the screen
                    d3ddev.Present ByVal 0, ByVal 0, 0, ByVal 0

                    start = GetTickCount
                    DoEvents
                End If


        Loop
    End Sub


    Public Sub DrawSurface( _
        ByRef source As Direct3DSurface8, _
        ByVal x As Long, _
        ByVal y As Long)

        Dim r As DxVBLibA.RECT
        Dim point As DxVBLibA.point
        Dim desc As D3DSURFACE_DESC

        'get the properties for the surface
        source.GetDesc desc

        'set dimensions of the source image
        r.Left = x
        r.Top = y
        r.Right = x + desc.width
        r.Bottom = y + desc.height

        'set the destination point
        point.x = 0
        point.y = 0

        'draw the scroll window
        d3ddev.CopyRects source, r, 1, backbuffer, point

    End Sub
```

```
Private Sub Form_Unload(Cancel As Integer)
    Shutdown
End Sub


Private Sub Form_KeyDown(KeyCode As Integer, Shift As Integer)
    If KeyCode = 27 Then Shutdown
End Sub
```

Having Some Fun with Sprites

Now that you have this really great source code for drawing sprites on the screen—transparently!—see what this code is really capable of. I want to explore scaling and translucency with you, because I know you will be interested in using these advanced features (made possible by the fact that sprites are actually Direct3D textures).

Sprite Translucency

The DrawSprite subroutine has a parameter called alpha that accepts the alpha color value that is used to render the sprite. I passed a value of &HFFFFFFFF for the color of the alpha color, and this is equivalent to a Red/Green/Blue color value of (255,255,255). This color causes the solid pixels in the sprite to be drawn with full opacity, while the transparent pixels are still ignored in the rendered image.

You can pass a different alpha to this subroutine to cause the sprite to be drawn with some weird special effects! Most notably, you can cause the sprite to become translucent by using a darker shade of gray. For instance, &HFFFFFFFF is a hexadecimal number that represents solid white. The sum total of this number is not important, because you are concerned with each digit of the number rather than what the value of the number is (which is insignificant).

Hexadecimal is a subject that I don't want to get into in this book, so let me give you a quick-and-dirty explanation: Hex numbers range from 0 to 9 and then from A to F, giving hex numbers a total of 16 digits. As you know, normal numbers use the *decimal* numbering system, which has 10 digits (0 to 9). Since hex numbers have 16 digits, a three-digit decimal number can be represented by just two hex digits.

To make a long story short, the Red/Green/Blue/Alpha (RGBA) values of a 32-bit color can be represented as 0 to 255 in decimal, or from 00 to FF in hexadecimal. Hex is more convenient than decimal when describing a 32-bit color, because you can tell *visually* what the color is just by looking at the digits: Red, Green, Blue, and Alpha.

- To make the sprite totally opaque, use &HFF000000 for the alpha parameter in DrawSprite.

- To make the sprite totally invisible, use &H0.
- To make the sprite partially translucent, use values from &H11111111 to &HFFFFFFFF. For example, 50-percent translucent is &H88888888 and is shown in Figure 9.6.

If you found this discussion of hexadecimal numbers daunting, don't worry about it! Remember, whatever you don't understand now eventually comes through experience. Just try to experiment with different hex values in the SpriteTest program to see the results. That is where the *science* in computer science comes in.

tip

I put sprite translucency to good use in Chapter 18, "Engaging In Combat with NPCs," by causing an enemy character to fade away when killed, and it looks really neat.

Sprite Scaling

Another fascinating effect you can use in your games with the help of Direct3D sprites: the ability to scale the sprite by any value from 0.0 to about 8.0. (Keep in mind that you

Figure 9.6 Drawing the sprite with partial translucency makes it see-through.

must not draw outside the border of the screen or the program could crash.) The
DrawSprite subroutine that you saw earlier had support for scaling using the ScaleFactor
variable in TSPRITE. Refer to the definition of TSPRITE earlier in this chapter (see the section
titled "The Sprite Handler Structure"). ScaleFactor is declared as a Single data type, which
is a floating-point number with a decimal place. By default, InitSprite sets ScaleFactor to
1.0. You can change the scale factor at any time by just accessing it in your sprite. Here is
an example:

```
sprite.ScaleFactor = 2.0
```

Calling DrawSprite with this sprite then draws it with a scaling factor of 200 percent! Take
a look at Figure 9.7 to see the tavern sprite drawn with a scale factor of 2.0.

Level Up

This chapter provided an introduction to sprites. You learned how to use a Direct3D texture to draw a transparent sprite on the screen. You learned how to create a basic sprite

Figure 9.7 Changing the scale factor of the sprite makes it bigger or smaller than the original
image.

handler, which lets you deal with numerous sprites by organizing the sprite data inside a custom sprite structure. One of the items on the "sprite to-do list" at this point is the coverage of sprite *movement* as well as *animation* on the screen, which were glaringly absent from this chapter. Now that you have the basic source code to draw a sprite on the screen, the sprite movement and animation is that much easier to accomplish in the next chapter. You can focus on those subjects with the basics out of the way.

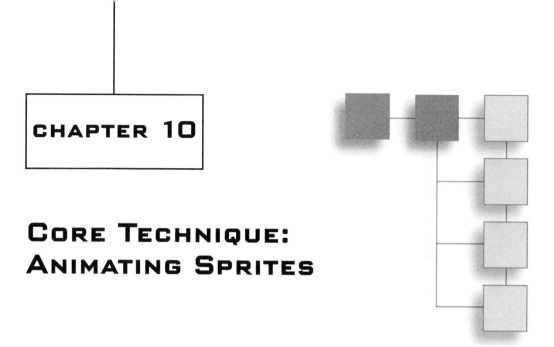

CHAPTER 10

CORE TECHNIQUE: ANIMATING SPRITES

This chapter continues the discussion of sprites brought up in the previous chapter, which developed the core source code for loading and drawing sprites. You take that core technique to the next level in this chapter by learning how to move sprites around on the screen, and then you learn how to animate sprites. This functionality was provided in the TSPRITE structure created in the previous chapter and is explained in this chapter now that you have the basic sprite functionality out of the way.

One might argue the point that with a tile-based scroller and transparent sprite functionality, you have all the tools necessary to create a killer game. Well, I would have to agree with that sentiment! You truly have all the information you need to develop a complete tile- and sprite-based game after finishing this chapter. Following this chapter, the book is about refinement; your learning process reaches the peak and, at that point, will be on the downhill slope. There are still a few things you need to learn in order to turn Celtic Crusader from concept to playable game.

Here is a breakdown of the major topics in this chapter:

- Creating animated sprites
- Getting a handle on animation sequences
- The AnimateSprite program

Moving Sprites

Moving sprites around on the screen is related to animating sprites, which is why the subject was reserved for this chapter rather than being covered in the previous chapter. As you may recall, a new Type called TSPRITE was created in the previous chapter. This structure contains all of the properties needed to draw and keep track of sprites on the screen:

```
Public Type TSPRITE
    spriteObject As D3DXSprite
    x As Long
    y As Long
    width As Long
    height As Long
    FramesPerRow As Long
    StartFrame As Long
    FrameCount As Long
    CurrentFrame As Long
    Animating As Boolean
    AnimSeq As Long
    AnimDelay As Long
    AnimCount As Long
    SpeedX As Long
    SpeedY As Long
    DirX As Long
    DirY As Long
    ScaleFactor As Single
End Type
```

The key variables of TSPRITE that are used to move the sprite are x, y, SpeedX, SpeedY, DirX, and DirY. The first two, x and y, are really all you need to move a sprite on the screen if you plan to directly control its movement. The other variables come in handy if you want to automate the movement of a sprite, and they also lend a sense of realism to sprites that can move in different directions and speeds that are not precisely controlled by your program's logic. For instance, I can set a sprite's SpeedX and SpeedY to a random number and have it wrap around the edges of the screen (or the game world, if a scroller is being used). Sometimes I use SpeedX or SpeedY as a general-purpose variable to control the overall speed of a sprite, regardless of the X or Y position on the screen. In other words, feel free to use the variables in TSPRITE however you want in order to accomplish your goals for a game, and feel free to add new variables to TSPRITE as well! It's not set in stone, after all.

After you have written a few games, you most likely find that many of the sprites in your games have similar behaviors, to the point of predictability. For instance, if you have sprites that just move around within the boundaries of the screen and wrap from one edge to the other, you can create a subroutine to produce this sprite behavior on call: Simply use that subroutine when you update the sprite's position. If you find that a lot of your sprites are doing other predictable movements, it is really helpful to create many different behavioral subroutines to control their actions.

Here is an example subroutine called MoveSprite. It keeps the sprite inside the boundary of the screen, and the sprite's movement is based entirely on the sprite's SpeedX and SpeedY variables.

```
Public Sub MoveSprite(ByRef spr As TSPRITE)
    spr.x = spr.x + spr.SpeedX
    If spr.x < 0 Then
        spr.x = 0
        spr.SpeedX = 0
    End If
    If spr.x > SCREENWIDTH - spr.width Then
        spr.x = SCREENWIDTH - spr.width - 1
        spr.SpeedX = 0
    End If

    spr.y = spr.y + spr.SpeedY
    If spr.y < 0 Then
        spr.y = 0
        spr.SpeedX = 0
    End If
    If spr.y > SCREENHEIGHT - spr.height Then
        spr.y = SCREENHEIGHT - spr.height - 1
        spr.SpeedX = 0
    End If
End Sub
```

This is just one simple example of a very primitive behavior, but you can create very complex behaviors by writing subroutines that cause sprites to react to other sprites or to the player, for instance, in different ways. You might have some behavior subroutines that cause a sprite to chase the player, or to run away from the player, or attack the player. The possibilities are truly limited only by your imagination, and generally, the most intelligent games are the most fun, because most players quickly figure out the patterns followed by so-called "dumb" sprites.

The AnimateSprite program later in this chapter demonstrates sprite movement as well as animation, so you may refer to that program for an example of how the sprite movement code is used.

Animating Sprites

Sprite animation goes back about three decades, when the first video game systems were being built for arcades. The earliest arcade games include classics such as Asteroids, and used vector-based graphics rather than bitmap-based graphics. A vector should sound familiar to you, since D3DVECTOR2 was introduced in Chapter 9, "Core Technique: Drawing Sprites." A *vector-based* graphics system uses lines connecting two points as the basis for all of the graphics on the screen. While a rotating vector-based spaceship might not be considered a sprite by today's standards, it is basically the same thing. In fact, any game object on the screen that uses more than one small image to represent itself might be considered a *sprite*. However, to be an *animated sprite*, the image must simulate a sequence of images that are drawn while the sprite is being displayed on the screen.

Animation is a fascinating subject because it brings life to a game and makes the objects in the game seem more realistic than static objects. An important concept to grasp at this point is that *every* frame of an animation sequence must be treated as a distinct image that is prerendered and stored in a bitmap file; as an alternative, some animation might be created on the fly if a technique such as rotation or translucency is used. (For instance, causing a sprite to fade in and out would be done at runtime.)

Creating Animated Sprites

Figure 10.1 shows a dragon sprite (provided courtesy of Reiner's Tilesets at http://www.reinerstileset.de) with 64 frames of animation. The dragon can move in any of eight directions of travel, and each direction has eight frames of animation. You learn to load this bitmap file into memory as a Direct3D texture and then draw it transparently on the screen with animation.

The trick to animating a sprite is keeping track of the current frame of animation along with the total animation frames in the animation sequence. This dragon sprite is stored in a single, large bitmap image, and was actually stored in 64 individual bitmaps before I converted it to a single bitmap using Pro Motion. (Pro Motion is an excellent sprite animation program available for download at http://www.cosmigo.com/promotion/.) You can see the dragon sprite loaded into Pro Motion in Figure 10.2.

You can load a sprite animation sequence as a series of individual bitmap files using one of Pro Motion's many awesome features: From the File menu, select Animation, Load as Single Images to bring up the Load Animation as Single Images dialog box in Figure 10.3.

Pro Motion displays a message telling you the resolution of the sequence of bitmaps along with the number of frames that will be added, allowing you to accept or cancel the import. After loading the individual files as a single animation sequence, you can then view the

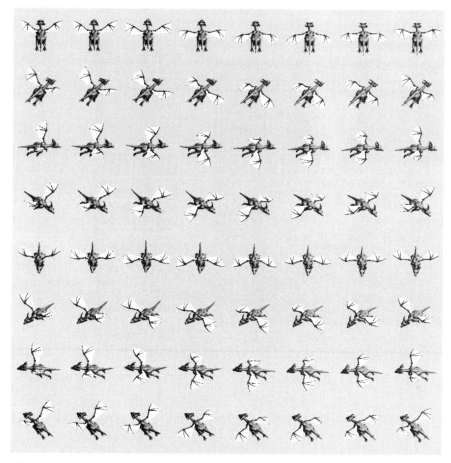

Figure 10.1 This dragon sprite has eight frames of animation for each of the eight directions that it can travel, resulting in 64 total frames of animation.

sprite animation using the Animation menu. The animation window can be scaled (see Figure 10.4) and the animation's speed can be slowed down or sped up so you can see what the sprite looks like in your game. In addition to these features, of course, you can edit the sprite images directly with the multifeatured pixel editing tools available in Pro Motion.

After importing a series of animation sequences and manipulating the animation and image sequence, you can then export the animation as a single, large bitmap file containing all the sprite animation frames. This is similar to the export feature of Mappy, which

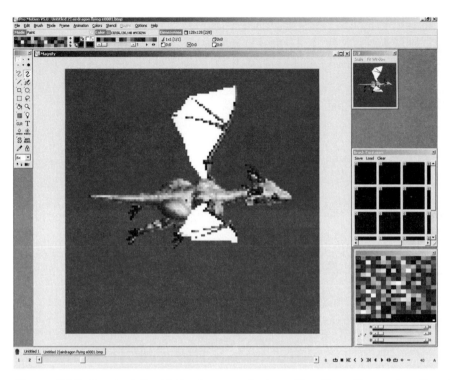

Figure 10.2 Cosmigo's Pro Motion is an excellent graphic editor with superb sprite animation tools.

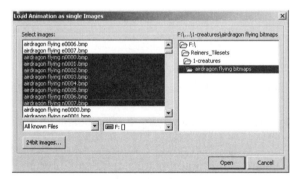

Figure 10.3 Loading a sprite animation as a series of individual bitmap files in Pro Motion.

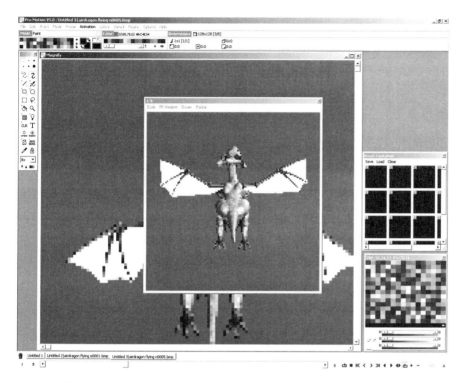

Figure 10.4 Saving a sprite animation sequence into a single bitmap file.

lets you save the tiles as a single bitmap file. Figure 10.5 shows the Save Animation dialog box. You can choose the type of file to save; AnimStrip as BMP is what you want.

Although I don't have room here to fully explore the many features of this terrific sprite animation program, I encourage you to experiment and learn how to use it. Pro Motion can be your close companion while working on a sprite-based game.

Getting a Handle on Animation Sequences

After you have exported an animation sequence to a file, the trick is to get a handle on animating the sprite correctly. Storing all the frames of animation inside a single file makes it easier to use the animation in your program. However, it doesn't necessarily make it easier to set up; you have to deal with the animation looping around at a specific point, rather than looping through all 64 frames. I have animated the dragon sprite by setting the TSPRITE.StartFrame variable to a specific frame depending on the user's keyboard input. That way the dragon flies around on the screen in any of the north, south, east, or west

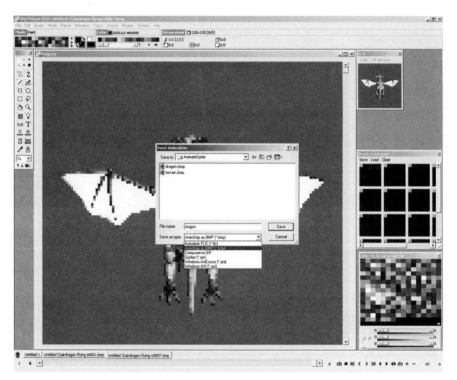

Figure 10.5 Saving a sprite animation sequence into a single bitmap file.

directions. Although the sprite images are available for all eight directions (including northwest, northeast, southwest, and southeast), I chose to stick to the four cardinal directions to keep the code simpler for this first example program in sprite animation. Here is how I handle the sprite based on user input:

```
Select Case KeyCode
    Case KEY_UP
        dragonSpr.StartFrame = 0
        dragonSpr.CurrentFrame = 0
        dragonSpr.SpeedX = 0
        dragonSpr.SpeedY = -DRAGONSPEED
    Case KEY_RIGHT
        dragonSpr.StartFrame = 16
        dragonSpr.CurrentFrame = 16
        dragonSpr.SpeedX = DRAGONSPEED
        dragonSpr.SpeedY = 0
```

```
    Case KEY_DOWN
        dragonSpr.StartFrame = 32
        dragonSpr.CurrentFrame = 32
        dragonSpr.SpeedX = 0
        dragonSpr.SpeedY = DRAGONSPEED
    Case KEY_LEFT
        dragonSpr.StartFrame = 48
        dragonSpr.CurrentFrame = 48
        dragonSpr.SpeedX = -DRAGONSPEED
        dragonSpr.SpeedY = 0
End Select
```

Note how this section of code handles both the movement and animation of the dragon sprite at the same time. This is usually the case, which is why these two subjects are being covered together in this chapter. The important part of this code to consider is how I set StartFrame to a specific value based on the keyboard input. When the up arrow key is pressed, then the first frame of animation is 0. For the left arrow key (which causes the dragon to move to the left), the first animation frame is 48. This corresponds with the number of frames inside the dragon.bmp file. Take a look at Figure 10.6 for a description of each row of images in this file.

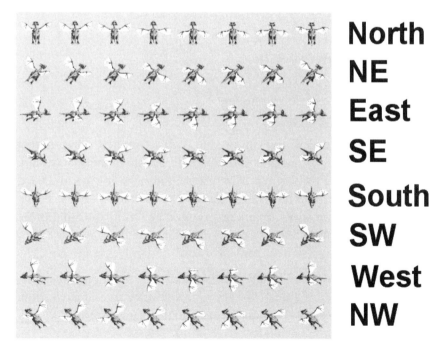

North
NE
East
SE
South
SW
West
NW

Figure 10.6 The dragon bitmap is made up of eight rows of animation.

After these variables have been set in the Form_KeyDown event, you can write a single sub-routine to cause the dragon to animate based on StartFrame:

```
Public Sub AnimateDragon()
    With dragonSpr
        'increment the animation counter
        .AnimCount = .AnimCount + 1

        'has the animation counter waited long enough?
        If .AnimCount > .AnimDelay Then
            .AnimCount = 0

            'okay, go to the next frame
            .CurrentFrame = .CurrentFrame + 1

            'loop through the frames
            If .CurrentFrame > .StartFrame + 7 Then
                .CurrentFrame = .StartFrame
            End If

        End If
    End With

    'draw the dragon sprite
    DrawSprite dragonImg, dragonSpr, &HFFFFFFFF
End Sub
```

The AnimateSprite Program

To demonstrate how sprite animation works, you need to write a complete program that draws a single sprite on the screen, animates it, and makes it possible to move it around. This could be autonomous, where the sprite just moves around randomly or in a fixed direction, but I wanted to demonstrate how user input can be used to direct the sprite. And in this case, since it is a dragon sprite, I thought it would be fun if you could move the dragon yourself. It looks really cool flapping its wings while you control where it goes. Figure 10.7 shows the output of the AnimateSprite program.

This would be an even better demonstration if the background were scrolling at the same time, but I am sticking to one thing at a time! You learn how to draw an animated sprite over the scrolling ground in Chapter 12, "Walking Around in the Game World."

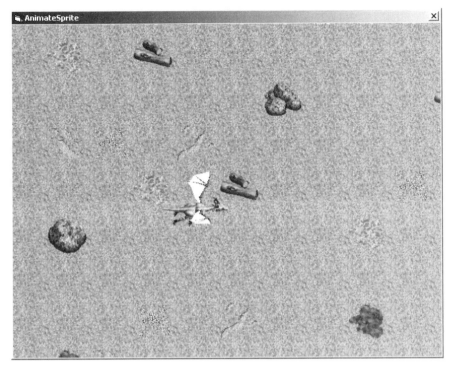

Figure 10.7 The user controls an animated dragon on the screen in the AnimateSprite program.

Creating the New Project

To create the AnimateSprite program, fire up Visual Basic and create a new Standard EXE project like usual. Add the reference to DirectX 8 for Visual Basic Type Library (also like you have done in the last few chapters). You need the DirectX.BAS and Sprite.BAS files from the previous chapter to run the AnimateSprite program, because it depends on these files for the core DirectX and sprite code that you have learned about so far.

The AnimateSprite Source Code

Here is the source code for AnimateSprite. You can load this project off the CD-ROM if you wish; it is located in \sources\chapter10\AnimateSprite. At the very least, copy the terrain.BMP and dragon.BMP files from the CD-ROM to your project folder so you can use the graphics for this program.

```vb
'----------------------------------------------------------
' Visual Basic Game Programming For Teens
' AnimateSprite Source Code File
'----------------------------------------------------------

Option Explicit
Option Base 0

'Windows API functions and structures
Private Declare Function GetTickCount Lib "kernel32" () As Long

Const C_BLACK As Long = &H0

Const KEY_ESC As Integer = 27
Const KEY_LEFT As Integer = 37
Const KEY_UP As Integer = 38
Const KEY_RIGHT As Integer = 39
Const KEY_DOWN As Integer = 40

'program constants
Const SCREENWIDTH As Long = 640
Const SCREENHEIGHT As Long = 480
Const FULLSCREEN As Boolean = False

Const DRAGONSPEED As Integer = 4

Dim dragonSpr As TSPRITE
Dim dragonImg As Direct3DTexture8

Dim terrain As Direct3DSurface8
Dim backbuffer As Direct3DSurface8

Private Sub Form_Load()

    'set up the main form
    Form1.Caption = "AnimateSprite"
    Form1.KeyPreview = True
    Form1.ScaleMode = 3
    Form1.width = Screen.TwipsPerPixelX * (SCREENWIDTH + 12)
    Form1.height = Screen.TwipsPerPixelY * (SCREENHEIGHT + 30)
    Form1.Show
```

```
'initialize Direct3D
InitDirect3D Me.hwnd, SCREENWIDTH, SCREENHEIGHT, FULLSCREEN

'get the back buffer
Set backbuffer = d3ddev.GetBackBuffer(0, D3DBACKBUFFER_TYPE_MONO)

'load the background image
Set terrain = LoadSurface(App.Path & "\terrain.bmp", 640, 480)
If terrain Is Nothing Then
    MsgBox "Error loading bitmap"
    Shutdown
End If

'load the dragon sprite
Set dragonImg = LoadTexture(d3ddev, App.Path & "\dragon.bmp")

'initialize the dragon sprite
InitSprite d3ddev, dragonSpr
With dragonSpr
    .FramesPerRow = 8
    .FrameCount = 8
    .DirX = 0
    .CurrentFrame = 0
    .AnimDelay = 2
    .width = 128
    .height = 128
    .ScaleFactor = 1
    .x = 150
    .y = 100
End With

Dim start As Long
start = GetTickCount()

'start main game loop
Do While True

    If GetTickCount - start > 25 Then

        'draw the background
        DrawSurface terrain, 0, 0
```

```
                    'start rendering
                    d3ddev.BeginScene

                    'move the dragon
                    MoveDragon

                    'animate the dragon
                    AnimateDragon

                    'stop rendering
                    d3ddev.EndScene

                    'draw the back buffer to the screen
                    d3ddev.Present ByVal 0, ByVal 0, 0, ByVal 0

                    start = GetTickCount
                    DoEvents
                End If


        Loop
End Sub

Public Sub MoveDragon()
    With dragonSpr
        .x = .x + .SpeedX
        If .x < 0 Then
            .x = 0
            .SpeedX = 0
        End If
        If .x > SCREENWIDTH - .width Then
            .x = SCREENWIDTH - .width - 1
            .SpeedX = 0
        End If

        .y = .y + .SpeedY
        If .y < 0 Then
            .y = 0
            .SpeedX = 0
        End If
```

```
        If .y > SCREENHEIGHT - .height Then
            .y = SCREENHEIGHT - .height - 1
            .SpeedX = 0
        End If
    End With

End Sub

Public Sub AnimateDragon()

    With dragonSpr
        'increment the animation counter
        .AnimCount = .AnimCount + 1

        'has the animation counter waited long enough?
        If .AnimCount > .AnimDelay Then
            .AnimCount = 0

            'okay, go to the next frame
            .CurrentFrame = .CurrentFrame + 1

            'loop through the frames
            If .CurrentFrame > .StartFrame + 7 Then
                .CurrentFrame = .StartFrame
            End If

        End If
    End With

    'draw the dragon sprite
    DrawSprite dragonImg, dragonSpr, &HFFFFFFFF

End Sub

Public Sub DrawSurface(ByRef source As Direct3DSurface8, _
ByVal x As Long, ByVal y As Long)
    Dim r As DxVBLibA.RECT
    Dim point As DxVBLibA.point
    Dim desc As D3DSURFACE_DESC

    source.GetDesc desc
```

```
    'set dimensions of the source image
    r.Left = x
    r.Top = y
    r.Right = x + desc.width
    r.Bottom = y + desc.height

    'set the destination point
    point.x = 0
    point.y = 0

    'draw the scroll window
    d3ddev.CopyRects source, r, 1, backbuffer, point

End Sub

Private Sub Form_Unload(Cancel As Integer)
    Shutdown
End Sub

Private Sub Form_KeyDown(KeyCode As Integer, Shift As Integer)

    Select Case KeyCode
        Case KEY_UP
            dragonSpr.StartFrame = 0
            dragonSpr.CurrentFrame = 0
            dragonSpr.SpeedX = 0
            dragonSpr.SpeedY = -DRAGONSPEED

        Case KEY_RIGHT
            dragonSpr.StartFrame = 16
            dragonSpr.CurrentFrame = 16
            dragonSpr.SpeedX = DRAGONSPEED
            dragonSpr.SpeedY = 0

        Case KEY_DOWN
            dragonSpr.StartFrame = 32
            dragonSpr.CurrentFrame = 32
            dragonSpr.SpeedX = 0
            dragonSpr.SpeedY = DRAGONSPEED
```

```
        Case KEY_LEFT
            dragonSpr.StartFrame = 48
            dragonSpr.CurrentFrame = 48
            dragonSpr.SpeedX = -DRAGONSPEED
            dragonSpr.SpeedY = 0

        Case KEY_ESC
            Shutdown
    End Select

End Sub
```

Level Up

This chapter rounded out the two-part discussion of sprites by explaining how to move and animate sprites on the screen. You learned a few tricks that can be done with the awesome sprite editing program Pro Motion, and learned how to use the key variables in the sprite handler structure to track a sprite's position and animation frames, even when dealing with a large animation sequence. The ability to incorporate many more sprites in a program is simply a matter of creating additional sprite handlers and then drawing them.

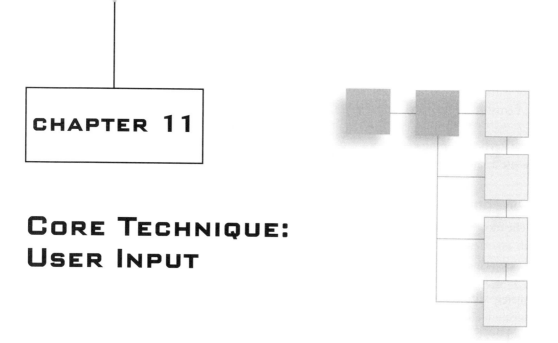

CHAPTER 11

CORE TECHNIQUE: USER INPUT

I n years past, programming the input devices for a game was an enormous task, requiring the programmer to write an interrupt service routine (often in assembly language) to handle multiple key presses, while mouse and joystick input required custom code depending on the make and model of input device. Today, DirectX is the dominant game development library in the world, and with it comes DirectInput, a comprehensive library for programming input devices such as the keyboard, mouse, and joystick. This chapter explores DirectInput in detail, providing all the code you need to handle the user input for a game written with Visual Basic. From a simple keyboard interface to multibutton mouse routines to an advanced joystick handler with support for digital buttons and analog inputs, this chapter should give you all the tools you need to handle the user input needs of any game. By necessity, this chapter leans on the complex side, because I want to completely cover DirectInput quickly. You will put it to use in later chapters.

Here is a breakdown of the major topics in this chapter:

- Choosing the best input device for a game
- Programming the keyboard
- Programming the mouse
- Programming the joystick

Choosing the Best Input Device for a Game

Visual Basic has built-in support for detecting mouse and keyboard events, but provides no support for game controllers, such as flight sticks, gamepads, and other types of joysticks. It is definitely possible to write a game without joystick support by using just the standard events that are part of a VB form. However, joysticks are becoming more popular as games are ported from advanced, next-generation video game consoles like the Microsoft Xbox, which features multifunction controllers with digital and analog inputs. Let me introduce you to DirectInput, the DirectX component that provides an interface to the keyboard, mouse, and joystick. To develop your understanding of DirectInput, you write a sample program to test each type of input device.

DirectInput Support

The most significant benefit to using DirectInput for keyboard, mouse, and joystick input in a game is that there is no need to use a VB form to detect input events (at least for the keyboard and mouse). There is the additional problem of transforming mouse movement events into a graphical, full-screen DirectX program, which may be running in a completely different resolution than the Windows desktop, which is where the VB form is located. Obviously, if you track a mouse click somewhere on the primary form in a game, and the game is actually running at a resolution of 320 × 240 pixels (just as an example), the mouse input events are unlikely to even show up! (Or more likely, such events have to be converted to the resolution being used by DirectX.)

Different types of games are suited for different input devices. *Real-time strategy (RTS)* games are not well suited for joysticks because such games involve detailed control (often called *micromanagement*) over the game that is only possible with the mouse.

The keyboard and mouse combination is the absolute best solution for *first-person shooter (FPS)* games like Doom 3 and Half-Life 2. As I'm sure most gamers have learned, any other form of input just does not work well enough in an FPS game. Sure, you can use an advanced joystick in an FPS game, but you aren't likely to score anywhere near the level of a player who is adept with a keyboard and mouse. The reason? A joystick is a single device. Even with multiple analog sticks and digital buttons, a joystick does not have the precision of a mouse pointer on the screen for targeting. The ability to quickly run, jump, and crouch by pressing closely coupled keys along with aiming and firing with a mouse simply cannot be beat.

But how does that relate to an RPG such as Celtic Crusader? I'm a big fan of console games, such as Fire Emblem for the Game Boy Advance. Games like this work really well with just a simple directional pad (D-pad) and a couple of buttons. You should keep this in mind when you are designing a PC game: Simpler is almost always better.

It is vitally important that you consider the best form of user input for any game you develop and then optimize the game for that form of input. Of course you must also provide an alternate means of input for those players who are not adept with your own favorite devices. No matter the argument, you should provide at least the two primary forms of input: keyboard and mouse. The keyboard can be used just like the joystick for player movement, while the mouse might be used in various parts of the game to select inventory and so on. Figure 11.1 shows you how the input devices break down.

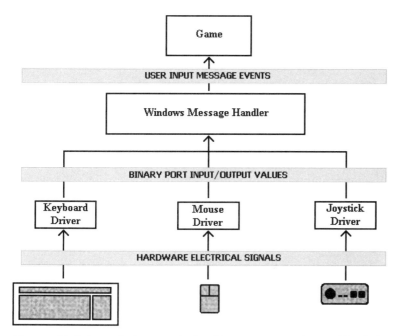

Figure 11.1 Input devices use device drivers to communicate with Windows and DirectX.

Understanding Keyboard Input

Keyboards have been around since the 1950s, at the dawn of the computer revolution. Supporting a keyboard might seem like a given until you actually start to consider how the keyboard should be utilized in a game. The keyboard is always available, while other devices like joysticks are not always available. Therefore, regardless of your input device of choice, you *must* support a keyboard in every game, at least minimally.

Most games provide a means to quickly end the game by pressing a simple key combination. This has been somewhat lacking in games of late, but is a feature I highly recommend. Back in the MS-DOS days, it was common for games to use Alt+X, Alt+Q, Ctrl+X, or Ctrl+Q to end the game (which might be precluded with a pop-up message asking for verification).

No matter how awesome you think your game is, and no matter if you believe users will just leave your game running 24/7, you must realize that some players try out the game and then uninstall it 5 minutes later with utmost urgency. The tastes of players vary widely. There are some players who think Doom 3 is the worst game ever, while at the same time believing that Pac-Man is the best game ever.

DirectX usually runs in full-screen mode, so you should provide a quick method for ending the game in a hurry, and be sure to use a common key combination to at least bring up a menu. (I recommend the Escape key.)

Understanding Mouse Input

The mouse is another user input device that has been around for decades and must be considered required hardware—something you can count on being present in a computer system. Building a game entirely around mouse input is acceptable, as long as basic keyboard functionality is provided as a supplement for power users (gamers who are experts with a game and prefer to use quick keyboard shortcut keys).

It is often tedious to use a mouse for absolutely everything in a game when shortcut keys may also be used. Power users demand it, so it is a good idea to provide at least minimal keyboard support, even if you plan to target the mouse as the primary means of input for your game. If you so choose, you may exclude keyboard input from such a game. I don't know anyone who uses a joystick to play Age of Mythology (in fact, I'm pretty sure the game does not support a joystick), but it would be novel to support a joystick in the games you develop as a matter of course.

Understanding Joystick Input

Joysticks have become extremely popular forms of game input in recent years, again due to the proliferation of consoles. With gaming at the top of software development in the computer industry and as the primary sales point for hardware companies, it is understandable how joysticks have become so popular. Quite often a game is ported from a console such as the Xbox to the PC (and vice versa), with the natural result of a game controller being the primary form of input.

Looking for the Input Devices

DirectInput provides a common interface to literally hundreds of different input devices that might be installed on a system. In the past, a game programmer would have needed to write a custom interface for each device separately. Most books and tutorials on DirectX (including the documentation that comes with DirectX) suggest that you enumerate the devices on a system before using them. The reasoning behind this is that DirectX components detect all installed devices on a system; it is then up to you to determine which device to use.

In every case I have seen, the default device is the correct one. Is there really a need to enumerate the keyboard and mouse? Of course not! I follow the same logic with joystick code. The only important thing to consider in a Visual Basic game is that a joystick exists. Any additional game controllers in a system are simply ignored.

Programming the Keyboard

DirectInput is the DirectX component responsible for providing a common interface for user input devices, allowing you to write the same code for many different types of devices (present or future). Like the other components of DirectX (such as Direct3D), Direct-Input is included when you install the DirectX runtime library.

The keyboard is definitely the easiest device to program with DirectInput, because it really does nothing but provide an event when a key is pressed and released. Multiple, simultaneous key presses are supported, allowing you to move a character (or space ship, for example) while shooting. Some games are naturally easier to control with a keyboard when a joystick is not available. Most arcade games do not work well with a mouse. There is a natural tendency to use two hands in an arcade game (which is most likely engendered through arcade or console experience).

The arrow keys and spacebar have been used in countless games as the primary means of user input. In a typical example like Asteroids, the left and right arrow keys would be used to rotate the ship. The up arrow key applies thrust to move the ship. The spacebar is a good candidate for firing a weapon.

Detecting DirectInput Keyboard Events

DirectInput uses a callback procedure for mouse and joystick events, but not for keyboard events. That makes programming the keyboard with DirectInput straightforward. I go over the most difficult part of setting up DirectInput and creating the keyboard interface here, so you understand how DirectInput works when you get to the mouse and joystick parts later in this chapter. There are four primary objects and structures needed to handle the keyboard:

```
Dim dx As New DirectX8
Dim dinput As DirectInput8
Dim diDevice As DirectInputDevice8
Dim diState As DIKEYBOARDSTATE
```

The DirectInput8 object handles the creation of DirectInputDevice8 objects through the CreateDevice function, which is called like this:

```
Set diDevice = dinput.CreateDevice("GUID_SysKeyboard")
```

The GUID_SysKeyboard string is an identifier that tells DirectInput to create a device interface to the system keyboard. After that is done, you must describe the properties of the keyboard device and then acquire it for exclusive use in your program:

```
diDevice.SetCommonDataFormat DIFORMAT_KEYBOARD
diDevice.SetCooperativeLevel Me.hWnd, _
    DISCL_BACKGROUND Or DISCL_NONEXCLUSIVE
diDevice.Acquire
```

The SetCommonDataFormat procedure provides this device object with an identifier that describes a keyboard. SetCooperativeLevel tells the device to acquire input for a specific program window. Finally, the Acquire procedure acquires the keyboard for exclusive use in your program.

In order to detect key presses, you have to check the keyboard status with a procedure called GetDeviceStateKeyboard, which returns data inside a DIKEYBOARDSTATE variable:

```
diDevice.GetDeviceStateKeyboard diState
```

Once you have filled diState with the state of all the keys, you can then check for keys that are being pressed. A single member of DIKEYBOARDSTATE, key, holds the status of every key on the keyboard as a byte. The definition of the key array looks like this:

```
key(0 To 255) As Byte
```

To scan the keyboard, you can loop through this key array and see which keys have been pressed (in which case the value is something other than 0). Most keyboards have 101 keys or fewer, so it seems logical that you might not need to scan every single element of this array. Unfortunately, the key codes do not map sequentially into this array, but are scattered throughout the array. Most of the consecutive keys (A, B, C, and so on) are sequential in the array, but many other keys (such as Page Up, Page Down, Home, and End) appear toward the end of the array.

Therefore, loop through the entire array to scan the entire keyboard. The following snippet scans through the keys and displays the scan code of each key that is currently being pressed to the Immediate window:

```
'scan the entire list for pressed keys
For n = 0 To 255
    If diState.Key(n) <> 0 Then
        Debug.Print "Key " & n & " was pressed"
    End If
Next
```

Testing Keyboard Input

To demonstrate how to write a keyboard handler using DirectInput, I walk you through a sample program called KeyboardTest. This simple program checks for key presses and then prints out the name of the key using VB's Immediate window. This window, which pops up at the bottom of the editor, displays messages that you can print using the Debug.Print command. An empty form pops up when you run the KeyboardTest program, but the real action takes place in the Immediate window, as shown in Figure 11.2.

The first section of the KeyboardTest program includes declarations for API functions, program user interface controls, and program variables:

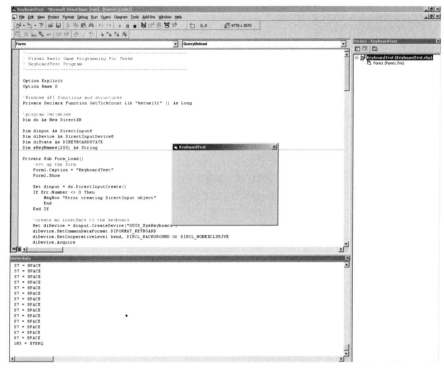

Figure 11.2 The KeyboardTest program displays key events in the Immediate window.

note

The KeyboardTest program *must* be run from within Visual Basic, because the only output in this program is displayed in the Immediate window in VB. You can open this window while the program is running by pressing Ctrl+G, or by using the View menu (although it opens by default when you run a program by pressing F5). Compiling this program to an executable wouldn't make sense because there's no output beyond the Immediate window. I just want to give you a short, quick example program that explains *just* how to detect DirectInput keyboard input.

```
'-------------------------------------------------------
' Visual Basic Game Programming For Teens
' KeyboardTest Program
'-------------------------------------------------------

Option Explicit
Option Base 0
```

```
'Windows API functions and structures
Private Declare Function GetTickCount Lib "kernel32" () As Long

'program variables
Dim dx As New DirectX8
Dim dinput As DirectInput8
Dim diDevice As DirectInputDevice8
Dim diState As DIKEYBOARDSTATE
Dim sKeyNames(255) As String
```

The next section of code for KeyboardTest includes `Form_Load` and `Form_QueryUnload`. `Form_Load` initializes DirectX and `DirectInput`, creates the keyboard interface, and initializes the keyname array.

```
Private Sub Form_Load()
    'set up the form
    Form1.Caption = "KeyboardTest"
    Form1.Show

    Set dinput = dx.DirectInputCreate()
    If Err.Number <> 0 Then
        MsgBox "Error creating DirectInput object"
        End
    End If

    'create an interface to the keyboard
    Set diDevice = dinput.CreateDevice("GUID_SysKeyboard")
    diDevice.SetCommonDataFormat DIFORMAT_KEYBOARD
    diDevice.SetCooperativeLevel hwnd, DISCL_BACKGROUND Or DISCL_NONEXCLUSIVE
    diDevice.Acquire

    'initialize the keyboard value array
    InitKeyNames

    'main game loop
    Do While True
        Check_Keyboard
        DoEvents
    Loop
End Sub

Private Sub Form_QueryUnload(Cancel As Integer, UnloadMode As Integer)
    Shutdown
End Sub
```

The next two procedures in the program listing are Check_Keyboard and Shutdown. The Check_Keyboard procedure, which is called from Form_Main by the game loop, retrieves the keyboard state array and then scans the array for active keys, which it then adds to the List-Box to show all the keys currently being pressed. Shutdown is a standard procedure in the sample programs so far and simply cleans up before ending the program.

```
Public Sub Check_Keyboard()
    Dim n As Long

    'get the list of pressed keys
    diDevice.GetDeviceStateKeyboard diState

    'scan the entire list for pressed keys
    For n = 0 To 255
        If diState.Key(n) > 0 Then
            Debug.Print n & " = " & sKeyNames(n)
        End If
    Next

    'check for ESC key
    If diState.Key(1) > 0 Then Shutdown

End Sub


Public Sub Shutdown()
    diDevice.Unacquire
    Set diDevice = Nothing
    Set dinput = Nothing
    Set dx = Nothing
    End
End Sub
```

The InitKeyNames subroutine sets up a string array with the names of the keys. Since DirectInput provides actual key codes for the physical location of keys (rather than scan codes or ASCII codes), this program is useful any time you need to check the code of a particular key. See, this is a multipurpose program! In addition to teaching how to program DirectInput, this program is also a useful keyboard code utility.

```
Private Sub InitKeyNames()
    sKeyNames(1) = "ESC"
    sKeyNames(2) = "1"
    sKeyNames(3) = "2"
    sKeyNames(4) = "3"
```

```
sKeyNames(5) = "4"
sKeyNames(6) = "5"
sKeyNames(7) = "6"
sKeyNames(8) = "7"
sKeyNames(9) = "8"
sKeyNames(10) = "9"
sKeyNames(11) = "0"
sKeyNames(12) = "-"
sKeyNames(13) = "="
sKeyNames(14) = "BACKSPACE"
sKeyNames(15) = "TAB"
sKeyNames(16) = "Q"
sKeyNames(17) = "W"
sKeyNames(18) = "E"
sKeyNames(19) = "R"
sKeyNames(20) = "T"
sKeyNames(21) = "Y"
sKeyNames(22) = "U"
sKeyNames(23) = "I"
sKeyNames(24) = "O"
sKeyNames(25) = "P"
sKeyNames(26) = "["
sKeyNames(27) = " ]"
sKeyNames(28) = "ENTER"
sKeyNames(29) = "LCTRL"
sKeyNames(30) = "A"
sKeyNames(31) = "S"
sKeyNames(32) = "D"
sKeyNames(33) = "F"
sKeyNames(34) = "G"
sKeyNames(35) = "H"
sKeyNames(36) = "J"
sKeyNames(37) = "K"
sKeyNames(38) = "L"
sKeyNames(39) = ";"
sKeyNames(40) = "'"
sKeyNames(41) = "`"
sKeyNames(42) = "LSHIFT"
sKeyNames(43) = "\"
sKeyNames(44) = "Z"
sKeyNames(45) = "X"
sKeyNames(46) = "C"
```

```
sKeyNames(47) = "V"
sKeyNames(48) = "B"
sKeyNames(49) = "N"
sKeyNames(50) = "M"
sKeyNames(51) = ","
sKeyNames(52) = "."
sKeyNames(53) = "/"
sKeyNames(54) = "RSHIFT"
sKeyNames(55) = "NUMPAD*"
sKeyNames(56) = "LALT"
sKeyNames(57) = "SPACE"
sKeyNames(58) = "CAPSLOCK"
sKeyNames(59) = "F1"
sKeyNames(60) = "F2"
sKeyNames(61) = "F3"
sKeyNames(62) = "F4"
sKeyNames(63) = "F5"
sKeyNames(64) = "F6"
sKeyNames(65) = "F7"
sKeyNames(66) = "F8"
sKeyNames(67) = "F9"
sKeyNames(68) = "F10"
sKeyNames(69) = "NUMLOCK"
sKeyNames(70) = "SCRLLOCK"
sKeyNames(71) = "NUMPAD7"
sKeyNames(72) = "NUMPAD8"
sKeyNames(73) = "NUMPAD9"
sKeyNames(74) = "NUMPAD-"
sKeyNames(75) = "NUMPAD4"
sKeyNames(76) = "NUMPAD5"
sKeyNames(77) = "NUMPAD6"
sKeyNames(78) = "NUMPAD+"
sKeyNames(79) = "NUMPAD1"
sKeyNames(80) = "NUMPAD2"
sKeyNames(81) = "NUMPAD3"
sKeyNames(82) = "NUMPAD0"
sKeyNames(83) = "NUMPAD."
sKeyNames(87) = "F11"
sKeyNames(88) = "F12"
sKeyNames(86) = "F13"
sKeyNames(84) = "F14"
sKeyNames(85) = "F15"
```

```
        sKeyNames(91) = "NUMPAD,"
        sKeyNames(116) = "PAUSE"
        sKeyNames(156) = "NUMPADENTER"
        sKeyNames(157) = "RCONTROL"
        sKeyNames(181) = "NUMPAD/"
        sKeyNames(183) = "SYSRQ"
        sKeyNames(184) = "RALT"
        sKeyNames(199) = "HOME"
        sKeyNames(200) = "UP"
        sKeyNames(201) = "PAGE UP"
        sKeyNames(203) = "LEFT"
        sKeyNames(205) = "RIGHT"
        sKeyNames(207) = "END"
        sKeyNames(208) = "DOWN"
        sKeyNames(209) = "PAGE DN"
        sKeyNames(210) = "INSERT"
        sKeyNames(211) = "DELETE"
        sKeyNames(219) = "LWIN"
        sKeyNames(220) = "RWIN"
        sKeyNames(221) = "APPS"
End Sub
```

That's the end of the KeyboardTest program. Run the program. If all goes well, when you press and hold multiple keys, the program lists those keys (along with DirectInput keyboard scan codes) in the Immediate window. The only drawback to this program is that it is useless when compiled into an .EXE file. You want to just run this program from within VB.

Programming the Mouse

Programming a mouse interface with DirectInput is not difficult at all, because DirectInput abstracts the mouse's motion. DirectInput abstracts the mouse events specifically for game programming, providing relative motion values for the mouse rather than absolute values. For instance, when tracking the mouse with DirectInput, if you move the mouse slowly to the right, the mouse X position is a small number (usually less than 5), but that number does not increase! When you stop moving the mouse, the X motion returns to 0.

Likewise, moving the mouse to the left generates a negative X motion, which returns to 0 when you stop moving the mouse. The process works in the same manner for vertical Y motion. The fascinating aspect of the DirectInput mouse handler is that the faster you move the mouse, the higher the X and Y motion values.

note

When you stop moving the mouse, `DirectInput` reports the mouse motion values to be 0 for both the X and Y axes.

Suppose you are writing a block-bashing game where the player controls a paddle at the bottom of the screen. By looking at the mouse motion values, you can move the paddle left or right using the mouse motion values *directly*—that is, without having to massage the numbers first! If you use VB events like `Form_MouseMove`, you have to convert the absolute position of the mouse into a relative motion value. `DirectInput` handles that automatically.

note

The MouseTest program also uses the Immediate window to display that status information about the mouse, including movement and button presses. This was intentional to keep the source code as short as possible so you will be able to easily paste it into your own games without wading through any other code.

This brings up a question: How do you figure out where the mouse is located on the screen without absolute values? The answer is that you must track the mouse pointer just like you would move a sprite on the screen. You have to make sure the pointer doesn't go off the edge of the screen, and you update the pointer position based on the mouse's motion. The hardware mouse cursor is not visible, so it is up to you to create and display a cursor using a simple sprite. You also have to keep track of the absolute position of the cursor (which is why a sprite is a good solution).

tip

One thing to keep in mind is that you should draw the mouse cursor after you have finished drawing all the other objects in the game. That way the mouse cursor always appears on top of the other images in the game.

Mouse Movement

The mouse handler works by using a `DirectXEvent8_DXCallback` callback procedure, which is required when you include the `DirectXEvent8` interface in the program. You can do that by including a single line of code at the top of the program:

```
Implements DirectXEvent8
```

That line of code tells your program to use a specific interface that DirectX understands (and which allows DirectX to send events directly into a VB program). In order to track mouse movement you need to look at the DirectXEvent8_DXCallback procedure. This procedure is detailed later in this chapter when I discuss joystick handling, so I only skim over it at this point. What I am more interested in showing you right now is how to call mouse events from within the callback procedure.

Look for two DirectInput constants inside the callback procedure when you need to read the mouse's relative position. These constants are DIMOFS_X and DIMOFS_Y.

Here is how you might write the code to detect mouse movement:

```
Case DIMOFS_X
    lMouseX = lMouseX + diDeviceData(n).lData
    Debug.Print "MouseX = " & lMouseX

Case DIMOFS_Y
    lMouseY = lMouseY + diDeviceData(n).lData
    Debug.Print "MouseY = " & lMouseY
```

This code makes more sense with all of the supporting code that goes along with it. However, it does demonstrate how the mouse movement values are relative. Look how the lMouseX and lMouseY variables are updated: These variables are incremented by the mouse motion values, rather than set directly to them! That is the key to converting relative mouse motion to absolute mouse position.

Mouse Buttons

The mouse button events are reported by DirectInput with the DIMOFS_BUTTONx events. Simply replace the x at the end of the constant with 0–7 to detect up to seven different button press and release events (in case you happen to have a very complex mouse!).

Here is how you write the code to detect the primary mouse-button press and release events:

```
Case DIMOFS_BUTTON0
    If diDeviceData(n).lData > 0 Then
        Debug.Print "Button 1 pressed"
    Else
        Debug.Print "Button 1 released"
    End If
```

I know this snippet of code doesn't make much sense without the Select . . . End Select statements wrapped around it, but I show you the whole procedure soon. Note that the button events are based on 0 for the first button.

Testing Mouse Input

Now put all of this fragmented knowledge into a cohesive program. The MouseTest program is interesting: It is a windowed program that captures the mouse. When DirectInput captures the mouse, it hides the mouse cursor. The result is that there is no way to click anywhere on the screen while this program is running! Rather, mouse events are completely captured by the MouseTest program, including mouse movement and button click events.

Figure 11.3 shows the MouseTest program running. If you think these programs are cheap in some way because nothing is really happening, then just wait until Chapter 12, "Walking Around in the Game World," for a complete demonstration of user input.

The MouseTest program is a Standard EXE project with a reference to the DirectX 8 for Visual Basic Type Library. This first section of code includes the DirectX objects and structures and the program variables.

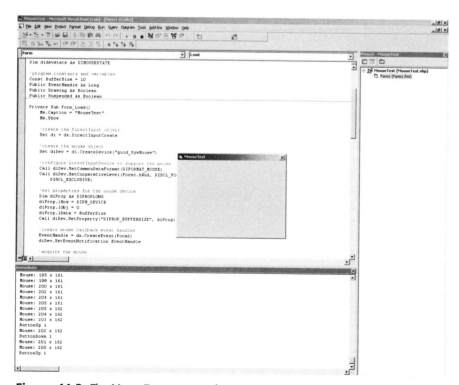

Figure 11.3 The MouseTest program demonstrates the mouse support in `DirectInput`.

```
'-------------------------------------------------------
' Visual Basic Game Programming For Teens
' MouseTest Program
'-------------------------------------------------------
Option Explicit
Option Base 0

Implements DirectXEvent8

'DirectX objects and structures
Public dx As New DirectX8
Public di As DirectInput8
Public diDev As DirectInputDevice8
Dim didevstate As DIMOUSESTATE

'program constants and variables
Const BufferSize = 10
Public EventHandle As Long
Public Drawing As Boolean
Public Suspended As Boolean
```

The Form_Load event sets up the program by creating the DirectInput and mouse objects.
Next, the mouse device properties are set and the event handler is created (which activates
the callback procedure). Finally, the mouse device is acquired for exclusive use.

```
Private Sub Form_Load()
    Me.Caption = "MouseTest"
    Me.Show

    'create the DirectInput object
    Set di = dx.DirectInputCreate

    'create the mouse object
    Set diDev = di.CreateDevice("guid_SysMouse")

    'configure DirectInputDevice to support the mouse
    Call diDev.SetCommonDataFormat(DIFORMAT_MOUSE)
    Call diDev.SetCooperativeLevel(Form1.hWnd, DISCL_FOREGROUND Or _
        DISCL_EXCLUSIVE)

    'set properties for the mouse device
    Dim diProp As DIPROPLONG
    diProp.lHow = DIPH_DEVICE
```

```
    diProp.lObj = 0
    diProp.lData = BufferSize
    Call diDev.SetProperty("DIPROP_BUFFERSIZE", diProp)

    'create mouse callback event handler
    EventHandle = dx.CreateEvent(Form1)
    diDev.SetEventNotification EventHandle

    'acquire the mouse
    diDev.Acquire
End Sub
```

The Form_KeyDown event simply checks for the ESC key, at which point it ends the program. The Shutdown subroutine is called by other routines to actually clean up and then end the program.

```
Private Sub Form_KeyDown(KeyCode As Integer, Shift As Integer)
    If KeyCode = 27 Then Shutdown
End Sub


Private Sub Shutdown()
    On Local Error Resume Next
    dx.DestroyEvent EventHandle
    Set diDev = Nothing
    Set di = Nothing
    Set dx = Nothing
    End
End Sub
```

DirectXEvent8_DXCallback is the callback procedure that reports the mouse events. This procedure shows the complete mouse handling code that I briefly touched upon earlier, and actually calls the mouse events that were shown earlier.

```
Private Sub DirectXEvent8_DXCallback(ByVal eventid As Long)
    Dim diDeviceData(1 To BufferSize) As DIDEVICEOBJECTDATA
    Static lMouseX As Long
    Static lMouseY As Long
    Static lOldSeq As Long
    Dim n As Long

    'loop through events
    For n = 1 To diDev.GetDeviceData(diDeviceData, 0)
        Select Case diDeviceData(n).lOfs
            Case DIMOFS_X
                lMouseX = lMouseX + diDeviceData(n).lData
```

```
    If lMouseX < 0 Then lMouseX = 0
    If lMouseX >= Form1.ScaleWidth Then
        lMouseX = Form1.ScaleWidth - 1
    End If

    If lOldSeq <> diDeviceData(n).lSequence Then
        Debug.Print "MouseMove: " & lMouseX & " x " & lMouseY
        lOldSeq = diDeviceData(n).lSequence
    Else
        lOldSeq = 0
    End If

Case DIMOFS_Y
    lMouseY = lMouseY + diDeviceData(n).lData
    If lMouseY < 0 Then lMouseY = 0
    If lMouseY >= Form1.ScaleHeight Then
        lMouseY = Form1.ScaleHeight - 1
    End If

    If lOldSeq <> diDeviceData(n).lSequence Then
        Debug.Print "Mouse: " & lMouseX & " x " & lMouseY
        lOldSeq = diDeviceData(n).lSequence
    Else
        lOldSeq = 0
    End If

Case DIMOFS_BUTTON0
    If diDeviceData(n).lData > 0 Then
        Debug.Print "ButtonDown 1"
    Else
        Debug.Print "ButtonUp 1"
    End If

Case DIMOFS_BUTTON1
    If diDeviceData(n).lData > 0 Then
        Debug.Print "ButtonDown 2"
    Else
        Debug.Print "ButtonUp 2"
    End If
```

```
        Case DIMOFS_BUTTON2
            If diDeviceData(n).lData > 0 Then
                Debug.Print "ButtonDown 3"
            Else
                Debug.Print "ButtonUp 3"
            End If


        End Select
    Next n
End Sub
```

That's the end of the MouseTest program! Go ahead and run it now. Remember that you can end the program by hitting the Escape key, since the mouse is not visible while the program is running. You can move the mouse around and press buttons to see how the program reports mouse input.

Programming the Joystick

What is a fast-paced arcade game without joystick support? Joysticks are suitably named because they add an enormous amount of fun factor to a game. Some games (such as an RTS game) are obviously not designed to support a joystick, but many games are designed to use a joystick, and such games are difficult to play with a keyboard or mouse. One such genre is the *role-playing game (RPG)*; rather, it is the controller or gamepad that works well with an RPG.

Joysticks range in price from $5 gamepads to $200 flight sticks with throttle and pedal controls. The best option is usually something closer to the low end of the pricing spectrum, since some very nice joysticks and gamepads are available—with force feedback—for a very affordable price. Some devices are difficult to categorize and fall somewhere between a joystick and a mouse.

The Microsoft Sidewinder Strategic Commander is one such device. This controller was designed for strategy games, with X and Y axes for scrolling the game map, while the player uses the mouse to manipulate units in the game. The Strategic Commander also includes a multitude of programmable buttons that can invoke macros in a game. For example, most mouse commands in an RTS game include keyboard shortcuts. By programming a sequence of keys into a macro for a button on the Strategic Commander, you could program a single key to perform a complicated task (such as equip a certain weapon from your player's inventory). The Strategic Commander allows you to store such macros in a profile that can be saved and recalled for different games.

Providing joystick support in a game is a decision that you should make early in the design process, because the game should be optimized for the preferred input device in development.

Using DirectInput to Program a Joystick

DirectInput dramatically simplifies joystick programming, making it relatively easy to support a wide variety of joysticks with a single code base. The key to programming a joystick with DirectInput lies with two objects called `DirectInputDevice8` and `DirectInputEnumDevices8`, as well as a structure called `DIDEVCAPS`. These three components provide the functionality to write a joystick handler:

```
Dim diDev As DirectInputDevice8
Dim diDevEnum As DirectInputEnumDevices8
Dim joyCaps As DIDEVCAPS
```

Reading the List of Game Controllers

The first thing you need to do is retrieve a list of available game controllers that are attached to the computer with a `DirectInput` function called `GetDIDevices`:

```
'enumerate the game controllers
Set diDevEnum = di.GetDIDevices(DI8DEVCLASS_GAMECTRL, _
    DIEDFL_ATTACHEDONLY)
```

You can then use the `diDevEnum` variable to see if a joystick is available:

```
If diDevEnum.GetCount = 0 Then
    MsgBox "No joystick could be found"
End If
```

Creating the Joystick Device Object

Once you have determined that a joystick is available, the next step is to create the joystick object, which is a `DirectInputDevice8` object. While `DirectInput` supports multiple joysticks, I show you how to work with the primary joystick attached to the computer, because that is all you are likely to need. Here is the code to create the joystick object:

```
'create the joystick object
Set diDev = di.CreateDevice(diDevEnum.GetItem(1).GetGuidInstance)
diDev.SetCommonDataFormat DIFORMAT_JOYSTICK
diDev.SetCooperativeLevel Me.hWnd, DISCL_BACKGROUND Or _
    DISCL_NONEXCLUSIVE
```

The Callback Procedure

The next step to writing a joystick handler is to set up the event handler and the callback procedure. The event handler is actually returned by the primary DirectX object, rather than the DirectInput object. Any VB program that needs to provide joystick support through DirectInput must implement the DirectX event object at the top of the program source code:

```
Implements DirectXEvent8
```

The actual callback procedure looks like this:

```
Private Sub DirectXEvent8_DXCallback(ByVal eventid As Long)
End Sub
```

To return the event handle for the joystick callback procedure, you can use the DirectX function called CreateEvent. You then pass the value to the DirectInputDevice8 procedure, which is called SetEventNotification. The code looks like this:

```
'create an event handler for the joystick
EventHandle = dx.CreateEvent(Me)
'ask for notification of events
diDev.SetEventNotification EventHandle
```

Detecting Joystick Motion

The key to reading joystick events in the DirectXEvent8_DXCallback procedure is a procedure called GetDeviceStateJoystick (which is a member of DirectInputDevice8). The procedure call looks like this:

```
'retrieve joystick status
Dim js As DIJOYSTATE
diDev.GetDeviceStateJoystick js
```

The DIJOYSTATE structure is filled with status information by this procedure, and this is where you need to look for joystick events. This structure contains values for the analog axes, D-pad, buttons, and sliders. To check on the joystick's analog motion, you can pick up the values for X and Y (with an additional value for the Z axis if you need it). In addition, there is an equivalent RX, RY, and RZ for an alternate analog stick (such as the second stick on a PlayStation 2 Dual-Shock controller, which is available on some PC gamepads now).

Handling Joystick Buttons

The buttons are read from the same DIJOYSTATE structure. Since joysticks come in various shapes and sizes, with anywhere from 1 to over 20 buttons, the button values are stored inside DIJOYSTATE as an enumeration (which looks like an array, for all practical purposes). The number of buttons on a joystick is stored in the DIDEVCAPS structure and is called lButtons. Since the button array is 0-based, use lButtons - 1 when processing the buttons. Here is a code snippet that checks the status of all the buttons on a joystick:

```
For n = 0 To joyCaps.lButtons - 1
    If js.Buttons(n) = 0 Then
        Debug.Print "Button " & n & " was released"
    Else
        Debug.Print "Button " & n & " was pressed"
    End If
Next n
```

Handling Joystick D-Pads

The D-pad is standard equipment on gamepads (note the name), but is not usually found on flight sticks. The DIJOYSTATE structure keeps track of the directional pad buttons in a separate array from the buttons. This array is called POV (which stands for *point of view*, since the D-pad is often used for movement).

Programming the POV buttons is similar to programming regular buttons. The strange thing about the D-pad support, however, is that DirectInput treats it as an array itself and returns the D-pad values as if it is an analog input button rather than a digital button. (Hence, the reason POV is separated from the buttons.) I have personally never seen a joystick or gamepad with two or more D-pads, so I'm not sure why there is an array of POVs available (unless perhaps the DirectInput team has aspirations for the library being used on real military aircraft with all kinds of different controls).

In the following code, note that I'm just using POV(0) to read the default D-pad. I think some joystick models treat the POV inputs as additional sliders for advanced flight simulator games that have a lot of complex controls. But back to the subject at hand—here is some example code to read the D-pad:

```
If js.POV(0) = -1 Then
    Debug.Print "D-pad is centered"
Else
    Debug.Print "D-pad = " & js.POV(0)
End If
```

Testing Joystick Input

Now I walk you through the process of creating a program that handles a joystick with DirectInput. The JoystickTest program is like the previous two programs in this chapter, simply displaying the device input values in the Immediate window using Debug.Print statements to keep the code as simple as possible, allowing you to focus all your attention on the joystick code and nothing else.

Now go over the source code for the JoystickTest program. This program, like usual, is a Standard EXE project with a single form and a reference to the "DirectX 8 for Visual Basic Type Library." The first part of the program includes the DirectX events and objects as well as the program variables.

```
'---------------------------------------------------------
' Visual Basic Game Programming For Teens
' JoystickTest Program
'---------------------------------------------------------


Option Explicit
Option Base 0


Implements DirectXEvent8


'DirectX objects and structures
Dim dx As New DirectX8
Dim di As DirectInput8
Dim diDev As DirectInputDevice8
Dim diDevEnum As DirectInputEnumDevices8
Dim joyCaps As DIDEVCAPS


'keep track of analog stick motion
Dim Analog(1 To 2) As D3DVECTOR


'program variables
Dim EventHandle As Long
```

The Form_Load event sets up the user interface for the JoystickTest program, creates the DirectInput object, initializes the joystick (by calling Joystick_Init), and then starts a small program loop running. Form_KeyDown and Form_QueryUnload are long-time favorites that should now be part of your game programming dictionary, and this section of code also includes Shutdown.

```
Private Sub Form_Load()
    On Local Error Resume Next

    'create the DirectInput object
    Set di = dx.DirectInputCreate()
    If Err.Number <> 0 Then
        MsgBox "Error creating DirectInput object"
        Shutdown
    End If
```

```
    'enumerate the game controllers
    Set diDevEnum = di.GetDIDevices(DI8DEVCLASS_GAMECTRL, DIEDFL_ATTACHEDONLY)
    If Err.Number <> 0 Then
        MsgBox "Error enumerating game controllers"
        Shutdown
    End If

    'check for the presence of a joystick
    If diDevEnum.GetCount = 0 Then
        MsgBox "No joystick could be found"
        Shutdown
    End If

    'initialize the joystick
    Joystick_Init

    'main polling loop
    Do While True
        diDev.Poll
        DoEvents
    Loop
End Sub

Private Sub Form_KeyDown(KeyCode As Integer, Shift As Integer)
    If KeyCode = 27 Then Shutdown
End Sub

Private Sub Form_QueryUnload(Cancel As Integer, UnloadMode As Integer)
    Shutdown
End Sub

Private Sub Shutdown()
    If EventHandle <> 0 Then
        dx.DestroyEvent EventHandle
    End If
    If Not (diDev Is Nothing) Then diDev.Unacquire
    Set diDev = Nothing
    Set di = Nothing
    Set dx = Nothing
    End
End Sub
```

The `Joystick_Init` subroutine sets up the joystick object, creates the callback procedure event, sets the analog stick ranges, and then acquires the joystick for exclusive use by the program. Then the procedure retrieves the joystick properties and displays some interesting information to the Immediate window with `Debug.Print` statements.

```
Private Sub Joystick_Init()
    On Local Error Resume Next

    'see if joystick was already acquired
    If Not diDev Is Nothing Then
      diDev.Unacquire
    End If

    'create the joystick object
    Set diDev = Nothing
    Set diDev = di.CreateDevice(diDevEnum.GetItem(1).GetGuidInstance)
    diDev.SetCommonDataFormat DIFORMAT_JOYSTICK
    diDev.SetCooperativeLevel Me.hWnd, _
        DISCL_BACKGROUND Or DISCL_NONEXCLUSIVE

    'create an event handler for the joystick
    EventHandle = dx.CreateEvent(Me)

    'ask for notification of events
    diDev.SetEventNotification EventHandle

    'set the analog response range
    SetAnalogRanges -1000, 1000

    'acquire joystick for exclusive use
    diDev.Acquire

    'manually poll joystick first time
    DirectXEvent8_DXCallback 0

    'retrieve joystick information
    diDev.GetCapabilities joyCaps

    'display information about the joystick
    Debug.Print diDevEnum.GetItem(1).GetInstanceName
    Debug.Print "Number of axes: " & joyCaps.lAxes
    Debug.Print "Number of buttons: " & joyCaps.lButtons
    Debug.Print "Device type: " & joyCaps.lDevType
```

```
        Debug.Print "Driver version: " & joyCaps.lDriverVersion
        Debug.Print "Time resolution: " & joyCaps.lFFMinTimeResolution
        Debug.Print "Sample period: " & joyCaps.lFFSamplePeriod
        Debug.Print "Firmware revision: " & joyCaps.lFirmwareRevision
        Debug.Print "Hardware revision: " & joyCaps.lHardwareRevision
        Debug.Print "Number of POVs: " & joyCaps.lPOVs
End Sub
```

The SetAnalogRanges subroutine sets up the range of motion for the analog stick (which would be the primary analog input for a flight stick, or may be an analog thumb stick on a gamepad). SetAnalogRanges uses two structures: DIPROPLONG and DIPROPRANGE. Rather than delve into the details of these structures, let me show you how to use.

The *analog range* is the range of values returned when you move the stick and can be as small or as large as you like (within reason). While you may be more comfortable with a range of, say, 0–10,000, I prefer to use a negative range for left or up, and a positive range for right or down on the analog stick. I have set up the range in the JoystickTest program for −1,000–1,000.

SetAnalogRanges also configures the joystick object's dead zone and saturation zone. The *dead zone* is the space at dead center that does not generate movement events; it should be a very small value. The *saturation zone* is the area of motion that is active and thus generates events.

```
Private Sub SetAnalogRanges(ByVal lMin As Long, ByVal lMax As Long)
    Dim DiProp_Dead As DIPROPLONG
    Dim DiProp_Range As DIPROPRANGE
    Dim DiProp_Saturation As DIPROPLONG
    On Local Error Resume Next

    'set range for all axes
    With DiProp_Range
        .lHow = DIPH_DEVICE
        .lMin = lMin
        .lMax = lMax
    End With
    'set the property
    diDev.SetProperty "DIPROP_RANGE", DiProp_Range

    'set deadzone for X and Y axes to 5 percent
    With DiProp_Dead
        .lData = (lMax - lMin) / 5
        .lHow = DIPH_BYOFFSET
        .lObj = DIJOFS_X
```

```
       diDev.SetProperty "DIPROP_DEADZONE", DiProp_Dead
       .lObj = DIJOFS_Y
       diDev.SetProperty "DIPROP_DEADZONE", DiProp_Dead
   End With


   'set saturation zone for X and Y axes to 95 percent
   With DiProp_Saturation
       .lData = (lMax - lMin) * 0.95
       .lHow = DIPH_BYOFFSET
       .lObj = DIJOFS_X
       diDev.SetProperty "DIPROP_SATURATION", DiProp_Saturation
       .lObj = DIJOFS_Y
       diDev.SetProperty "DIPROP_SATURATION", DiProp_Saturation
   End With
End Sub
```

The next section of code in the JoystickTest program includes the joystick events that are called by the callback procedure. These joystick events are just normal subroutines that make it easier to deal with joystick events. The only complicated piece of code in this section involves an array called Analog, which was declared at the top of the program as a D3DVECTOR (which was just a convenient structure to use). The Analog array simply holds the values of the analog sticks.

```
Private Sub Joystick_AnalogMove(ByVal lNum As Long, ByRef vAnalog As D3DVECTOR)
    Debug.Print "Analog stick " & lNum & " = " & _
        vAnalog.x & "," & vAnalog.y & "," & vAnalog.z
End Sub


Private Sub Joystick_SliderMove(ByVal lSlider As Long, ByVal lValue As Long)
    Debug.Print "Slider " & lSlider & " = " & lValue
End Sub
```

Now for the callback procedure that I have been promoting throughout this section of the chapter! The DirectXEvent8_DXCallback procedure was implemented as an interface at the top of the program with the Implements keyword. Remember earlier, when I covered the CreateEvent function? That function was passed the window handle for the JoystickTest program, which is actually Form1.hWnd. When you tell the event to look at this form, it calls the DXCallback subroutine automatically.

I have already covered most of the key ingredients to this procedure, so I do not focus on the details again. One important factor to consider, however, is how this procedure fires off the joystick events. Regardless of the state of the joystick, these events are being called. That's not a good way to do it in a real game, because there are several hundred joystick events per second, even when nothing has changed! Therefore, you may want to check to see if the value of the stick or button has actually changed before doing anything inside these subroutines.

```
Private Sub DirectXEvent8_DXCallback(ByVal eventid As Long)
    Static Analog1 As D3DVECTOR
    Static Analog2 As D3DVECTOR
    Dim js As DIJOYSTATE
    Dim n As Long
    On Local Error Resume Next

    'retrieve joystick status
    diDev.GetDeviceStateJoystick js
    If Err.Number = DIERR_NOTACQUIRED Or Err.Number = DIERR_INPUTLOST Then
        diDev.Acquire
        Exit Sub
    End If

    'fire off any joystick analog movement events
    For n = 1 To 8
        Select Case n
            Case 1
                Analog1.x = js.x
                Joystick_AnalogMove 1, Analog1
            Case 2
                Analog1.y = js.y
                Joystick_AnalogMove 1, Analog1
            Case 3
                Analog1.z = js.z
                Joystick_AnalogMove 1, Analog1
            Case 4
                Analog2.x = js.rx
                Joystick_AnalogMove 2, Analog2
            Case 5
                Analog2.y = js.ry
                Joystick_AnalogMove 2, Analog2
            Case 6
                Analog2.z = js.rz
                Joystick_AnalogMove 2, Analog2
            Case 7
                Joystick_SliderMove 1, js.slider(0)
```

```
            Case 8
                Joystick_SliderMove 2, js.slider(1)
        End Select
    Next n


    'fire off any button events
    For n = 0 To joyCaps.lButtons - 1
        If js.Buttons(n) = 0 Then
            Debug.Print "Joystick ButtonUp: " & n
        Else
            Debug.Print "Joystick ButtonDown: " & n
        End If
    Next n


    'fire off any direction-pad button events
    If js.POV(0) = -1 Then
        Debug.Print "DPAD: -1"
    Else
        Debug.Print "DPAD: " & js.POV(0) / 4500
    End If
End Sub
```

That's the end of the JoystickTest program! Give it a spin and see what happens. If you have a joystick plugged in, you should see several messages printed in the Immediate window in VB. If not, you get an error message that a joystick could not be found.

Level Up

This chapter explained how to use DirectInput to handle keyboard, mouse, and joystick devices. While Visual Basic has rudimentary user input events that are available with a form, these events pale in comparison to what is provided with DirectInput. In addition to covering the keyboard and mouse, this chapter explored how to read the analog controls and digital buttons on a joystick.

User input is such a critical part of a game that it deserves adequate attention during design. It is important that you consider what the game's optimum input device is and then optimize the game for that particular device. While DirectInput provides a means to support input through a callback procedure, it is more useful to poll the user input devices directly.

CHAPTER 12

WALKING AROUND IN THE GAME WORLD

This chapter combines the tile-based scroller engine with the texture-based sprite handler to let you take a "walk about" in the game world using an animated character sprite. This is the next logical step in the RPG engine that is coming together in this book and is a significant step forward from the simple example programs you have seen up to this point. This chapter combines the scroller, player sprite, and DirectInput source code to allow your character to literally walk around in the game world. The subjects of collision detection, combat with *non-player characters (NPCs)*, inanimate objects, and so on are covered in later chapters.

Here is a breakdown of the major topics in this chapter:

- Mapping the game world
- Loading a binary Mappy file
- The animated character artwork
- The WalkAbout program

Mapping the Game World

The first thing I discovered when attempting to create 9th-century Ireland using Mappy was that this game world is *huge*. As the WalkAbout program that you develop later in this chapter demonstrates, it took 4.5 minutes for me to walk from the left to the right side of the map (including water tiles). From the very top to the very bottom of the map, it took just over 6 minutes! What is even more surprising is that the WalkAbout program scrolls at twice the normal speed at which the game should move. Instead of 2 pixels at a time (per screen update), it scrolls at 4 pixels, which means that in the realistic version of the running game, it takes you about 12 minutes to walk the entire map north to south, and 9 minutes from west to east.

note

___

If this map were represented in memory rather than being stored virtually as a tile map (with the scrolling view generated on the fly), it would be a bitmap image with a resolution of 96,000 × 128,000 pixels, and would require about 50 gigabytes of memory. Instead, the tile engine only requires a couple megabytes. This is an interesting fact because some data compression algorithms use a similar method to compress data.

___

Refamiliarizing Yourself with the Ireland Map

Why does the game need such a large map? For one thing, to demonstrate clearly that Visual Basic is fully capable of handling a large-scale game; secondly, to prove that the tile-based scroller engine, in theory as well as practice, is simply incredible at rendering a huge game world. Take a look at Figure 12.1, which shows the original map of 9th-century Ireland first introduced back in Chapter 3, "Designing the Game." As you may recall, this is a map that was drawn by hand, scanned with a full-page scanner, and then cleaned up and enhanced using Paint Shop Pro.

Now take a look at Figure 12.2. This figure shows the map of Ireland with a small box up near the ruins of Bangor. That small box represents the portion of the map rendered on a 640 × 480 screen.

The sheer magnitude of the game world's scale in Celtic Crusader should be very encouraging to you, especially if you are the sort of person with a wild imagination who would like to create a massive RPG with a long, complex storyline and intense, varied character-development features. Figure 12.3 shows the WalkAbout program with the player centered at the very same spot that was highlighted on the map. The tiles you see in this screenshot are *raw*; that is, no cosmetic tiles have been used yet to transition from the land to the water. (These tiles are available in the Ireland.FMP map file as well as in the Ireland.BMP file included in the \sources\chapter12 folder on the CD-ROM.)

Digitizing the Real World

Creating the map of Ireland with Mappy was no small undertaking, as it required many hours of work to make it look right, along with a custom program written just to display the entire map scaled down so that it is visible in its entirety. The ViewMap program is

Figure 12.1 The original digitized and enhanced map of 9th-century Ireland.

Figure 12.2 The actual size of the screen compared to the entire map.

available in the folder for this chapter on the CD-ROM. Figure 12.4 shows the program displaying a very early version of the Ireland map with a small border of water tiles and some reference points added to the map to help orient myself while editing.

Figure 12.3 A tiny portion of the game world is displayed by the WalkAbout program.

Figure 12.4 The ViewMap program draws the entire Mappy file like a satellite view.

Although ViewMap can view any Mappy map that you create (and save in the binary .MAR format; more on that later), you need to modify the program if you are using a map with different dimensions, as it is currently configured for Ireland.MAR, which is a huge map of 1,500 tiles across and 2,000 tiles down. Just modify the MAPWIDTH and MAPHEIGHT constants and perhaps the STEP values in the SatelliteView subroutine for your own map. (As is often the case, custom-written utility programs are not always versatile because such programs are meant to solve problems quickly. My goal was to view the whole map while I was creating it in Mappy.) The reference points are inserted into the bitmap image and in the Mappy file using tiles to help keep track of the map's scale while editing with tiles. Figure 12.5 shows the Ireland.BMP file loaded into Paint Shop Pro, revealing some of the reference points. The darker dots represent towns. (Refer to the original map in Chapter 3.)

The map was originally 4,000 × 3,000 tiles, but I quickly realized that this would be utterly daunting to edit and not really necessary, so I settled on 1,500 × 2,000. I realized that the game world would be very difficult, if not impossible, to create in Mappy without very specific coordinates from the original map image.

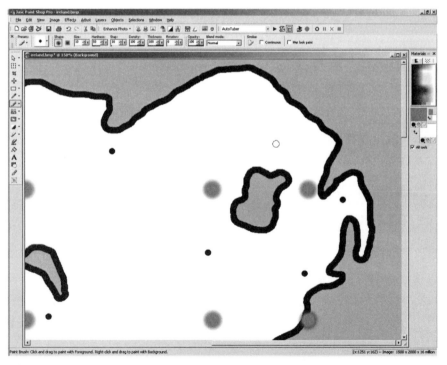

Figure 12.5 The Ireland.BMP file has the same dimensions as the Mappy file.

I decided to take the original bitmap and resize it so that it has the same dimensions as the tile map in Mappy. In other words, if my Mappy map is 1,500 tiles across, then my bitmap image is 1,500 pixels across; likewise for the height of the tile map and the bitmap image. This makes it possible to model the "real" map with great precision. Using Mappy's line tool, I clicked on a point in the map that corresponds to a point on the border of the island in the bitmap image. Then, locating a new spot, I highlighted the spot with the mouse (I'm still in Mappy here) and pressed the L key to draw a line of tiles from the previous click spot to the current highlighted spot.

note

When I say I am making the bitmap version of the map the same size as the Mappy version of the map, what I mean is that 1 tile = 1 pixel.

By carefully following the contour of the terrain in the bitmap, I painstakingly created a map of Ireland in Mappy. You can see the smaller reference points around the contour of the island in Figure 12.6, as well as around the lakes (which *are* included in the Mappy file). The large dots on the image were only used early on, and were not needed once the contour had been digitized.

The next screenshot of ViewMap (see Figure 12.7) shows the completed tile map of Ireland used in the Celtic Crusader game. You can now see why this program was needed; otherwise it's impossible to see what the tile map really looks like, as you usually see a small portion of it at a time.

Loading a Binary Mappy File

Of course, the ability to load the map back into memory and render it onscreen using the tile engine is the key to this large map being usable. This tile map is a thousand times bigger than any sample tile map you have used in previous chapters. Therefore, you must assume that Visual Basic would take a very long time to load this file if it is stored in the same manner—using an exported text file of comma-separated values (a .CSV file). The answer to this very serious problem is to use a binary file format instead of a text file format.

Exporting to Binary

Mappy can export a lot of different files, and this is one of its best features, since you aren't required to use the .FMP format if you don't want to. Mappy can export your tile map into a very simple binary file that contains *nothing but* the tile numbers, in sequential order, as short integers. This means Mappy writes 2 bytes into the binary file for every tile numbered in order, just like the text file format but without all the wasted space associated with

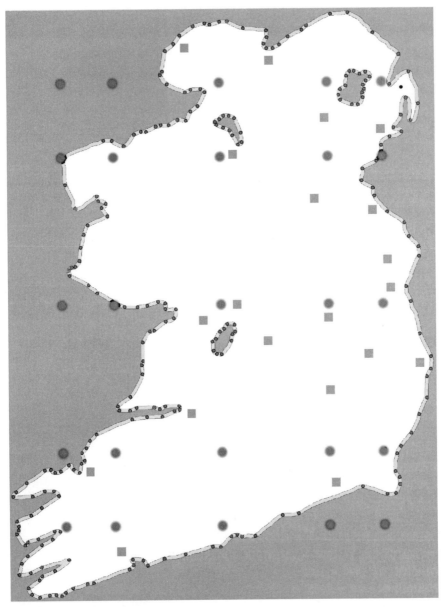

Figure 12.6 Mappy creates an accurate representation of Ireland by breaking down the outline of the island into reference points.

a text file. In my testing, it took over 30 seconds to load a text map exported from this map of Ireland. In contrast, the binary version of the file takes only about 5 seconds to load (on an Athlon 1.2-GHz system).

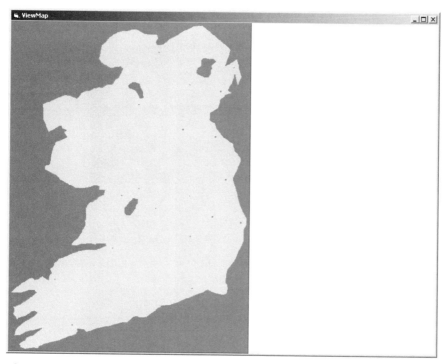

Figure 12.7 The entire island of Ireland has been converted to a very large tile map.

First, you need to know how to export a tile map to the binary file format. As you have already learned, you can export a file in Mappy using the File, Export option, which brings up the dialog box shown in Figure 12.8.

Just select the first option, Map Array (?.MAR) to save the tile map as a binary file. The .MAR format (which is short for *map array*) is the format I just described, where each tile is saved as a 2-byte short integer, which can be read in Visual Basic using the regular Integer data type (which is 2 bytes in Visual Basic 6.0).

Loading Binary Data in Visual Basic

I have written a new subroutine LoadBinaryMap to load a binary map file, which should complement the LoadMap subroutine already in the TileScroller.bas file you have been using. I recommend adding this subroutine to that file so that it is available whenever you need it.

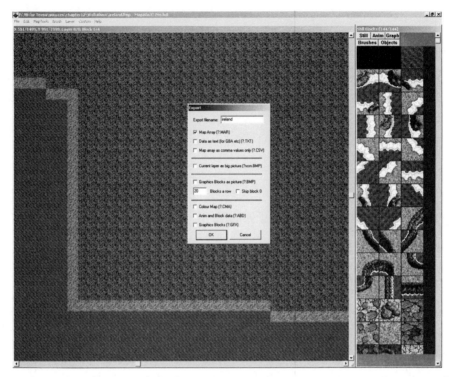

Figure 12.8 The Export dialog box in Mappy is where you can export a tile map as a binary file.

```
Public Sub LoadBinaryMap( _
    ByVal filename As String, _
    ByVal lWidth As Long, _
    ByVal lHeight As Long)

    Dim filenum As Integer
    Dim n As Long
    Dim i As Integer

    'open the map file
    filenum = FreeFile()
    Open filename For Binary As filenum

    'prepare the array for the map data
    ReDim mapdata(lWidth * lHeight)
```

```
'read the map data
For n = 0 To lWidth * lHeight - 1
    Get filenum, , i
    mapdata(n) = i / 32 - 1
Next n

'close the file
Close filenum

End Sub
```

The Animated Character Artwork

Now I'd like to discuss how you can prepare a sprite for use in this game. Each sprite is somewhat different, in the number of frames it uses for each type of animation, as well as the types of animation available. All of the character sprites that I'm using in Celtic Crusader have the full eight-direction walking animation sequences, as well as frames for attacking with a weapon. Some sprites have a death animation, and some have running and falling. To keep the game as uniform as possible, you should use character sprites that have the exact same number of animation frames for the key animation that takes place in the game. That way you can switch character classes (Warrior, Paladin, Archer, and so on) without changing any source code.

I have based my work in the WalkAbout program on the Paladin version of the Hero sprite, as shown in Figure 12.9.

The source artwork from Reiner's Tilesets does not come in this format, but comes with each frame of animation stored in a separate bitmap file. As I explained in Chapter 10, you can combine these frames into an animation strip using Cosmigo's awesome Pro Motion graphic editor and animation program. Since Pro Motion works best with single animation strips, I decided to import each group of bitmaps for the character's walking animation in all eight directions. Using Pro Motion, I exported all into individual bitmap files and combined them into a single, large file using Paint Shop Pro. Figure 12.10 shows the individual animation strips for the Paladin Hero character.

Nothing beats experimentation, so it is up to you to use the freely available sprites provided by Reiner's Tilesets to enhance Celtic Crusader to suit your own imagination. We can only accomplish so much in this book, so I want to give you as many tools, tips, and tricks as I can possibly squeeze in at this time. All you need is Pro Motion, Mappy, and Paint Shop Pro to create the artwork for your own RPG. There are so many sprites and tiles available at www.reinerstilesets.de that it would take a whole book just to list them all! There is a sprite for everything you can possibly imagine adding to an RPG, including fireballs and other types of magic spells, with both casting animation as well as

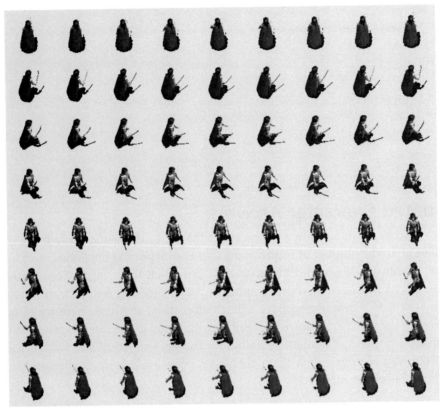

Figure 12.9 The sword-wielding Paladin sprite is the Hero figure in the WalkAbout program.

the projectile animation of the fireball itself! That is but one example of something really awesome I would love to explore here, but must cut the discussion short over the next few chapters.

The WalkAbout Program

You have already received a complete tutorial on how to use tile-based scrolling as well as how to draw transparent, animated sprites. The only thing left to do is combine these two techniques into a single program while using DirectInput (which you learned how to use in the previous chapter). Sounds easy, doesn't it? As a matter of fact, once the map is actually ready to go, it is rather easy to get this program going. Figure 12.11 shows the Walk-About program running. Note that the player sprite has all eight directions of travel (while the dragon sprite was limited to just four directions back in Chapter 10, as you recall). The WalkAbout program is a fully functional prototype of the player walking around on the map.

Hero - Paladin (Sword) - AnimSeq 1

Hero - Paladin (Sword) - AnimSeq 2

Hero - Paladin (Sword) - AnimSeq 3

Hero - Paladin (Sword) - AnimSeq 4

Hero - Paladin (Sword) - AnimSeq 5

Hero - Paladin (Sword) - AnimSeq 6

Hero - Paladin (Sword) - AnimSeq 7

Hero - Paladin (Sword) - AnimSeq 8

Figure 12.10 There are eight animation strips to give the Paladin Hero full eight-way movement.

In addition, this program displays the current ScrollX and ScrollY values in the window caption bar, along with the current tile that the player is standing on. This is an exceptionally good thing to know, particularly given that you learn about collision detection two chapters from now! Collision in this game is extremely fun to learn about now that you have a working prototype of the game.

Figure 12.11 This is supposed to be Dubh Linn; obviously more work needs to be done on the towns!

---

tip

Remember, the black bar at the bottom of the screen is an issue of tile boundaries, which must be maintained to keep the scrolling engine running at top speed. You don't want to deal with the special case of drawing partial tiles at the right and bottom edges, because that slows down the scrolling.

This screenshot also shows how the player remains stationary at the center of the screen. The sense of movement is just simulated by scrolling the ground underneath the player, which adds to the effect by using a walking animation. Figure 12.12 shows another screenshot of the program running. As you can see, much work remains to be done on the collision detection and terrain parts of the game, which you start to learn about in Chapter 14, "Core Technique: Collision Detection."

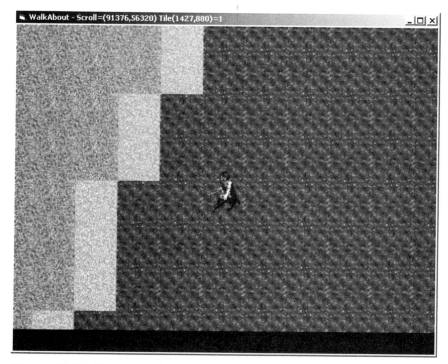

Figure 12.12 The player either has a lot of faith or used a walk-on-water spell.

Creating the Project

Create a new Standard EXE project called WalkAbout and add a reference to DirectX 8 for Visual Basic Type Library to the project. This project takes a slightly different approach than previous programs. Rather than using Form_Load for all of the initialization code and the game loop, this program uses Sub Main instead. The benefits to using a modular subroutine instead of Form_Load is that you can call subroutines and functions in the main module from other modules, which isn't possible when most of your important game code is in Form1.

Of course you can access the variables, functions, subroutines, and everything else inside a form by using the dot operator (as in Form1.Caption), but the form generally is not where the game's code should be located. The form is basically just a window for DirectX to attach to, as a window handle is required by most DirectX components. By moving the bulk of your code into a module, such as Game.bas, your source code is actually easier to maintain. You can set Sub Main as the project's startup code by going into the Project menu and selecting Properties to bring up the Project Properties dialog box. As Figure 12.13 shows, you want to select Sub Main from the Startup Object drop-down list.

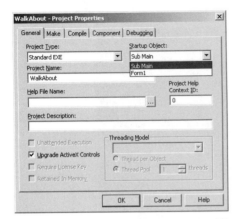

Figure 12.13 Changing the startup object from `Form1` to `Sub Main`.

Adding the Support Files for DirectX

You need some support files for this program that you have developed in previous chapters. Here is a list of the files you need to add to this project. Just copy the files to your new project folder and then add them using the Project, Add File option.

- Direct3D.bas
- DirectInput.bas
- TileScroller.bas
- Sprite.bas

Remember, all of the normal source code that you are used to typing into `Form_Load` now belongs in the Game.bas file, which I go over shortly.

tip

Form1 is not even used in this project! The form is only used by DirectX components that need a window handle. Type all code into Game.bas and use Globals.bas for global variables.

Adding the Globals.bas File

The Globals.bas file contains the constants and global variable definitions and any other items that need to be visible throughout the whole project.

```
'-----------------------------------------------------
' Visual Basic Game Programming for Teens
' Globals File
'-----------------------------------------------------

Option Explicit
Option Base 0

'Windows API functions
Public Declare Function GetTickCount Lib "kernel32" () As Long

'colors
Public Const C_BLACK As Long = &H0

'customize the program here
Public Const FULLSCREEN As Boolean = False
Public Const SCREENWIDTH As Long = 800
Public Const SCREENHEIGHT As Long = 600
Public Const STEP As Integer = 8

'tile and game world constants
Public Const TILEWIDTH As Long = 64
Public Const TILEHEIGHT As Long = 64
Public Const MAPWIDTH As Long = 1500
Public Const MAPHEIGHT As Long = 2000
Public Const GAMEWORLDWIDTH As Long = TILEWIDTH * MAPWIDTH
Public Const GAMEWORLDHEIGHT As Long = TILEHEIGHT * MAPHEIGHT

'scrolling window size
Public Const WINDOWWIDTH As Integer = (SCREENWIDTH \ TILEWIDTH) * TILEWIDTH
Public Const WINDOWHEIGHT As Integer = (SCREENHEIGHT \ TILEHEIGHT) * TILEHEIGHT

'scroll buffer size
Public Const SCROLLBUFFERWIDTH As Integer = SCREENWIDTH + TILEWIDTH
Public Const SCROLLBUFFERHEIGHT As Integer = SCREENHEIGHT + TILEHEIGHT
```

Adding the Game.bas File

The main source code file for the WalkAbout program is now stored in a file called Game.bas instead of in the Form_Load event of Form1. I did this primarily to support the DirectInput event, KeyPressed, but also because I prefer to get the code out of Form1 and into a real module where it is visible to other modules. *Forms* are similar to classes in that you can access them from a module without declaring a variable to use them (at which point the variable becomes an *object*).

As you can see in the Game.bas source code listing, I actually do create a variable called frm, which is created from a new instance of Form1, oddly enough. This allows me to initialize the form and get it ready for DirectX.

```
'--------------------------------------------------------
' Visual Basic Game Programming for Teens
' Chapter 12 - WalkAbout program
'
' Requires the following files:
'   Direct3D.bas, DirectInput.bas, Globals.bas, TileScroller.bas,
'   Sprite.bas, and an empty Form1.
'--------------------------------------------------------


Option Explicit
Option Base 0

Const HEROSPEED As Integer = 4
Dim heroSpr As TSPRITE
Dim heroImg As Direct3DTexture8
Dim SuperHero As Boolean

Dim frm As New Form1

Public Sub Main()

    'set up the main form
    frm.Caption = "WalkAbout"
    frm.AutoRedraw = False
    frm.BorderStyle = 1
    frm.ClipControls = False
    frm.ScaleMode = 3
    frm.width = Screen.TwipsPerPixelX * (SCREENWIDTH + 12)
    frm.height = Screen.TwipsPerPixelY * (SCREENHEIGHT + 30)
    frm.Show

    'initialize Direct3D
    InitDirect3D frm.hwnd

    InitDirectInput
    InitKeyboard frm.hwnd
```

```
'get reference to the back buffer
Set backbuffer = d3ddev.GetBackBuffer(0, D3DBACKBUFFER_TYPE_MONO)

'load the bitmap file
Set tiles = LoadSurface(App.Path & "\ireland.bmp", 1024, 576)

'load the map data from the Mappy export file
LoadBinaryMap App.Path & "\ireland.mar", MAPWIDTH, MAPHEIGHT

'load the dragon sprite
Set heroImg = LoadTexture(d3ddev, App.Path & "\hero_sword_walk.bmp")

'initialize the dragon sprite
InitSprite d3ddev, heroSpr
With heroSpr
    .FramesPerRow = 9
    .FrameCount = 9
    .CurrentFrame = 0
    .AnimDelay = 2
    .width = 96
    .height = 96
    .ScaleFactor = 1
    .x = (SCREENWIDTH - .width) / 2
    .y = (SCREENHEIGHT - .height) / 2
End With

'create the small scroll buffer surface
Set scrollbuffer = d3ddev.CreateImageSurface( _
    SCROLLBUFFERWIDTH, _
    SCROLLBUFFERHEIGHT, _
    dispmode.Format)

'start player in the city of Dubh Linn
ScrollX = 1342 * TILEWIDTH
ScrollY = 945 * TILEHEIGHT

'this helps to keep a steady framerate
Dim start As Long
start = GetTickCount()

'clear the screen to black
d3ddev.Clear 0, ByVal 0, D3DCLEAR_TARGET, C_BLACK, 1, 0
```

```
        'main loop
        Do While (True)
            'poll DirectInput for keyboard input
            Check_Keyboard

            'update the scrolling window
            UpdateScrollPosition
            DrawTiles
            DrawScrollWindow
            Scroll 0, 0
            ShowScrollData

            'reset scroll speed
            SuperHero = False

            'set the screen refresh to about 50 fps
            If GetTickCount - start > 20 Then

                'start rendering
                d3ddev.BeginScene

                'animate the dragon
                If heroSpr.Animating Then
                    AnimateSprite heroSpr, heroImg
                End If

                'draw the hero sprite
                DrawSprite heroImg, heroSpr, &HFFFFFFFF

                'stop rendering
                d3ddev.EndScene

                d3ddev.Present ByVal 0, ByVal 0, 0, ByVal 0
                start = GetTickCount
                DoEvents
            End If
        Loop
    End Sub
```

```
Public Sub ShowScrollData()
    Static old As point
    Dim player As point
    Dim tile As point
    Dim tilenum As Long

    player.x = ScrollX + SCREENWIDTH / 2
    player.y = ScrollY + SCREENHEIGHT / 2
    tile.x = player.x \ TILEWIDTH
    tile.y = player.y \ TILEHEIGHT

    If (tile.x <> old.x) Or (tile.y <> old.y) Then
        old = tile
        tilenum = mapdata(tile.y * MAPWIDTH + tile.x)
        frm.Caption = "WalkAbout - " & _
            "Scroll=(" & player.x & "," & player.y & ") " & _
            "Tile(" & tile.x & "," & tile.y & ")=" & tilenum
    End If
End Sub

'This is called from DirectInput.bas on keypress events
Public Sub KeyPressed(ByVal key As Long)
    Select Case key
        Case KEY_UP, KEY_NUMPAD8
            heroSpr.AnimSeq = 0
            heroSpr.Animating = True
            Scroll 0, -HEROSPEED

        Case KEY_NUMPAD9
            heroSpr.AnimSeq = 1
            heroSpr.Animating = True
            Scroll HEROSPEED, -HEROSPEED

        Case KEY_RIGHT, KEY_NUMPAD6
            heroSpr.AnimSeq = 2
            heroSpr.Animating = True
            Scroll HEROSPEED, 0

        Case KEY_NUMPAD3
            heroSpr.AnimSeq = 3
            heroSpr.Animating = True
            Scroll HEROSPEED, HEROSPEED
```

```
            Case KEY_DOWN, KEY_NUMPAD2
                heroSpr.AnimSeq = 4
                heroSpr.Animating = True
                Scroll 0, HEROSPEED

            Case KEY_NUMPAD1
                heroSpr.AnimSeq = 5
                heroSpr.Animating = True
                Scroll -HEROSPEED, HEROSPEED

            Case KEY_LEFT, KEY_NUMPAD4
                heroSpr.AnimSeq = 6
                heroSpr.Animating = True
                Scroll -HEROSPEED, 0

            Case KEY_NUMPAD7
                heroSpr.AnimSeq = 7
                heroSpr.Animating = True
                Scroll -HEROSPEED, -HEROSPEED

            Case KEY_LSHIFT, KEY_RSHIFT
                SuperHero = True

            Case KEY_ESC
                Shutdown

    End Select

    'uncomment this when you want to find new key codes
    'Debug.Print "Key = " & key

End Sub

Public Sub Scroll(ByVal horiz As Long, ByVal vert As Long)
    SpeedX = horiz
    SpeedY = vert

    If SuperHero Then
        SpeedX = SpeedX * 4
        SpeedY = SpeedY * 4
    End If
End Sub
```

Level Up

This chapter produced perhaps the first real prototype of the game that you have seen so far, by pulling together the tile-based scroller, the texture-based sprite code, and the `DirectInput` code. These technologies work in tandem to produce a scroller with an animated sprite at the center, which moves in a direction specified using the arrow keys and numeric keypad for motion. You can literally walk anywhere in the map now using a fully animated sprite for the *player's character (PC)*. Although the map of Ireland is sparse at this point, that was intentional, because now you have a large game world that you can customize to suit your own imagination. Although this island resembles Ireland, your game players need not know that detail, as you could just as easily call it by another name. Without seeing the satellite view, so to speak, the player has no real sense of the shape of the world because it is so immense. Furthermore, you could build several games out of the single map by using different parts of it. As you learn in the coming chapters, adding scenery and inanimate objects, as well as NPCs, make an otherwise spartan world come to life.

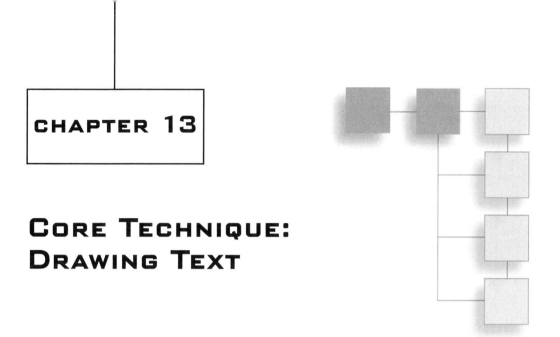

CHAPTER 13

CORE TECHNIQUE: DRAWING TEXT

This chapter covers the solitary subject of drawing text on the screen. Since you have already used surfaces and textures, you should be able to understand how a font is created and printed on the screen. It is treated like a sprite with many animation frames—except there is no animation, just a series of characters. The ability to draw a bitmapped font on the screen is crucial in any game, which is why this core technique is now being covered. The subroutines developed in this chapter are very valuable in your game projects.

Here is a breakdown of the major topics in this chapter:

- Creating a bitmapped font
- Printing the bitmapped font

Creating a Bitmapped Font

The bitmapped font that I use in this chapter (and in the following chapters as well) is shown in Figure 13.1. The characters in this bitmap file are 16 × 24 pixels per character, with 20 characters across in each row. Set up the font sprite for 20 columns.

You can create any type of bitmapped font that you want by drawing each character yourself, and it is usable in your games as long as each character has the same size. You may want a larger font with better details, so you might opt for a character size of 32 × 24 or so. Keep in mind that the characters are treated as a texture in memory, meaning that you can scale your font at runtime to produce a variety of sizes (although spacing must be accommodated because the original width and height of each character is used, regardless of the scale factor).

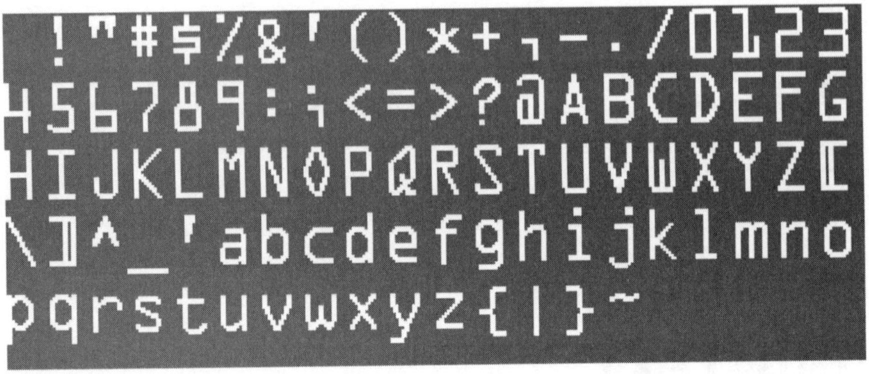

Figure 13.1 The bitmapped font includes only the most commonly needed text characters.

Printing the Bitmapped Font

Now I show you how to print this font on the screen via reusable `PrintText` and `PrintChar` subroutines. You can paste these subroutines into one of your DirectX module files (I recommend Sprite.BAS) for later use.

The Text Printing Subroutines

I have written two subroutines that work together to print out a text message on the screen. There are a lot of parameters in these two subroutines because I want them to be completely reusable and capable of supporting multiple fonts (which you can load, each from a different bitmap file). Since this code is all based on the sprite code you have seen in previous chapters, I don't think it's necessary to explain what each line of code does here.

```
Private Sub PrintText( _
    ByRef fontImg As Direct3DTexture8, _
    ByRef fontSpr As TSPRITE, _
    ByVal X As Long, _
    ByVal Y As Long, _
    ByVal color As Long, _
    ByVal sText As String)

    Dim n As Long
    For n = 1 To Len(sText)
        PrintChar fontImg, fontSpr, X + (n - 1) * fontSpr.width, _
            Y, color, Asc(Mid$(sText, n, 1))
    Next n

End Sub
```

Basically, the `PrintText` subroutine looks at each character in the passed string and passes it to the `PrintChar` subroutine, which does the real work of drawing the sprite to the screen. The important things are that you have already loaded a bitmap into a texture that is passed to these subroutines, and that you have already created a `TSPRITE` variable describing the font.

```
Private Sub PrintChar( _
    ByRef fontImg As Direct3DTexture8, _
    ByRef fontSpr As TSPRITE, _
    ByVal X As Long, _
    ByVal Y As Long, _
    ByVal color As Long, _
    c As Byte)

    fontSpr.X = X
    fontSpr.Y = Y
    fontSpr.CurrentFrame = c - 32
    DrawSprite fontImg, fontSpr, color
End Sub
```

The PrintText Program

The PrintText program demonstrates how to use the two text-printing subroutines that you just learned about. Figure 13.2 shows the program running. Note the variety of sizes and colors. By simply adjusting the alpha component of the 32-bit RGBA color, the font appears in a different color. Therefore, you need not create a custom font for each color that you want to use.

This program is a Standard EXE project with a reference to the DirectX 8 for Visual Basic Type Library. The project needs the following additional modules to run:

- Direct3D.bas
- Sprite.bas

In addition to the following code, paste the `PrintText` and `PrintChar` subroutines to the end of the code listing. You may also want to just type these routines into the Sprite.bas file.

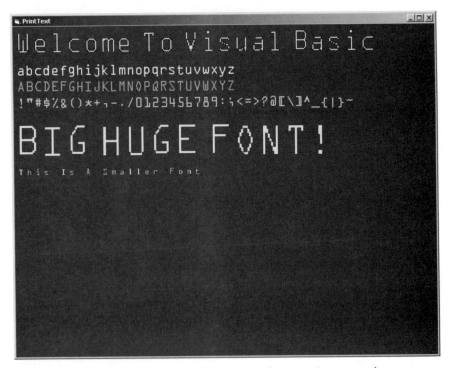

Figure 13.2 The PrintText program demonstrates how to print text on the screen with a bitmapped font.

```
'-------------------------------------------------------
' Visual Basic Game Programming for Teens
' PrintText Program
'-------------------------------------------------------

Option Explicit
Option Base 0

Const SCREENWIDTH As Long = 800
Const SCREENHEIGHT As Long = 600

Const C_PURPLE As Long = &HFFFF00FF
Const C_RED As Long = &HFFFF0000
Const C_GREEN As Long = &HFF00FF00
Const C_BLUE As Long = &HFF0000FF
Const C_WHITE As Long = &HFFFFFFFF
Const C_BLACK As Long = &H0
Const C_GRAY As Long = &HFFAAAAAA
```

```vb
Dim fontImg As Direct3DTexture8
Dim fontSpr As TSPRITE

Private Sub Form_Load()
    'set up the main form
    Me.Caption = "PrintText"
    Me.ScaleMode = 3
    Me.width = Screen.TwipsPerPixelX * (SCREENWIDTH + 12)
    Me.height = Screen.TwipsPerPixelY * (SCREENHEIGHT + 30)
    Me.Show

    'initialize Direct3D
    InitDirect3D Me.hWnd

    'get reference to the back buffer
    Set backbuffer = d3ddev.GetBackBuffer(0, D3DBACKBUFFER_TYPE_MONO)

    'load the bitmap file
    Set fontImg = LoadTexture(d3ddev, App.Path & "\font.bmp")

    InitSprite d3ddev, fontSpr
    fontSpr.FramesPerRow = 20
    fontSpr.width = 16
    fontSpr.height = 24
    fontSpr.ScaleFactor = 2

    'clear the screen to black
    d3ddev.Clear 0, ByVal 0, D3DCLEAR_TARGET, &H0, 1, 0

    d3ddev.BeginScene

    PrintText fontImg, fontSpr, 10, 10, C_BLUE, _
        "W e l c o m e   T o   V i s u a l   B a s i c"

    fontSpr.ScaleFactor = 1
    PrintText fontImg, fontSpr, 10, 70, C_WHITE, _
        "abcdefghijklmnopqrstuvwxyz"
    PrintText fontImg, fontSpr, 10, 100, C_GRAY, _
        "ABCDEFGHIJKLMNOPQRSTUVWXYZ"
    PrintText fontImg, fontSpr, 10, 130, C_GREEN, _
        "!""#$%&()*+,-./0123456789:;<=>?@[\]^_{|}~"
```

```
        fontSpr.ScaleFactor = 3
        PrintText fontImg, fontSpr, 10, 180, C_RED, _
            "B  I  G    H  U  G  E    F  O  N  T  !"

        fontSpr.ScaleFactor = 0.6
        PrintText fontImg, fontSpr, 10, 260, C_PURPLE, _
            "This Is A Smaller Font"

        d3ddev.EndScene
End Sub

Private Sub Form_KeyDown(KeyCode As Integer, Shift As Integer)
    If KeyCode = 27 Then Shutdown
End Sub

Private Sub Form_Paint()
    d3ddev.Present ByVal 0, ByVal 0, 0, ByVal 0
End Sub
```

Level Up

This chapter provided a core technique in the ability to print text on the screen, which has been ignored up to this point (although displaying status information on the screen in previous sample programs would have been very useful). The ability to display a message on the screen is absolutely crucial, so you are likely to find yourself using the code provided in this chapter more than any other.

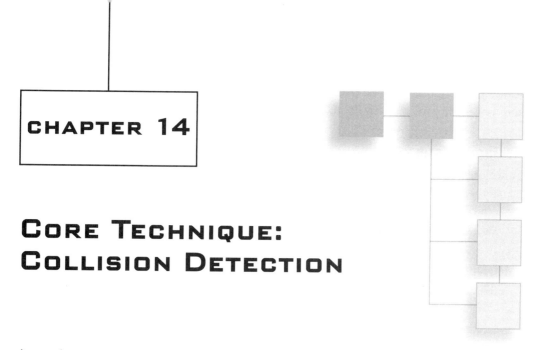

CHAPTER 14

CORE TECHNIQUE: COLLISION DETECTION

T his chapter explains the core technique of detecting collisions between two sprites in a game. This is a higher-level technique than previous topics you have learned so far, which have focused more on the key aspects of just getting something on the screen. Now that you have a complete prototype for the game up and running (per Chapter 12, "Walking Around in the Game World"), you can focus on these higher-level things. This chapter shows you how to identify when the player has hit a tile that is impassable (such as an ocean square), and this technique is refined over the next three chapters when dealing with *non-player characters (NPCs)*.

Here is a breakdown of the major topics in this chapter:

- Rectangle intersection
- Writing a reusable collision function
- Keeping track of "bad" tiles
- Checking for tile collisions
- Revising the scroll data display
- The CollisionTest program

Reacting to Solid Objects

Collision detection is an important technique that you should learn. It is an absolute requirement for every game ever made. I can't think of any game that does not need collision detection, because it is such an essential aspect of gameplay. Without collisions, there is no action, goal, or purpose in a game. There is no way to die without collisions taking place. In other words, collision detection makes the sprites in a game come to life, and makes the game believable.

Rectangle Intersection

Traditional collision detection involves the comparison of two rectangles on the screen, usually representing the bounding boxes around two sprites. A function available within the Windows API gives you a quick answer to the question of a collision between two sprites. This function is called IntersectRect:

```
Public Declare Function IntersectRect _
Lib "user32" Alias "IntersectRect" ( _
lpDestRect As RECT, _
lpSrc1Rect As RECT, _
lpSrc2Rect As RECT) _
As Long
```

IntersectRect returns the intersection rectangle, lpDestRect, with the union of the two other rectangles (although this information is not usually needed). Two additional RECT structures are required in the call to this function, and they contain the location and size of each sprite.

Writing a Reusable Collision Function

It is helpful to write a support function that sets up the two RECT structures by representing the two sprites that need to be checked for a collision. By encapsulating this support code inside a function, you can reduce the amount of code that you must write to check for multiple collisions in your game (which can become quite tedious if you have to set up the structures for every single instance). I recommend adding this Collision function to the Sprite.bas file:

```
Public Function Collision( _
    ByRef sprite1 As TSPRITE, _
    ByRef sprite2 As TSPRITE) As Boolean

    Dim dest As RECT
    Dim rect1 As RECT
    Dim rect2 As RECT

    'set up the first rect
    rect1.Left = sprite1.x
    rect1.Top = sprite1.y
    rect1.Right = sprite1.x + sprite1.width
    rect1.Bottom = sprite1.y + sprite1.height
```

```
    'set up the second rect
    rect2.Left = sprite2.x
    rect2.Top = sprite2.y
    rect2.Right = sprite2.x + sprite2.width
    rect2.Bottom = sprite2.y + sprite2.height

    'check for collision
    If IntersectRect(dest, rect1, rect2) <> 0 Then
        Collision = True
    Else
        Collision = False
    End If
End Function
```

Keeping Track of "Bad" Tiles

For the purposes of detecting collisions within the Celtic Crusader game, it is important first to check tile numbers for valid movement regions on the map. Water tiles, solid object tiles, and so on should be impassable; in other words, these are *blocking tiles* that the player should not be able to cross.

The whole process of limiting the player's movement in the game world is done by making use of a list of impassable tiles. You can store these tile numbers in a data file to be loaded at runtime or just set an array containing the tile numbers that you know are impassable.

I created a simple Integer array to keep track of the bad tiles:

```
Dim badtiles() As Integer
```

Then initialize the bad tiles with just a few tile numbers for testing purposes. In the complete game I fill this array with *all* of the impassable tiles. This really shouldn't be a very large number in the end, because most of the tiles in Mappy *are*, in fact, for creating terrain that the player can walk on. Just as an example, tile 2 is the water tile, which certainly should not be walked on!

```
Public Sub BuildTileCollisionList()
    ReDim badtiles(5)
    badtiles(0) = 2
    badtiles(1) = 34
    badtiles(2) = 44
    badtiles(3) = 54
    badtiles(4) = 79
End Sub
```

When it comes time to actually check the list of bad tiles, you can use the following function. Do you see how unfriendly this function is, with the hard-coded array range (0 to 4)? You need either to modify this value when adding new items to the bad tiles array or create a constant that specifies the number of bad tiles. I am keeping it simple so you can focus mainly on the subject of collision and not on support code.

```
Public Function IsBadTile(ByVal tilenum As Long) As Boolean
    Dim n As Long
    For n = 0 To 4
        If badtiles(n) - 1 = tilenum Then
            IsBadTile = True
            Exit Function
        End If
    Next n
    IsBadTile = False
End Function
```

Checking for Tile Collisions

The main tile collision subroutine called from within the game loop is called Check-TileCollisions. This subroutine scans the current tile under the player's feet and then runs it by the IsBadTile function to determine if the current tile number is on the black list. If that is true, then the next step is to prevent the player from moving over that tile. By calling this CheckTileCollisions subroutine *before* the tiles are drawn and *before* the scroll window is drawn, you can cause the player to actually take a step back to counter the movement that triggered the tile collision. As far as the player is concerned, the sprite just stopped at the edge of the impassable tile. What actually happened is that the sprite moved onto the tile and was moved off it by the same amount of space. By the time the scene is rendered, it appears that the sprite just stopped.

```
Public Sub CheckTileCollisions()
    Dim tilenum As Long

    tilenum = CurrentTile()
    If IsBadTile(tilenum) Then
        Scroll 0, 0

        Select Case heroSpr.AnimSeq
            Case 0
                ScrollY = ScrollY + HEROSPEED
            Case 1
                ScrollY = ScrollY + HEROSPEED
                ScrollX = ScrollX - HEROSPEED
```

```
            Case 2
                ScrollX = ScrollX - HEROSPEED
            Case 3
                ScrollX = ScrollX - HEROSPEED
                ScrollY = ScrollY - HEROSPEED
            Case 4
                ScrollY = ScrollY - HEROSPEED
            Case 5
                ScrollX = ScrollX + HEROSPEED
                ScrollY = ScrollY - HEROSPEED
            Case 6
                ScrollX = ScrollX + HEROSPEED
            Case 7
                ScrollX = ScrollX + HEROSPEED
                ScrollY = ScrollY + HEROSPEED
        End Select
    End If
End Sub
```

Revising the Scroll Data Display

At this point, I need to show you some of the code I changed in the program to accommodate the tile collision routines. This code was originally found back in Chapter 12 in the WalkAbout program, which is the game's first prototype. The following code includes some support routines that I wrote to provide the current player's position and tile number (which were programmed in the ShowScrollData subroutine previously).

```
Public Function TileAt(ByVal x As Long, ByVal y As Long) As Long
    Dim tile As point
    tile.x = x \ TILEWIDTH
    tile.y = y \ TILEHEIGHT
    TileAt = mapdata(tile.y * MAPWIDTH + tile.x)
End Function

Public Function CurrentTile() As Long
    CurrentTile = TileAt(PlayerPos.x, PlayerPos.y)
End Function

Public Function PlayerPos() As point
    'get tile pos at center of screen
    PlayerPos.x = ScrollX + SCREENWIDTH / 2
    PlayerPos.y = ScrollY + SCREENHEIGHT / 2
End Function
```

```
Public Sub ShowScrollData()
    Static old As point
    Dim tile As point

    tile.x = PlayerPos.x \ TILEWIDTH
    tile.y = PlayerPos.y \ TILEHEIGHT

    If (tile.x <> old.x) Or (tile.y <> old.y) Then

        'erase the background
        DrawSurface wood, 0, 0, 639, 30, backbuffer, 0, 449

        old = tile

        PrintText fontImg, fontSpr, 5, 452, C_WHITE, _
            "Scroll=(" & PlayerPos.x & "," & PlayerPos.y & ") "
        PrintText fontImg, fontSpr, 5, 466, C_WHITE, _
            "Tile(" & tile.x & "," & tile.y & ")=" & CurrentTile()
    End If
End Sub
```

Another thing this code does is make use of the new PrintText subroutine that was provided in the previous chapter for printing text on the screen. I modified the ShowScrollData subroutine so that it would print the scrolling and tile numbers at the bottom of the screen rather than in the window caption. Along the way, I came up with a nice image to fill the space at the bottom of the screen. This is a wood-grain bitmap image, loaded into a surface and drawn at the bottom of the screen during each screen update. I created and loaded this image using the following code in Sub Main:

```
Dim wood As Direct3DSurface8
Set wood = LoadSurface(App.Path & "\bottom.bmp", 644, 32)
```

The CollisionTest Program

A lot of changes were made to the WalkAbout program during the development of collision-detection code, with the resulting program for this chapter (CollisionTest). I do not want to list the source code for the project in each chapter because the source code is starting to get somewhat complex, and I prefer that you focus on the algorithms and individual functions and subroutines that are covered in each chapter.

I encourage you, therefore, to load the current project that you copied from the CD-ROM to your hard drive and examine the program running. At this point, I am confident that you have gained enough experience entering code that it is no longer necessary for me to include complete listings of each program. In each chapter from here on out I use the

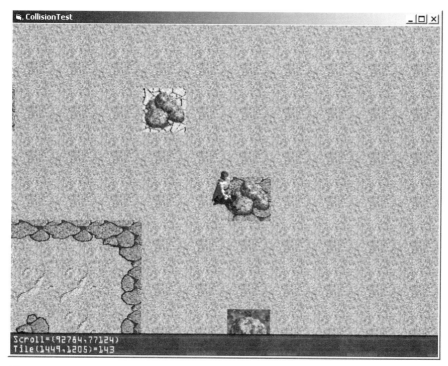

Figure 14.1 The CollisionTest program demonstrates tile-collision checking within the game.

same code that was originally developed for the WalkAbout program, with incremental updates and improvements along the way.

With the tile-collision code added to the original WalkAbout program, the resulting new program has been called CollisionTest and is available on the CD-ROM in \sources \chapter14. Figure 14.1 shows the new version of the game running. Note the player is standing next to a solid, impassable tile.

Level Up

This chapter provided an introduction to collision detection. You learned about the basic collision between two sprites—or more accurately, between two rectangles—using the IntersectRect function available in the Windows API (and greatly simplifies the collision code that you would otherwise have to write yourself). You then learned how to implement tile collision in the game so you can specify a certain tile number as impassable. By modifying some of the code in the game, it is now possible to prevent the player from walking on specific tiles.

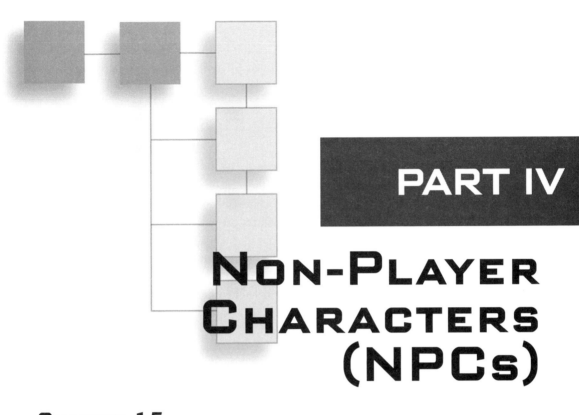

PART IV

NON-PLAYER CHARACTERS (NPCs)

The fourth part of this book covers the subject of *non-player characters (NPCs)* for the most part, although the subject of character classes is applicable to the primary *player's character (PC)*. This part starts off with a chapter on creating character classes, explaining how to load and save character classes from binary data files. The next three chapters focus on adding NPCs to the game world. Just getting NPCs into the game world is the first issue; following that, you expand on the idea by making it possible to interact with the NPCs by communicating and—when necessary—engaging in combat with them. By the time you have finished with this part of the book, you have a very playable game in Celtic Crusader.

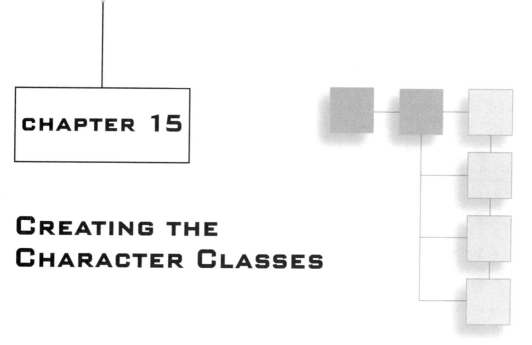

CHAPTER 15

CREATING THE
CHARACTER CLASSES

This chapter provides a discussion of player attributes and the creation of character classes. You learn how to take the designs of the character classes and make use of them in the game itself—at the source code level. I am unable to provide a complete tutorial on constructing a player generation system (with randomly generated attributes, an attractive screen, and so forth) due to the time involved in building a user interface. However, I point you in the right direction and give you the essentials for creating each of the five character classes described in Chapter 3, "Designing the Game." This important chapter fills a sorely needed discussion on this topic, which has been put aside until this point by the necessity of creating the game engine itself. Now you can finally get into player creation and begin to populate the game world.

Here is a breakdown of the major topics in this chapter:

- Character classes and attributes
- Gaining experience and leveling up
- The base character classes
- Character data files
- The character class data type
- Loading and saving binary character data files
- The character-editor program

Character Classes and Attributes

All of the previous chapters have focused on the difficult task of getting a player, fully animated, to walk around in the game world. Both the animation and the movement should be realistic, and tile-collision detection should prevent the player from walking through solid and impassable tiles (such as water). Now that these basic problems have been solved, you can get more into the game's design and into the nuances of combat and NPC interaction.

As you may recall from Chapter 3, the player attributes are as follows:

- **Strength** represents the character's ability to carry a weight and swing a weapon. It is generally good for the warrior and knight classes, which carry blunt weapons. Strength is used to calculate the attack value for the character.

- **Dexterity** represents the agility of the character, the ability to manipulate objects (like a weapon), and the skill with which the player uses his or her hands in general. A very low dexterity means the character is clumsy, while a very high dexterity means the character can perform complex actions.

- **Intellect** represents the character's ability to learn, remember things, and solve problems. A very high intellect is required by the mage class, while relatively low intellect is common in fighter classes, where brute force is more important than mental faculties.

- **Charisma** represents the character's attractiveness and generally affects how others respond to the character. A character with very high charisma attracts others, while very low charisma repels others.

- **Stamina** represents a character's *endurance*, the ability to continue performing an activity for a long period of time. Very high stamina provides a character with the ability to engage in lengthy battles without rest, while a character with low stamina tires quickly (and is likely to fall in battle).

Gaining Experience and Leveling Up

One of the most rewarding aspects of a *role-playing game (RPG)* is gaining experience by performing actions in the game (usually combat) and leveling up your character. When you start the game, the character is also just starting out as a level 1 with no experience. This reflects the player's own skill level with the game, and that is the appeal of an RPG: *You*, the player, gain experience with the game while your PC gains experience at the same time.

Both you and your character improve as you play the game, so you transfer some of your own identity to the character, and in some cases, younger players even assume some of the identity of their inspiring characters. This fascinating give-and-take relationship can really draw someone into your game if you design it well! Like I have said, cut back on the magic and let players really get out in the game world and experience some good, solid combat to make the whole experience feel more real.

The Base Character Classes

The standard, or *base*, classes can be used for the player as well as for the *non-player characters (NPCs)*. You should feel free to create as many classes as you want to make your game world diversified and interesting. The classes I have described here are just the usual classes you find in an RPG, which you might consider the stock classes. Each class also has subclasses, or specialties within that class. For instance, Paladins are really just a subclass of the Knight, which may include Teutonic Knight, Crusader, and so on.

When you are designing a game, you can make it as historically accurate or as fictional as you want; don't feel compelled to make every class realistic or historically based. You might make up a completely fictional type of Knight subclass, such as a Dark Knight or Gothic Knight, with some dark magic abilities. However, I want to encourage you to shy away from overdoing the magic system in a game. Many RPGs I have played use character classes that might be thought of as wizards on steroids, because the whole game boils down to upgrading spells and magic, with little emphasis on "realistic" combat.

You would be surprised by how effective an RPG can be with just a few magic abilities. You can really go overboard with the hocus pocus, and that tends to trivialize a well-designed storyline and render interesting characters into fireball targets. No warrior should be able to do *any* magic whatsoever. Think about it: The warriors are basically barbarians—massive, hulking fighters who use brute force to bash skulls on the battlefield. That this type of character can become civilized and educated is ludicrous.

Of course, don't limit yourself on my account. I'm just pointing out some obvious design concerns with characters. If you really want a world of magic, then go ahead and create magical characters; that sounds like a really fun game, as a matter of fact! If you are designing a traditional RPG, then be realistic with your classes and keep the magic reasonable. Think about *The Lords of the Rings*; these stories are the sole source of inspiration for every RPG ever made. Everything since J.R.R. Tolkien has been derivative!

Tables 15.1 through 15.5 present my idea of a character class structure that you can use in the game.

In addition to these combat classes, you might want to create some base classes for some of the regular people in the world, like townsfolk, peasants, farmers, and so on. These non-combat NPCs might all just share the same character class (with weak combat skills, poor experience, and so on). See Table 15.6.

One design consideration that you might use is the concept of *class modifiers*. Say you have a set of stock classes like those listed in the preceding tables. Instead of re-creating a class from scratch using similar values, you can create a subclass based on the parent class, but that modifies the attributes by a small amount to produce the new class with custom attributes.

Table 15.1 Warrior

Attribute	Value
Strength	+8
Dexterity	+4
Intellect	-3
Charisma	0
Stamina	+6

Table 15.2 Knight

Attribute	Value
Strength	+6
Dexterity	+4
Intellect	-3
Charisma	+5
Stamina	+3

Table 15.3 Rogue (Thief)

Attribute	Value
Strength	-1
Dexterity	+7
Intellect	+3
Charisma	+1
Stamina	+5

Table 15.4 Scout (Archer)

Attribute	Value
Strength	+3
Dexterity	+8
Intellect	-2
Charisma	+1
Stamina	+5

Table 15.5 Mage

Attribute	Value
Strength	-6
Dexterity	+3
Intellect	+9
Charisma	+4
Stamina	+5

Table 15.6 Peasant

Attribute	Value
Strength	+1
Dexterity	+1
Intellect	0
Charisma	+1
Stamina	+1

Say, for instance, that you want to create a new type of Warrior called the Berserker, which is an extremely stupid and ugly character with immense strength and stamina. Sounds a little bit scary, doesn't it? By setting the base class of the Berserker to Warrior, you can then modify the base class at any time and the Berserker automatically is changed along with the base class (Warrior). This works great for balancing the game play without requiring that you modify *every single* subclass that you have used in the game.

Class modifiers must be dealt with in code rather than in a character-editor program, therefore I don't use subclass modifiers (although the idea is a good one).

Using Character Classes in the Game

You know what type of data you want to use in the game based on the descriptions of the various classes. How, then, do you make use of those classes in the game? Among the many ways that you could approach this problem, two solutions immediately come to mind:

- You can hard code all of the character classes using source code.
- You can load character classes from data files.

The first option seems to be more reasonable, especially when you are just getting started. It does help to have a custom data type ready for use before deciding which method you would prefer to use in the game. Ultimately, I think it is best to use the second option, which means you store character class information outside the program in data files. This is a good idea because it allows you to make changes to the character classes to balance the gameplay and enhance the game, all without requiring you to edit source code and recompile.

Character Data Files

I would definitely store the character classes in a separate data file and use a binary file format along with VB's Get and Put statements to read and save records (these commands give VB the ability to work with binary files). Isn't it easier to use a text file for character data? I agree this is a good idea for development, but text files are a pain. Seriously. Not only are they a pain to open and parse out the data you need, but text files can be edited by *anyone* using Notepad! At least with a binary character data file you have one layer of protection over your data—and I'm fully aware of how easy it is to edit data using a hex editor program. The second reason for using binary data files is that they are *extremely* easy to use in source code. You can create a custom structure for your characters and then load and save an entire record using that structure, automatically, using VB's binary data file input/output routines.

In contrast, using a text file format means you must load the text data into the program and then parse it into the appropriate variables, which is a lot of unnecessary code when the binary format fills your character data automatically.

If you plan to create a full-featured RPG on your own, then you may want to write a simple VB program that uses VB's file input/output routines to load and save character data files, with the ability to create new files and edit existing characters. I give you an example of that code following the next section. First, let's talk about the character class data type.

The Character Class Data Type

The character class data type is a structure (Type) that is used in the game as well as in the binary data files. This custom data type includes the character's name, class, experience, and level, as well as the five attributes. In addition, this data type is future proof (in that it is expandable with the use of filler strings and integers at the end of the data type). You can add new attributes to the character class by taking away from the filler arrays and filling in the same number of bytes. This is important because without the filler data, you would have to type in all the character class records *again* every time you changed the record format.

```
Public Type TCHARACTER
    name As String * 20
    classtype As String * 20
    experience As Integer
    level As Integer
    strength As Integer
    dexterity As Integer
    intellect As Integer
    charisma As Integer
    stamina As Integer
    fillerstr As String * 80
    fillerint(10) As Integer
End Type
```

By using filler fields, you can take an item out of one of the filler arrays to add new fields, and then the character-editor program and the data files still work. For instance, suppose you want to add a new field to the characters that tracks their total number of kills. (That is a pretty neat field to add to the character's data, come to think of it!) To do this, you take one value out of the fillerint array and add the field *immediately before or after* the array. You must make the change so that the data file still looks exactly the same in memory, which means you have to add fields directly before or after the array itself. The same goes for the fillerstr string, which is defined as 80 bytes long. Suppose you want to add a new text field to the character classes, such as a Hometown field, for instance. Decide how many bytes to use for this new field, define the field with that number, and then take away from the filler array. Here is what the changes might look like:

```
    Hometown As String * 20
    fillerstr As String * 60
    TotalKills As Integer
    fillerint(9) As Integer
End Type
```

Loading and Saving Binary Character Data Files

You can open a file to read or write a record of the TCHARACTER type using the following code. The first function is called LoadCharacterBinaryFile. This function opens the specified filename and reads the first record from the file into a temporary TCHARACTER variable. It then closes the file and returns the record. You could store all of your game's characters in a single data file with multiple records stored in the file; feel free to do this if you want, although you will have to write an editor program that supports multiple records per file. I think it is simpler to just store one character per file.

```
Public Function LoadCharacterBinaryFile( _
    ByVal filename As String) As TCHARACTER

    Dim filenum As Integer
    Dim dude As TCHARACTER

    filenum = FreeFile()
    Open filename For Binary As filenum Len = Len(dude)
    Get filenum, , dude
    Close filenum

    LoadCharacterBinaryFile = dude
End Function
```

A similar routine saves a character record to a binary data file using the custom TCHARACTER structure:

```
Public Sub SaveCharacterBinaryFile( _
    ByVal filename As String, _
    ByRef dude As TCHARACTER)

    Dim filenum As Integer

    filenum = FreeFile()
    Open filename For Binary As filenum Len = Len(dude)
    Put filenum, , dude
    Close filenum
End Sub
```

The only problem with this technique is that you have to write your own character-editor program that saves the information into the binary data file. One weird way to do it is to create the character classes in code and then call SaveCharacterBinaryFile with each one to save the characters. As you might imagine, this is a very time-consuming task that is totally unnecessary. What you need is an editor program.

The Character-Editor Program

Luckily for you, I have already made such a program. It's called Simple Character Editor and is located in \sources\chapter15 on the CD-ROM for your convenience. This program should be considered an example, not a complete character-editor program. It does, how-ever, succeed in dealing with the key attributes of the PCs and NPCs. Using this editor program, you can create a whole multitude of different NPCs for the game just to give the player some level-up fodder: peasants, evil creatures, Viking explorers, Viking warlords, and random NPCs of various classes.

The idea behind the character data files is not to create a separate file for every single char-acter in the game, but only for the different character *classes*. You might have many NPCs that are Warriors, Knights, Rogues, Scouts, and Mages, all using the same classes available to your player's character. Remember that you can create as many characters in the game as you want, all based on the *same* classes. While you can create as many different classes as you want, just remember that you aren't editing *individuals*, just classes.

The five classes have been created using the Simple Character Editor program, as shown in Figure 15.1. I recommend loading up the CharacterEditor project yourself and modi-fying the program to suit your needs. Since there is a user interface involved, I won't bother listing the source code for the editor program here. (The source code is short, but doesn't account for the controls on the form.)

Level Up

This chapter filled in the details of character attributes and classes. Now that things are looking pretty good in the game department, you can focus some attention again on char-acter design. The last few chapters have focused on designing the game world and inter-acting with the world in general. After having read this chapter, I'm sure you are eager to add some characters to the world and give the player something to do! Stay tuned, because the next chapter gets into that subject.

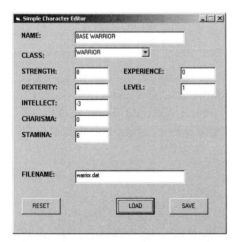

Figure 15.1 The Simple Character Editor program is a prototype character-class editor for an RPG.

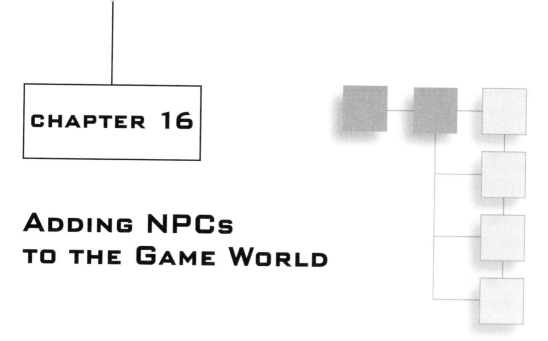

CHAPTER 16

ADDING NPCs
TO THE GAME WORLD

A role-playing game is only fun if the game world is sufficiently populated to allow interaction and fighting with computer-controlled players. These *non-player characters*, or *NPCs* for short, are a vital element of a *role-playing game (RPG)*. Although some types of RPGs prefer to reserve NPC for human characters, I simplify the issue and define an NPC as any type of character in the game other than the *player's character (PC)* and animals. Animals are defined as the native fauna of the game world, and do not necessarily have to be recognizable creatures. You might have alien-type animals in your game, but the difference is that fauna do not engage in combat, and therefore should not be grouped with NPCs.

This chapter fills the role of explaining how to add NPCs to the game world, and also squeezes in a sorely needed discussion of player attributes and the entire player-creation process. Although I am unable to provide a complete tutorial on constructing a player-generation system for this game, I point you in the right direction and provide the essentials for creating each of the five character classes described in Chapter 3, "Designing the Game." Throughout this chapter, you have NPCs with which the player may engage in battle; therefore, the discussion of player attributes (and NPC attributes) is called for.

Here is a breakdown of the major topics in this chapter:

- Introduction to NPCs
- Creating reusable NPCs
- Initializing the NPCs
- Moving the NPCs
- Setting a random destination
- Drawing the NPCs

Introduction to NPCs

I focus all of my remaining attention on building up the Leinster Region of the game world. (You may recall that Leinster is one of the four regions in 9th-century Ireland and consists of the most towns and ruins on the map.) As you might imagine, the creation of an entire game world is a daunting task that requires attention to detail and an investment of time, and it should be directed toward your game's overall storyline. Since I'm limited by the scope of this book, I have to give you the tools you need to take this game to the level you want, according to your own imagination. In essence, I am giving you the game engine and the tools, rather than a completely polished game—without apology, as this is how it should be. I do not want to limit your creative potential with my particular vision for a game. Take this as far and wide as you possibly can!

By the time you have finished this chapter, you have a new, improved version of the Celtic Crusader game (which is still more of a game engine at this point than a complete game) available. The version that you see developed in this chapter is shown in Figure 16.1. The game has basic NPC support by the time you finish this chapter.

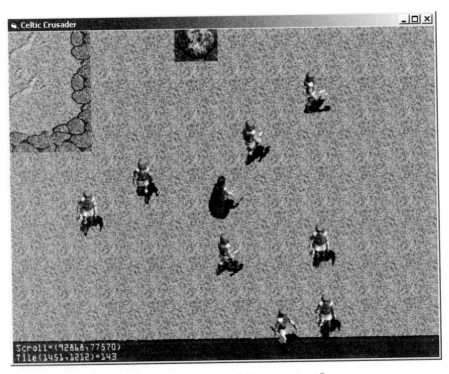

Figure 16.1 Hero: "Help, I'm surrounded by Viking warriors!"

Starting Position and Range of Movement

The most important thing to consider (after loading the NPC's images, that is) is the starting position. Where does the NPC start off in the game? After this, the next most important thing to consider is this NPC's behavior: What does this character do in the game world? The starting position is an actual pixel X,Y location in the game world. Depending on the behavioral subroutine being used by each NPC, you may want to set the starting position in the middle of a town, so that when the NPC reaches a new destination after walking around for a while, it is basically centered on a town. (Most of the population should be near towns.)

The starting position also specifies where NPCs respawn after being killed (with additional randomness applied along with, perhaps, a different name). The NPC's range should keep that character relatively close to his or her starting point, and the character's behavior is then based on the movement state (which might be stopped, walking, running, and so on). By respawning an NPC, perhaps at the other side of the game world, you can keep the game flowing smoothly without allowing a rampaging player to decimate your plans for challenging gameplay! Indeed, one thing you might consider is increasing the experience and level of each NPC that is killed, so that over time the game world gets more and more challenging for the player. You explore these issues in the next two chapters.

A Simple State Engine

At this early stage in the game, I have created a very simple subroutine (which is called a "state engine" because it reacts to the character's current state). This subroutine directs the behavior of the NPCs. You can add behavioral subroutines and states to the game as you learn how to control the NPCs. For starters, I have an enumerated list called NPCSTATES that the TNPC type uses to keep track of an NPC's location and behavioral properties (such as the starting, current, and destination points in the game world).

```
'keeps track of NPC state
Public Enum NPCSTATES
    NPC_STOPPED = 0
    NPC_WALKING = 1
End Enum
```

As you learn in the next two chapters, you can add new states to the list, such as NPC_FLEEING, NPC_TALKING, and NPC_ATTACKING.

Benevolent Versus Malevolent NPCs

You want to use basically two types of NPCs in the game (in addition to animals, perhaps, for scenery). *Benevolent NPCs* are harmless people like villagers, townsfolk, peasants, and perhaps even local law enforcement. (Have you considered the possibility of having local guards attack the player if you harm any local peasants? That would be a fascinating aspect of the game.) The other type of NPC is *malevolent* in nature—that is, characters opposed to the player, including evil creatures, outlaws, bandits, and of course in the context of this game: Vikings (which should be particularly tough to fight, given the theme of the game).

Creating Reusable NPCs

The NPCs are based on the standard character classes (created with the Simple Character Editor program that you saw in the previous chapter), but a little bit of randomness applied to the characters makes them interesting, while not requiring you to creating custom characters with the editor. The randomness might affect the attributes if you want, but I prefer to just give each NPC a random experience and level to make them more or less powerful than the player (but not beyond reason). Keep the random NPCs within a certain range of the player's experience and level to keep the game interesting.

The previous chapter also introduced you to the custom TCHARACTER structure used by the binary data files and that keeps track of characters in memory. The TNPC structure (in the next section) works in tandem with TCHARACTER to let you add NPCs to the game world and move them around (which is the best you can hope for at this stage, but stay tuned).

The Custom NPC Data Types and Arrays

The custom data type that tracks each individual NPC is called TNPC. This structure allows you to keep tabs on every NPC in the game, with variables that track the NPC's state, starting position, current position, destination, and so on.

```
'keeps track of each character
Public Type TNPC
    name As String
    state As NPCSTATES
    startpos As point
    curpos As point
    destpos As point
    classindex As Integer
    SpeedDelay As Integer
    SpeedCount As Integer
    Facing As Integer
End Type
```

The game actually uses a series of arrays to manage the NPCs (that is, to move, animate, and draw them on the screen). NUMCHARS defines the number of unique character classes being used in the game. This is an important distinction to make, because this constant doesn't refer to the total number of NPCs in the game, just the number of available *classes* (presumably classes that you have loaded from the binary data files, per the Simple Character Editor program).

The charImages array is unique only to the classes and is not used by every single NPC. This is a shared array. The charClasses array is of type TCHARACTER and is also limited to the distinct classes.

On the other hand, two arrays keep track of every single NPC in the game. These two arrays, charStates and charSprites, are of types TNPC and TSPRITE, respectively, and have an array size specified by the NUMNPCS constant. The important thing to remember here is that these last two arrays are what you work with. A variable in TNPC, classindex, specifies the index into the charImages and charClasses arrays that are shared.

The end result is that you can load a Warrior class from warrior.DAT, open a bitmap image containing the animated sprite of this warrior, and then create 1, 10, 50, or 100 individual NPCs that share this bitmap and class data. Those individual NPCs use charStates and charSprites. If you are at all confused on this point, then just go ahead and start poring through the source code in the completed project on the CD-ROM (located in \sources\chapter16\CelticCrusader1), run the project, and observe how these array variables are being used. You also gain more familiarity with them over the next two chapters.

```
'generic data for the character classes
'images and data are shared by the NPCs
Const NUMCHARS As Long = 1
Dim charImages(NUMCHARS) As Direct3DTexture8
Dim charClasses(NUMCHARS) As TCHARACTER

'unique data for each individual NPC
Const NUMNPCS As Long = 10
Dim charStates(NUMNPCS) As TNPC
Dim charSprites(NUMNPCS) As TSPRITE
```

Initializing the NPCs

I have written a subroutine called InitCharacters that initializes all of the NPCs in the game. This subroutine is what you modify when you want to load new characters designed with the Simple Character Editor program (in addition to putting together the animated sprite frames using a tool such as Pro Motion). The subroutine is somewhat hard coded at present because the game is using just a single class of NPC, but you modify it over the next two chapters as the game comes to life.

```
Public Sub InitCharacters()
    Dim p As point
    Dim n As Long
```

```
'set up all the base character classes, sprites, and images
'so far we're only using a single type of character—Viking Warrior
charClasses(0) = LoadCharacterBinaryFile(App.Path & "\warrior.dat")
Set charImages(0) = LoadTexture(d3ddev, App.Path & "\viking_walking.bmp")

'now create the individual characters used in the game
'all of these will share the base data above
For n = 0 To NUMNPCS - 1

    'initialize sprite data
    InitSprite d3ddev, charSprites(n)
    With charSprites(n)
        .FramesPerRow = 8
        .FrameCount = 8
        .AnimDelay = 2
        .width = 96
        .height = 96
    End With

    'start NPCs at the player's location
    '(to test NPC movement at this stage)
    p.x = PLAYERSTARTX * TILEWIDTH
    p.y = PLAYERSTARTY * TILEHEIGHT

    'customize the Viking character
    With charStates(n)

        'this is the key! points to the base image/sprite/data
        .classindex = 0

        .name = "Viking"
        .startpos = p
        .curpos = p
        .SpeedDelay = 1
        .SpeedCount = 0
        .state = NPC_WALKING
        SetRandomDestination n

    End With
Next n


End Sub
```

Moving the NPCs

The MoveNPCs subroutine is called by the main game loop, but I recommend calling it *before* the screen is updated between the BeginDraw and EndDraw calls. You want the NPCs to move around without being limited by the game's timer (which causes the game to run at a consistent frame rate). Instead of relying on the frame rate timer, use the SpeedCount and SpeedDelay variables in TNPC to adjust the movement speed of each NPC.

```
Public Sub MoveNPCs()
    Dim n As Long

    'loop through all of the NPCs and move them
    For n = 0 To NUMNPCS - 1
        MoveNPC n
    Next n
End Sub
```

I was tempted to break up this MoveNPC subroutine into two subroutines because it is on the lengthy side. However, the code herein is completely logical and linear, making it easier to read as one block of code rather than as separate subroutines. As the code comments show, each part deals with a direction that the NPC is facing. Surprise, surprise: The directional code is the most difficult part of moving an NPC!

If all you had to do is move a sprite, that would be a few lines of code at most! Since these sprites have 64 frames each (*at least*), with 8 directions of travel, this requires some forethought. When you see the CelticCrusader1 program demonstration running, I think you may be floored with how cool it is! If you are expecting a full-featured game at this point, I just want to help you tone down your expectations because the game *is* coming along. You have to realize the limited amount of space in this book prevents a thorough treatment of the subject, so what you see here is hard-core RPG action! All of the bells and whistles are up to you. The text discusses the most difficult aspects of the game, so I hope you manage many of the smaller details of the game on your own. Consider it a challenge and a learning experience.

```
Public Sub MoveNPC(ByVal num As Long)
    'moves a single NPC
    With charStates(num)

        'update movement rate--exit if not there yet
        .SpeedCount = .SpeedCount + 1
        If .SpeedCount < .SpeedDelay Then Exit Sub

        'okay, time to move, reset move counter
        .SpeedCount = 0
```

```
'check to see if destination reached
If .curpos.x = .destpos.x And .curpos.y = .destpos.y Then
    'yes! set a new destination then exit
    .state = NPC_STOPPED
    SetRandomDestination num
    Exit Sub
Else
    .state = NPC_WALKING
End If

'time to set the NPC's "facing" direction
'and update the X,Y position
If .curpos.x < .destpos.x Then

    'needs to walk westward
    .curpos.x = .curpos.x + 1

    If .curpos.y < .destpos.y Then
        'facing SE
        .curpos.y = .curpos.y + 1
        .Facing = 3
    ElseIf .curpos.y > .destpos.y Then
        'facing NE
        .curpos.y = .curpos.y - 1
        .Facing = 1
    Else
        'facing EAST
        .Facing = 2
    End If

ElseIf .curpos.x > .destpos.x Then

    'needs to walk eastward
    .curpos.x = .curpos.x - 1

    If .curpos.y < .destpos.y Then
        'facing SW
        .curpos.y = .curpos.y + 1
        .Facing = 5
```

```
            ElseIf .curpos.y > .destpos.y Then
                'facing NW
                .curpos.y = .curpos.y - 1
                .Facing = 7
            Else
                'facing WEST
                .Facing = 6
            End If


        Else 'must be facing due NORTH or SOUTH

            If .curpos.y < .destpos.y Then
                'facing SOUTH
                .curpos.y = .curpos.y + 1
                .Facing = 4
            ElseIf .curpos.y > .destpos.y Then
                'facint NORTH
                .curpos.y = .curpos.y - 1
                .Facing = 0
            End If

        End If


    End With
End Sub
```

Setting a Random Destination

Now I show you a behavioral subroutine that makes the NPCs come to life! This should be just one of many such routines that you eventually have in your own game, adjusting the behavior of NPCs based on events (usually in response to the player). This subroutine should be considered just a demonstration of NPC behavior, giving you some ideas about what you can really do with the NPCs. This subroutine gives the player a new, random destination based on its starting position when the game began. Setting a random destination at a certain distance from the starting position ensures that NPCs stay near their homes in the game world.

```
Public Sub SetRandomDestination(ByVal num As Long)
    With charStates(num)

        'set random X near the starting position
        '(the NPC will never wander away from his "home")
        .destpos.x = .startpos.x + Random(600)
```

```
        If .destpos.x > GAMEWORLDWIDTH Then
            .destpos.x = GAMEWORLDWIDTH - 1
        End If


        'set random Y near the starting position
        .destpos.y = .startpos.y + Random(600)
        If .destpos.y > GAMEWORLDHEIGHT Then
            .destpos.y = GAMEWORLDHEIGHT - 1
        End If
    End With
End Sub
```

This is just one example of a behavior, and the range of the NPC has been hard coded to 600 (that's in pixel units, not tiles). So, the range is very small. I wanted it this way to demonstrate that the NPCs are not only working, but moving around within close proximity to the player. At this early stage in NPC development, you want to keep your test subjects nearby, so you can observe them. I had to do quite a bit of debugging to get them to face the right direction when moving from one point to another on the map. The result as it is now, I think, is really cool!

I was just thinking about how many different behaviors I would love to give to these NPCs, and I started thinking about the game The Sims. You know, if you spend enough time on your NPCs, you could give them realistic behaviors similar to the characters in The Sims, only perhaps more closely related to the game at hand. Instead of doing dumb things like going to the bathroom and taking a shower—what's that all about, anyway?— you can program your NPCs to use one of several behaviors based on the conditions in the game.

One thing I show you here is how to implement behavior modifications using the state property (within the TNPC structure). This is an example that you can implement fairly easily. (I actually get into this in the next two chapters, so I talk about behavior quite a bit more there.) By adding additional states to the NPCSTATES enumerated list, you can then cause NPCs to react to the player realistically. Suppose you attack a peasant villager. Should that NPC just stand there? Of course not! You need to give the NPC some options in the form of state behaviors. One behavior might be to flee the current location at twice normal speed (which could be equivalent to running). Another state might be to fight back! As you learn in the next two chapters, all it takes is a few behavioral subroutines, used collectively, to give NPCs a wide range of behaviors.

Drawing the NPCs

The DrawNPCs subroutine is called by the main game loop and simply iterates through all of the NPCs in the game world, calling on the DrawNPC helper routine to get the job done.

```
Public Sub DrawNPCs()
    Dim n As Long

    'loop through all of the NPCs and draw them
    For n = 0 To NUMNPCS - 1
        DrawNPC n
    Next n
End Sub
```

The actual subroutine that draws an NPC onto the screen is DrawNPC. It is called by DrawN-PCs, which should be placed inside the main game loop between the BeginDraw and EndDraw statements.

The bulk of the code in DrawNPC is just an algorithm that figures out whether the sprite is even supposed to be drawn at this time. Based on the ScrollX and ScrollY variables, this subroutine checks to see if the sprite should be visible, and if it is, then it is displayed with the current direction and animation frame.

```
Public Sub DrawNPC(ByVal num As Long)
    Dim r As RECT
    Dim classindex As Long

    'grab a shortcut to these long variable names
    r.Left = charStates(num).curpos.x
    r.Top = charStates(num).curpos.y
    r.Right = r.Left + charSprites(num).width
    r.Bottom = r.Top + charSprites(num).height

    'remember, images/data are referred to using the NPC's classindex!
    'the sprite and state arrays are for every single unique NPC,
    'but the bitmap image and class data are shared by all NPCs
    classindex = charStates(num).classindex

    'now check to see if the sprite is within the scrolling viewport
    'sprite's position is actually global, so this determines if it's visible
    If r.Left > ScrollX - 1 And r.Right < ScrollX + SCREENWIDTH + 1 And _
       r.Top > ScrollY - 1 And r.Bottom < ScrollY + SCREENHEIGHT + 1 Then

        'update animation frame if walking
        If charStates(num).state = NPC_WALKING Then
            AnimateSprite charSprites(num)
        End If
```

```
'draw the sprite--remember, it's using the shared image (texture)
charSprites(num).x = charStates(num).curpos.x - ScrollX
charSprites(num).y = charStates(num).curpos.y - ScrollY
charSprites(num).AnimSeq = charStates(num).Facing
DrawSprite charImages(classindex), charSprites(num), C_WHITE


        End If


End Sub
```

The New and Improved Game

This new version of Celtic Crusader is located on the CD-ROM in \sources\chapter16 \CelticCrusader1. I encourage you to load up the project and run it, because I don't include complete source code listings in this chapter. (My focus at this point is on the algorithms and helping you understand how the game works, so you can modify it yourself.)

Before diving into the new source code for the game, which is starting to look more and more like a functional RPG with each new chapter (refer back to Figure 16.1), create the custom sprite artwork for each new character in the game. Fortunately, as you have seen in previous chapters, you have these wonderful 3D modeled and rendered sprites available from Reiner's Tilesets at http://www.reinerstilesets.de.

Figure 16.2 shows the Viking sprite loaded into Pro Motion and ready to be exported as a series of eight animation strips. Each strip contains eight frames of animation for one of the directions of travel. This is the same process that you observed in action back in Chapter 14, "Core Technique: Collision Detection."

After saving the animation strips into eight individual bitmap files, you can combine them into a single bitmap using a graphic editor like Paint Shop Pro. You can see how I combined the images into one large bitmap in Figure 16.3. Note that the transparent pixels in the background should be pink, which is a color with an RGB value of (255,0,255).

Level Up

This chapter introduced you to the rather complex issues involved in adding NPCs to the game. Although an RPG is playable without a big population of NPCs, it is a good idea to have a large variety of people with whom the player can interact (and fight). Otherwise, the game becomes slow and boring. This chapter gave you the logistical code to get an NPC up on the screen, moving around, and realistically facing in the right direction when walking. The next steps, covered in Chapters 17 and 18, add behaviors to the NPCs allowing them to talk with the player, as well as engage in combat!

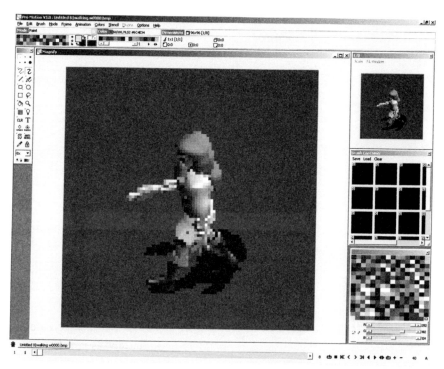

Figure 16.2 The individual Viking Warrior sprites are saved as animation strips by Pro Motion.

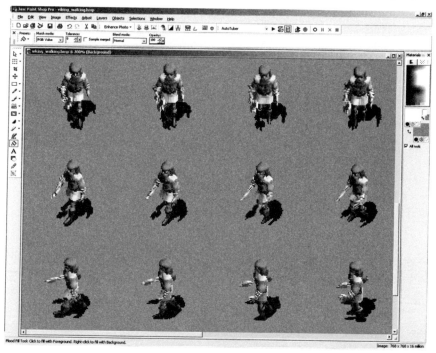

Figure 16.3 This redheaded Viking Warrior is ready to do your player some damage!

Figure 16-2.—

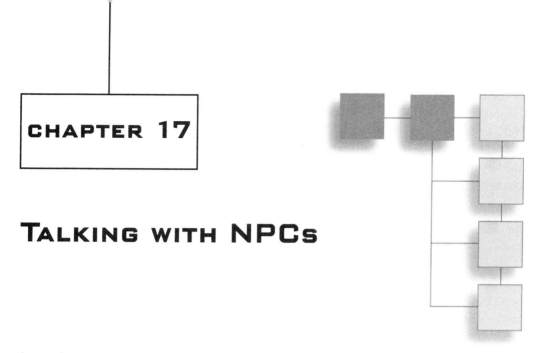

CHAPTER 17

TALKING WITH NPCs

T his chapter adds another level of realism to the game by making it possible to interact with the *non-player characters (NPCs)* you added in the previous chapter. Although it is mainly up to you to create a dialog between the player and various NPCs, I show you how to get started doing so in this chapter. The main aspect of NPC communication is adding another state item to the TNPC structure, so that when the player engages an NPC in dialog, the NPC pauses and faces the player. After the dialog is complete, the NPC should go about his business. That is the primary goal of this chapter.

Here is a breakdown of the major topics in this chapter:

- Behavioral states
- Encountering the player
- Talking to the player
- Modifying the Celtic Crusader project

Behavioral States

Turning some of the code over to an event-driven state-management system is the key to progressing from a tile-based scroller and animated sprite demo, which is essentially what Celtic Crusader might be called by a critical person at this early stage. Such a system takes into account the current state of the NPCs in the game—most notably, those in close proximity to the player—and effect change in that behavior based on events the player creates.

For one thing, an event such as a near collision with the player should not be treated as a collision at all, but rather as an *encounter* that precedes some sort of dialog. In the version of Celtic Crusader that you will see in this chapter, I have enhanced the NPC code in Characters.bas so that the NPCs do, in fact, react to an encounter with the player. As each NPC is being moved (which is a separate process from the code that animates and draws the NPC's sprite image) the current state of the NPC is considered. The state is also examined when the NPC is being drawn. Therefore, you have two opportunities to effect changes to the behavior of an NPC.

What I want to do quickly here is show you the goals I set out to accomplish in this chapter, and then go over the code that you need to study in order to achieve those goals. The current problem with the game is that the NPCs do nothing short of wandering around within close proximity of their starting positions. This, of course, is good for testing during the development. To take this game to the next level, populate regions of the game world with NPCs; of course you want to add many more NPCs and disperse them in the major population centers (as well as a few out and about for chance encounters in the wilderness).

Encountering the Player

Figure 17.1 shows the first example of how the NPCs react when the player is nearby due to the new code developed in this chapter. The key is setting the current state of the NPC

Figure 17.1 NPCs slow down and face the player when the player is nearby.

when a certain event occurs. In this example, the event occurs when the player is close by (in other words, when there is a *collision* between the two sprites). As you can see in this figure, the collision works very well, as the NPC is facing the player in exactly the right direction; one might even assume that they are having a conversation based on this image.

That was the primary goal of the player collision code—to set the NPC to a new state called NPC_TALKING anytime the player is close by. The normal state of the NPC is called NPC_WALKING, because the characters in the game are always moving. If you would like to have some NPCs who stop once in a while without *having* to move all the time, that would be a fun project. You might use the existing NPC_PAUSED state (which I am not using for anything at present) to mean that the character has stopped to admire the scenery or perhaps to chat with another NPC. Now that would be fun! Can you imagine that NPCs might say "Hello" to each other in passing? I don't know about you, but I am fascinated by possibilities such as these.

note

Don't get hung up on the fact that only one type of NPC is being shown in these screenshots. I have chosen to use just this one NPC sprite so I can focus on bringing the NPCs to life (by building the state engine, among other things). It is a very simple matter to add the other NPC classes and additional sprite images to the game, but doing so would add complexity to the code, and I want you to focus on how the NPC code works at this point.

Figure 17.2 shows another image where a group of NPCs have walked toward the player. The state engine sets the state of each NPC to NPC_TALKING at this point ("talking" is basically just a term I use to describe an encounter). The NPCs are basically moving slowly in their original directions, but facing the player while doing so to show that they are responding to your character's sprite.

Talking to the Player

The next logical step after you have managed to convince the NPCs to respond to the player is to teach them to participate in a dialog (which requires a lot of coercion—or rather, debugging—until you grasp the concept of a state-driven game). That response can be literally anything. As soon as one of these fellows changes state, you can jump in and have your custom code do something like attack or run from the player.

I have chosen to start the work on a simple dialog system. That system works by engaging the nearby NPCs using the spacebar key. As you can see in Figure 17.3, the NPCs respond to the player's input during the encounter by displaying a Hello message on the screen.

At this point, you can create a more robust and full-featured dialog system with the NPCs. What I have provided you here is the game state that produces a dialog event that makes communication possible. Unfortunately, I don't have the time or space to fully develop the

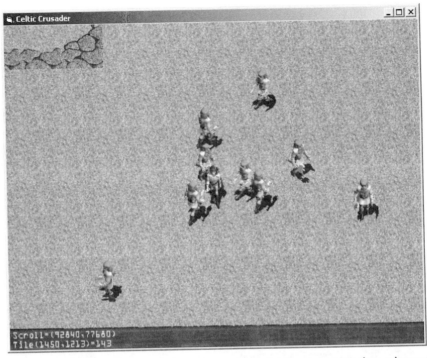

Figure 17.2 A small group of Vikings have surrounded the player! But they only want to talk . . . .

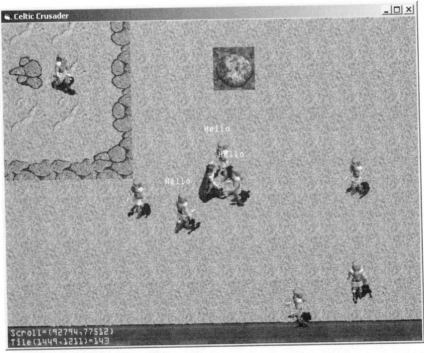

Figure 17.3 Engaging the NPCs in dialog is possible *after* the encounter has occurred (but not before).

potential for true in-game dialog, so I encourage you to take it to the next level on your own. If you are at a loss as to how you might accomplish that, I have a suggestion: Just start by having the NPCs display a random quote out of a list of possible quotes. You can then expand on the dialog by allowing the player to select from a list of things to say (perhaps using the mouse or arrow keys).

One thing that can accomplish that is to pause all animation on the screen and bring up perhaps a window on the screen with some dialog options. The usual thing to do here is create some standard dialog for each character class. For instance, if the Viking characters are always going to be hostile toward your player, then you can easily accommodate a simple dialog between the player and any Viking NPCs with very few options. You might just have the Viking NPCs ignore the player, or say something rude, or perhaps even attack! As for other NPCs, once you have a simple dialog window working, use the arrow keys to scroll down a list of possible things that you would like to say to the NPCs and track responses and reactions using another simple state engine for dialog. (You might do something as simple as keep track of the attitude of each NPC toward the player.)

Modifying the Celtic Crusader Project

Now I show you how the encounter and limited dialog system works from the source code point of view. I encourage you to load up the project for this chapter, which is provided on the CD-ROM in \sources\chapter17\CelticCrusader2. The project is too big to modify in each chapter at this point, so I am just showing you the key subroutines and functions that make the biggest splashes in each chapter, and then refer you to the game's current work-in-progress version. Note that many parts of the project (I estimate about 10 percent of the code) that were introduced to you in previous chapters have been modified for the most recent versions of the game to accommodate the changes needed to interact with NPCs and so on.

New States

In order to change the behavior of an NPC when an event occurs, it is best to change the state of that NPC rather than directly calling a subroutine to cause an event at that very instant. By setting a state value, you can then deal with an event at a more appropriate point in the game loop. Here is the new NPCSTATES:

```
'keeps track of NPC state
Public Enum NPCSTATES
    NPC_STOPPED = 0
    NPC_WALKING = 1
    NPC_PAUSED = 2
    NPC_TALKING = 3
End Enum
```

Utilizing the new states requires a change to the MoveNPCs and the DrawNPCs subroutines. Here is the new version of MoveNPCs, which is called by the main game loop. This new version of the subroutine now does more than just loop through all of the NPCs and move each character. The routine checks the state of each NPC before taking any action. As an example, take note of the case where an NPC's state equals NPC_TALKING. There is a subroutine call to FacePlayer. This is a new subroutine that I introduce to you shortly.

```
Public Sub MoveNPCs()
    Dim n As Long

    'loop through all of the NPCs and move them
    For n = 0 To NUMNPCS - 1

        Select Case charStates(n).state
            Case NPC_TALKING
                FacePlayer n

            Case NPC_PAUSED
                SetRandomDestination n

            Case NPC_WALKING
                MoveNPC n

            Case NPC_STOPPED
                SetRandomDestination n

        End Select
    Next n
End Sub
```

Facing the Player

The FacePlayer subroutine is similar to the MoveNPC subroutine in that one position is compared to another position in order to turn one object toward another. In this case, however, the goal is to cause one of the NPCs to face the player. Since this is the second time a facing routine has been needed, I think it is a good idea to convert this basic algorithm into a reusable function that accepts two points, compares their positions, and then returns a value representing one of the eight directions used in the game.

```
Public Sub FacePlayer(ByVal num As Long)
    Dim a As point
    Dim b As point
```

```
a.x = heroSpr.x + heroSpr.width / 2
a.y = heroSpr.y + heroSpr.height / 2

b.x = charSprites(num).x + charSprites(num).width / 2
b.y = charSprites(num).y + charSprites(num).height / 2

With charStates(num)

    If b.x < a.x - 5 Then
        If b.y < a.y - 5 Then
            .Facing = 3
        ElseIf b.y > a.y + 5 Then
            .Facing = 1
        Else
            .Facing = 2
        End If

    ElseIf b.x > a.x + 5 Then
        If b.y < a.y - 5 Then
            .Facing = 5
        ElseIf b.y > a.y + 5 Then
            .Facing = 7
        Else
            .Facing = 6
        End If

    Else
        If b.y < a.y - 5 Then
            .Facing = 4
        ElseIf b.y > a.y + 5 Then
            .Facing = 0
        End If
    End If

End With
End Sub
```

State-Based Drawing

In addition to a state-based movement routine, I have also modified the DrawNPCs subroutine so it is also based on the state of an NPC. The reason state is checked in both of these routines is because the move routine occurs before any screen updates, while the draw routine occurs inside the BeginScene and EndScene block of code.

```
Public Sub DrawNPCs()
    Dim n As Long

    'loop through all of the NPCs and draw them
    For n = 0 To NUMNPCS - 1

        Select Case charStates(n).state
            Case NPC_TALKING
                DrawNPC n
                charStates(n).state = NPC_WALKING

                If diState.key(KEY_SPACE) > 0 Then
                    TalkToPlayer n
                End If

            Case NPC_PAUSED
                DrawNPC n
                charStates(n).state = NPC_WALKING

            Case NPC_WALKING
                DrawNPC n

            Case NPC_STOPPED
                DrawNPC n
                charStates(n).state = NPC_WALKING

        End Select

    Next n
End Sub
```

Encountering the Player

In order to accommodate the new state engine and, in particular, the encounter state that is to take place, I wrote a new subroutine called CheckNPCCollisions that is called by the main game loop. (The name is consistent with the last collision routine, which is called

`CheckTileCollisions`.) This routine looks for a close encounter between any one NPC and the player, at which point the NPC's state is set to `NPC_TALKING`.

```
Public Sub CheckNPCCollisions()
    Dim n As Long

    'check all NPCs for collisions
    For n = 0 To NUMNPCS - 1

        If Collision(charSprites(n), heroSpr) Then
            charStates(n).state = NPC_TALKING
        End If
    Next n
End Sub
```

Talking to the Player

The `DrawNPCs` routine calls `TalkToPlayer` when the user chooses to talk to an NPC. To do this, you press a certain key during an encounter to engage the NPC in dialog. I chose the spacebar in this example, but you may feel free to use any key you wish (and this is also a good time to add joystick support to the game, in which case you could then use a joystick button to chat with an NPC).

```
Public Sub TalkToPlayer(ByVal num As Long)
    Dim x As Long
    Dim y As Long

    x = charSprites(num).x + charSprites(num).width / 4
    y = charSprites(num).y
    PrintText fontImg, fontSpr, x, y, C_WHITE, "Hello"
End Sub
```

Level Up

This chapter discussed the possibilities that you might use to deal with NPCs, with an emphasis on switching to a state-based event system in the game. By using the state of an NPC, you create the appearance of behavior where very little (or none) exists. State is a powerful concept in a game where interaction with computer-controlled players might otherwise be a daunting task. This chapter also explained and presented an example of how you might add a dialog system to the game, which may or may not be part of your vision for the game. (After all, do you really need to talk to zombies and giant spiders?) However, with the code now available, you can add dialog to the game based on an encounter with an NPC.

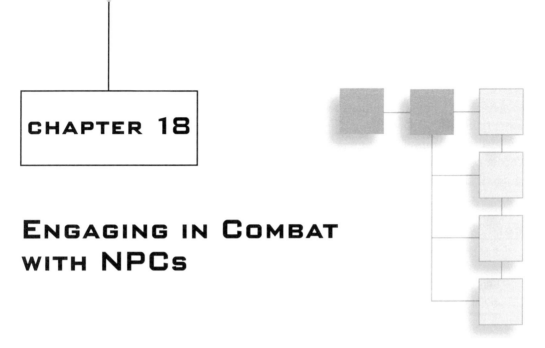

CHAPTER 18

ENGAGING IN COMBAT WITH NPCs

This chapter is the last major discussion of working with *non-player characters (NPCs)* in the book, so my goal here is to develop a working combat system within the game. This requires the use of a complete set of combat animation sequences for the player and NPCs. Fortunately, the sprites available from Reiner's Tile-sets (http://www.reinerstileset.de) also include the attack animations that you use in this chapter. Combat requires another layer of logic added to the state engine that controls the NPCs. Although higher, more advanced interaction with the player should make the game more realistic, at this point a simple state-based reactionary system has to be used, where the NPCs fight back when attacked by the player.

Here is a breakdown of the major topics in this chapter:

- State-based combat
- Dealing with the player's death
- Combat animations
- Introducing the Skeleton Knight
- Engaging in combat
- Managing the player's state
- Managing the NPC states

Contemplating the Combat System

The Celtic Crusader project, as of the last chapter, is basically a template game that has most of the functionality you need to actually create a *role-playing game (RPG)*, but is lacking most of the finer details. One thing you can do with a basic dialog system (which was started in the last chapter) is move toward incorporating the game's story into the gameplay. You can add subtle clues in the dialog with NPCs (most notably, noncombatants) that lead the player toward a goal. For instance, suppose you follow the classic "save the girl" plot. You might use this as one of several subquests to lead the player from one corner of the world to the other, seeking out maidens to rescue. These subquests not only progress the storyline of the game, but also provide the player with much-needed experience points.

note

This chapter does not provide the complete code changes needed to add the combat system. The key source code routines are explained, but the changes to the project are too numerous to list, so I encourage you to just load up the project from the CD-ROM in \sources\chapter18 and follow along while looking at the completed project.

There is just an enormous amount of detail that must be put into even the simplest of RPGs, so what I'm getting at is that I don't want you to expect this game to be a finished product by the time you are done with this book. As you might imagine, the size and scope of this book is nowhere near enough to completely build the game (something that I deeply regret, but cannot help), and I do not want to add functionality that I have not explained in each chapter. What I'm providing you here is a working RPG engine with all the tools you need to complete it. By describing it so, I want you to realize that the creative work, the use of your imagination, and the finishing touches should come from you, because this is *your* game. I believe that with the addition of the combat system in this chapter, you have what you need to turn out a complete game.

State-Based Combat

The previous chapter developed the ability for the player to have encounters with NPCs, which is an important first step in the game's NPC interaction. From this point, you can engage the NPCs in dialog or combat, and the game responds appropriately. Every NPC should behave, in some manner, to attack by the player. A higher level of behavior over the NPCs is also needed to turn this skeleton game into a polished game, a system of behavior that causes NPCs to seek out and engage the player, rather than always *responding* to the player. At the very least, you can add the ability for NPCs to fight back.

Fighting Back

The goal of this chapter is to add combat animations in such a way that it is easy for you to add new NPCs to the game without requiring much extra work. The hostile NPCs need attack animations, while the peasantry do not, so if the player attacks a peasant or any other nonfighting NPC, then you have to add behavior that causes the character to run away or die, depending on your style. (I recommend adding a state that causes nonfighting NPCs to flee.)

Respawning NPCs

When you are fighting with an NPC and kill that character, there should be a death animation. These are not always possible in every case, due to a limited number of sprites. You are limited overall by the availability of artwork, without which you have to get creative with your sprites. Rather than dealing with a whole slew of death animations for each NPC, I have seen some games use the fade effect, where a character blinks out of existence or fades away. You might use the alpha color parameter in `DrawSprite` to cause a character to fade out of existence after dying, which requires some sort of death state.

The important thing is that you recycle your sprites in the game, which means recycling the NPCs. You don't want the NPCs to just respawn at the same place every time, because then the player can see the spawning taking place (which seriously ruins the realism of the game). In addition, if a player learns where some of the NPCs are respawning on the map, he or she will be able to *spawn camp* (which refers to hiding out near a spawn point and killing new players that appear) and rack up a ridiculous amount of experience, which also ruins the game.

Simulating Damage

One aspect of combat you need is some sort of status display showing the hero's health and other attributes. I think it is a good idea to use the main game window for chatting and combat, which means that most of the bottom toolbar is unused. I recommend using it to display the hero's attributes, including health (which is calculated using strength and stamina).

The best way to show damage is to cause a character to flicker on the screen—and keep in mind, this is only my opinion based on my experience with RPGs. Some of the most successful RPGs used the flicker/fade method of showing hits. Since that can also be used for a death animation, it makes sense that enough hits cause a character to flicker out completely (which implies death). It also keeps you, the programmer, from having to keep track of dead bodies in the game world. Although a combat-focused game might benefit from showing the carnage of bodies on the ground, it requires a lot of extra work on your part. You basically have to keep all of those sprites in memory just to draw their dead bodies and then create new sprites to respawn the NPCs. This is all just a lot of unnecessary work; the player is plowing through a lot of enemies in the game, anyway. The flicker/fade technique works well overall.

Attack Rolled Against Defense

What really happens when you attack another character in the game? That is the basis of the game's combat system and it has to do with each player's attributes, including weapon and armor class. Usually, the defender's defensive value is compared to the attacker's attack value, and a simulated "roll" of dice is made to determine if the attack even succeeded (before calculating damage).

If the attack value is less than the defense value, then basically you can do no damage to your opponent! So, say you are a new Warrior with an axe that does +10 damage, and you attack a level-10 Viking Berserker with 93 defense points. What happens in this situation? You can stand there and bang against this fellow's armor all day long with your pathetic little axe and do *no damage* to him whatsoever! If you don't like this aspect of game play, maybe you should go back to playing Zelda. (Sorry, I actually love Zelda, especially Link To The Past, but it has a primitive combat system.) In a situation like this, you are helplessly outclassed by this character, who swiftly and easily kills you with a single blow.

This is called the *to-hit roll* and it adds a nice layer of realism to the game (as opposed to some games where just swinging your sword kills enemies nearby). Knowing that not every swing does damage requires you to use some tactics in your fighting method, and this gives players the ability to be somewhat creative in how they fight enemies. You can swing and run or swing several times in a row, hoping to get a hit. But in general, it's a hit-or-miss situation (sorry, bad pun).

Many RPGs allow the player to equip modifiers such as rings and special weapons with bonuses for the to-hit value. These modifiers increase your chances of scoring a hit when you attack. Since this game is still a work in progress, I have not had a chance to talk with you about inventory items and equipping your character. This very challenging aspect of the game to program requires you to create an item editor program and use an array of items in the game to display items on the ground that the player can pick up. Items in the player's inventory (which probably means the player's backpack) also have modifiers that the player can use in the game, so your forethought on item management is important. Not only is it essential for a good RPG, but working with miscellaneous items as well as different types of swords, shields, armor, helmets, and so on, is an extremely fun part of the game!

Factoring Weapon Values

After the to-hit roll determines that the player did hit his target, determine how much damage was done to the target. This is where the weapon attributes come into play. But wait—I haven't even talked about weapons yet! Well, now is as good a time as any. Since the inventory system is not possible in this prototype game, I propose basing all attack values directly on the player's attributes and using a fixed damage value for each character class. The Warrior should do more damage with his axe than a Mage does with his staff.

Default weapon damage values make the combat system functional until a proper inventory system is added to the game.

If the game features real items that you can give your character to use in combat, then it makes a big difference in the game play. For one thing, you can scatter treasure chests around the game world that contain unique quest items (like magical swords, shields, and armor), as well as valuable jewels and gold. These types of items are all modeled and available in the sprites provided by Reiner's Tilesets. The artwork department is finished and it's just a matter of adding this feature to the game.

Dealing with the Player's Death

One drawback to combat is that you can die. It's a cold, hard, truth, I realize, but it can happen. What should you do, as the game's designer and programmer, when the *player's character (PC)* dies? That is a tough decision that requires some thought and should be based on the overall design of your game. You might let the player save and load games, but that takes away from the suspension of disbelief. Remember that concept that I introduced to you back in Chapter 3, "Designing the Game"? You want the player to be completely immersed in the game and unaware of a file system, an operating system, or even of the computer. You want your players to be mesmerized by the content on the screen, and something as cheesy as a load/save feature takes away from that. I'll admit, though, most players abuse the save/load game feature and complain if you don't have one. After all, you want the player to be able to quit at a moment's notice without going through any hassle. Let's face it: Sometimes the real world asserts itself into the reverie you are experiencing in the game, and you have to quit playing.

But just for the sake of game play, what is the best way to deal with the PC's death, aside from having a save/load feature? I recommend just respawning the PC at a nearby town at this point. You don't want the player to get too frustrated with having to walk clear across the world again after dying, so respawning at the starting point is a *bad* idea. (Remember how big this world is!)

Implementing the Combat System

I have made some changes to the Celtic Crusader project that you find on the CD-ROM in \sources\chapter18. The player/hero code has been moved to a separate module called Hero.BAS and the main game loop has been cleaned up as a result. I have also added some new sprites to the game for this chapter.

Combat Animations

Before you can engage in combat, one might argue that you need a weapon first. Granted, the hero in this game has been carrying a sword around for quite a while. The problem is that he doesn't know how to use it, so it's what you might call a decorative sword at present. What this hero needs is the ability to swing away at the bad guys, and that calls for some new animations!

Wait a second. I want to do something a little different this time. Take a look at one of the other character classes for this chapter. What do you say? I really like the Mage character's artwork, so look into using the Mage in this chapter. He won't have any magic spells and just swings his staff like a blunt weapon, but it is cool to see a different character this time.

tip

The fully prepared sprites for several character classes of the player are available on the CD-ROM in the \bitmaps folder, available in both walking and fighting animations.

First, like usual, I downloaded from Reiner's Tilesets the character animations of the Mage character (which Reiner calls "staffstan"). Take a look at one of the character frames in Pro Motion shown in Figure 18.1.

After the eight animation strips have been saved (from the original bitmap images) by Pro Motion, I then combine the strips and set the background to pink in Paint Shop Pro, which you can see in Figure 18.2.

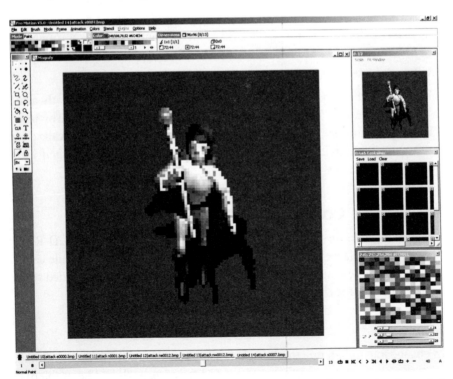

Figure 18.1 The animated Mage character is being converted to an animation strip in Pro Motion.

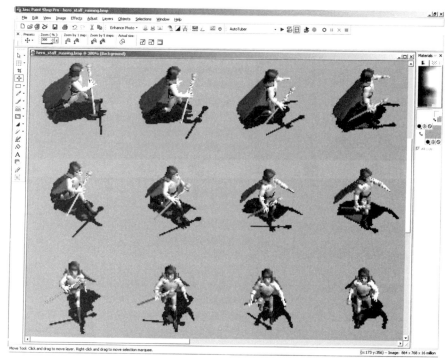

Figure 18.2 The Mage animation strips are combined into a single bitmap file.

In addition to the walking animation, I need a combat animation of the Mage. I have also exported the animation strips for the Knight Hero character, but want to use the Mage Hero in the updated version of Celtic Crusader for this chapter. The combat animations are really good for the Mage sprite, with 13 frames for each direction for a total of 104 animation frames—just to swing the staff! See for yourself in Figure 18.3.

While I'm on the subject of combat animations, I've got the attack frames for the Viking ready to go in this chapter as well! Figure 18.4 shows this really cool character that I totally love; check out his huge battle axe! While you can't tell from the figure here, this character has red hair and is a very imposing-looking figure (which is perfect for a Viking).

Introducing the Skeleton Knight

In addition to the attack animations for the Hero and Viking, I have added a skeleton to the mix to demonstrate how the game looks with different NPCs present. Figure 18.5 shows the Skeleton Knight walking animation in Pro Motion.

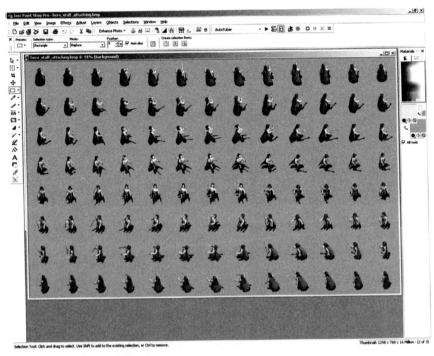

Figure 18.3 The combat animations for the Mage character.

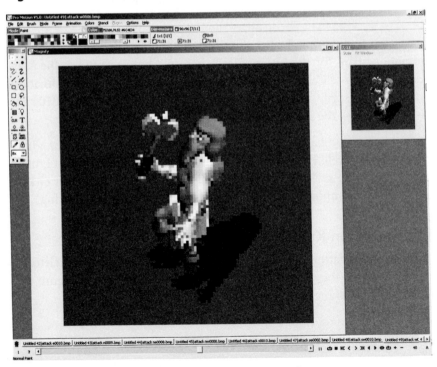

Figure 18.4 A combat animation for the Viking Warrior character.

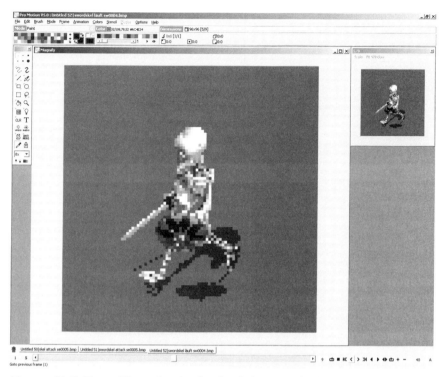

Figure 18.5 The walking animation for the Skeleton Knight character.

Since this chapter now includes the ability to engage in combat, the Skeleton Knight needs some attack animations. Figure 18.6 shows one of the attack frames for this character.

I had to combine the animation strips for the two versions of the Skeleton Knight into individual bitmap files using Paint Shop Pro. Again, this is technically something you can do in Pro Motion, but I find it more time consuming to insert frames into Pro Motion rather than just combining the images in Paint Shop Pro (shown in Figure 18.7).

Engaging in Combat

There are two basic things you need to do to allow the player to fight with NPCs:

- Make sure the player is close enough to an enemy to hit him.
- Make sure the player is facing an enemy while attacking.

If you can take care of these two problems, then you can create a combat system for the game. Tackle these two key problems in order. Figure 18.8 shows the general goal. You want to be able to acknowledge that a hit has occurred when the player is in attack mode and also facing the enemy.

Figure 18.6 The attack animation for the Skeleton Knight character.

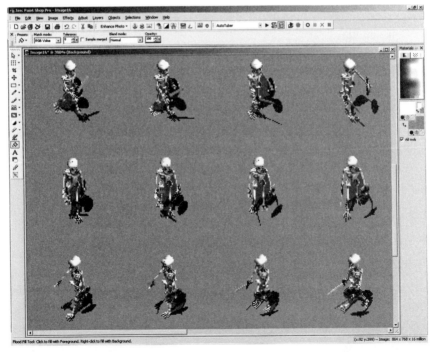

Figure 18.7 The Skeleton Knight character animation strips are being combined in Paint Shop Pro.

Figure 18.8 Dealing damage to the enemy occurs only if you are facing the enemy character.

The first thing you need to check on before you can handle a combat strike is whether the player is close enough to an enemy character to actually hit him. That is accomplished with a simple call to the Collision function (a technique that you learned back in Chapter 14, "Core Technique: Collision Detection"). If there is no collision between the two sprites, then there definitely can't be an attack, and the swing misses! After determining if the two sprites are close enough for an attack, see if the attacker is at least facing the enemy.

The code that checks whether the player is facing an enemy is like the code that sets the player's animation sequence based on its direction. It is important that the player actually faces an enemy before you start to tally the attacks. Otherwise it's possible to hit the enemy by just swinging a weapon anywhere in close proximity to him (using the earlier collision routine).

I wrote a function called IsFacing that returns True or False depending on whether one sprite is facing another sprite. This is also useful for pitting NPCs against each other, not just for the player.

```
Public Function IsFacing( _
    ByRef spr1 As TSPRITE, _
    ByRef spr2 As TSPRITE) As Boolean
```

```
Dim n As Long
Dim a As point
Dim b As point

'are both sprites in range of each other?
If Not Collision(spr1, spr2) Then
    IsFacing = False
    Exit Function
End If

a.x = spr1.x + spr1.width / 2
a.y = spr1.y + spr1.height / 2
b.x = spr2.x + spr2.width / 2
b.y = spr2.y + spr2.height / 2

Select Case spr1.AnimSeq
    'looking up
    Case 7, 0, 1
        If b.y < a.y Then IsFacing = True

    'looking down
    Case 5, 4, 3
        If b.y > a.y Then IsFacing = True

    'looking left
    Case 6
        If b.x < a.x Then IsFacing = True

    'looking right
    Case 2
        If b.x > a.x Then IsFacing = True
End Select

End Function
```

Managing the Player's State

After you have the combat code ready to go, there's just one little problem: The source code written in the game so far just draws the walking version of the player. With combat, the player has to swing his weapon too. The main game loop has to be modified so that you can check the player's state and then draw either the walking or the attacking animations based on what the player is doing.

I modified the game loop so that all the player update code is replaced with a single call to UpdateHero, which is listed here:

```
Public Sub UpdateHero()
    Dim state As String

    Select Case PlayerData.state

        Case HERO_STOPPED
            state = "STOPPED"
            DrawSprite heroImgWalk, heroSprWalk, C_WHITE

        Case HERO_WALKING
            state = "WALKING"

            'animate the walking hero
            If heroSprWalk.Animating Then
                AnimateSprite heroSprWalk
            End If

            'draw the walking hero
            DrawSprite heroImgWalk, heroSprWalk, C_WHITE

        Case HERO_ATTACKING
            state = "ATTACKING"

            'animate the attacking hero
            If heroSprAttack.Animating Then
                AnimateSprite heroSprAttack

                'done attacking? go back to walking
                If heroSprAttack.Animating = False Then
                    PlayerData.state = HERO_STOPPED
                End If
            End If

            'draw the walking hero
            DrawSprite heroImgAttack, heroSprAttack, C_WHITE

            'check for a hit
            CheckForHits
```

```
            Case Else
                Debug.Print "Hero state error!"

        End Select

        'display hero state
        PrintText fontImg, fontSpr, 400, 452, C_WHITE, state

End Sub
```

Managing the NPC States

As you can see for yourself, there is a lot more to drawing the Hero's sprite now that combat is involved. Before, it was easy because just one type of animation was being used—walking. Now, though, two different states have to be monitored and the correct sprite has to be animated. State engines are very helpful when you need to keep track of a complicated series of conditions in a game, because each condition is isolated from the rest, allowing you to write code for each condition separately.

Here is the new list of states being used for each NPC:

```
Public Enum NPCSTATES
    NPC_STOPPED = 0
    NPC_WALKING = 1
    NPC_PAUSED = 2
    NPC_TALKING = 3
    NPC_DYING = 4
    NPC_KILLED = 5
    NPC_ATTACKING = 6
End Enum
```

The arrays that keep track of character classes, images, and sprites have also been changed to accommodate the new combat system:

```
Public Const NUMCHARS As Long = 2
Public charWalk(NUMCHARS) As Direct3DTexture8
Public charAttack(NUMCHARS) As Direct3DTexture8
Public charClasses(NUMCHARS) As TCHARACTER

'unique data for each individual NPC
Public Const NUMNPCS As Long = 10
Public charStates(NUMNPCS) As TNPC
Public charWalkSpr(NUMNPCS) As TSPRITE
Public charAttackSpr(NUMNPCS) As TSPRITE
```

Checking for Attack Hits on NPCs

The section of code under the HERO_ATTACKING state includes a call to a subroutine called CheckForHits:

```
Public Sub CheckForHits()
    'this is temporary--replace with weapon attack value
    Const ATTACKVALUE As Long = 1
    Dim n As Long

    For n = 0 To NUMNPCS - 1
        If IsFacing(heroSprAttack, charWalkSpr(n)) Then
            AttackNPC charStates(n), ATTACKVALUE
            Exit For
        End If
    Next n

End Sub
```

CheckForHits looks at all of the NPCs in the game and then calls IsFacing on each one to see if the player is close to and facing the NPC. If these two conditions are met, then the player hits the NPC with the weapon swing. If no NPC is in range (in front of the player) then the swing doesn't hit anything! See how easy it is when a state engine is being used?

Doing Damage to an NPC

Now take a look at the AttackNPC subroutine that is called from the preceding routine you just looked at. This new routine is actually only called when the player has definitely hit an NPC. When this happens, the NPC's health needs to be cut down by an appropriate amount, and he dies if health is 0! AttackNPC has some test code that prints a message above the player, and a message above the target NPC during an attack, to tell you that the game registered the hit. When the NPC's health reaches 0, the state of the character is set to NPC_DYING.

```
Public Sub AttackNPC(ByRef target As TNPC, ByVal attack As Long)

    'fight back!
    target.state = NPC_ATTACKING

    'decrease health
    target.health = target.health - attack
    If target.health < 1 Then
        target.state = NPC_DYING
    End If
```

```
'display a message to indicate the NPC was hit!
PrintText fontImg, fontSpr, _
    heroSprAttack.x, heroSprAttack.y, C_WHITE, _
    "Take that! (" & attack & " pts)"


'make the target respond to the hit
Dim p As point
p.x = target.curpos.x - ScrollX
p.y = target.curpos.y - ScrollY
PrintText fontImg, fontSpr, _
    p.x, p.y, C_WHITE, _
    "Argh, I've been hit! (" & target.health & ")"


End Sub
```

Death Sequence

There is a death sequence where the NPC is frozen and fades into nothingness (a simple way to show that the NPC has died). If this happens, then the NPC's state takes over the death, allowing your player's code to continue without worrying about dealing with the NPC's resting place. The state engine in Characters.bas manages the state of the NPCs. When the dying state has played out (using a simple counter to keep the faded body visible for a short time), then the state of the bad guy is set to NPC_KILLED. This state triggers the calling of KillNPC, which respawns the character. Figure 18.9 shows an example of the dying sequence for an NPC.

```
Public Sub KillNPC(ByRef dude As TNPC)
    Dim p As point

    p.x = PLAYERSTARTX * TILEWIDTH + Random(1000)
    p.y = PLAYERSTARTY * TILEHEIGHT + Random(1000)

    With dude
        .startpos = p
        .curpos = p
        .SpeedDelay = 1
        .SpeedCount = 0
        .health = 20    'added in chapter 18
        .state = NPC_WALKING
    End With
    SetRandomDestination dude
End Sub
```

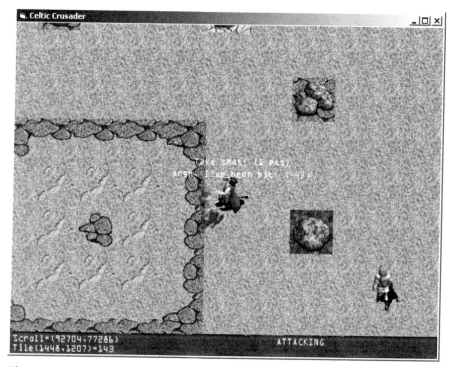

Figure 18.9 This NPC's health has reached 0, so he is about to die.

Moving the State-Based NPC

With all of these different states to handle walking, attacking, and dying, the code that moves and draws the NPCs has to be modified to take them into account. Here is the current `MoveNPCs` subroutine, which is called by the main game loop:

```
Public Sub MoveNPCs()
    Dim n As Long

    'loop through all of the NPCs and move them
    For n = 0 To NUMNPCS - 1

        Select Case charStates(n).state

            Case NPC_ATTACKING
                'stop attacking if the player leaves or if I'm dead...
                If charStates(n).health < 0 Then
                    charStates(n).state = NPC_STOPPED
                End If
```

```
                        If Not Collision(charWalkSpr(n), heroSprWalk) Then
                            charStates(n).state = NPC_STOPPED
                        End If

                    Case NPC_TALKING
                        FacePlayer n

                    Case NPC_PAUSED
                        SetRandomDestination charStates(n)

                    Case NPC_WALKING
                        MoveNPC n

                    Case NPC_STOPPED
                        SetRandomDestination charStates(n)

                    Case NPC_DYING
                        charStates(n).destpos = charStates(n).curpos
                        charStates(n).health = charStates(n).health - 1
                        If charStates(n).health < -100 Then
                            charStates(n).state = NPC_KILLED
                        End If

                    Case NPC_KILLED
                        KillNPC charStates(n)

            End Select
        Next n
End Sub
```

Drawing the State-Based NPC

In addition to moving the NPCs differently based on state, the drawing code also has to take into account the character's state. Different sequences for the walking and attacking animations have to be accounted for in the draw routine. This is where the dying sequence takes place as well. Figure 18.10 shows a skeleton that has been dealt the fatal blow. When the state is NPC_DYING, the sprite is drawn using a gray color that renders the sprite with about 50-percent translucency. (The color is &H99FFFFFF, which has an RGB for white, but a 50-percent alpha or thereabouts.)

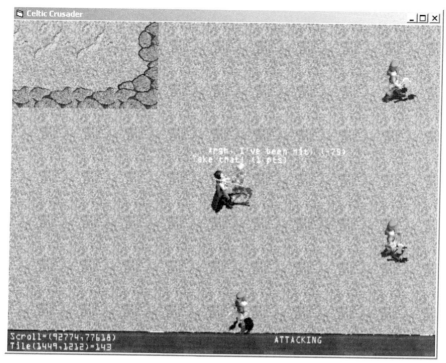

Figure 18.10 Alpha blending is used to draw a sprite with partial translucency.

```
Public Sub DrawNPCs()
    Dim n As Long

    'loop through all of the NPCs and draw them
    For n = 0 To NUMNPCS - 1

        Select Case charStates(n).state
            Case NPC_ATTACKING
                DrawNPC n, C_RED
                charStates(n).state = NPC_WALKING

            Case NPC_TALKING
                DrawNPC n, C_WHITE
                charStates(n).state = NPC_WALKING

                If diState.key(KEY_SPACE) > 0 Then
                    TalkToPlayer n
                End If
```

```
            Case NPC_PAUSED
                DrawNPC n, C_WHITE
                charStates(n).state = NPC_WALKING

            Case NPC_WALKING
                DrawNPC n, C_WHITE

            Case NPC_STOPPED
                DrawNPC n, C_WHITE
                charStates(n).state = NPC_WALKING

            Case NPC_DYING
                DrawNPC n, &H99FFFFFF
        End Select
    Next n
End Sub
```

The DrawNPCs routine calls on the more specific DrawNPC subroutine to do the actual work. This routine also checks the state to draw the attack animation. When you attack an NPC, that character goes into the NPC_ATTACKING state to fight back. The NPCs are still pretty dumb, because they go about their business as if nothing happened if you stop fighting with them. As long as you're attacking them, though, the NPCs fight back. Figure 18.11 shows a Viking taking swings at the player's sprite.

The alpha channel support is utilized by drawing the NPC in red when the NPCs are engaging the player in combat (as shown in Figure 18.12). I wanted to clearly show when an NPC is attacking your player because the attack animations are so similar to the walking animations; it's hard to tell exactly which NPC is fighting back. The red coloration of the sprite is a fantastic effect! In fact, I like it so much that I think it should be a part of the game and left in place! It would be cool to use this coloring effect for other states, and you can use it with some great results for things like spells and so on.

As you know, the NPCs need to be drawn even when they aren't just walking or attacking, because the other states (such as NPC_TALKING) must have the sprite being updated on the screen. DrawNPC checks for new states and then assumes NPC_WALKING for any state that is not explicitly programmed to handle everything else that the NPC might be doing. If you add animations to the NPCs, you need to add the state condition here to account for it.

```
Public Sub DrawNPC(ByVal num As Long, ByVal color As Long)
    Dim r As RECT
    Dim classindex As Long
```

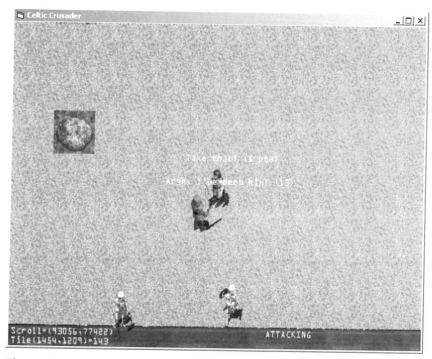

Figure 18.11 This Viking Warrior is attacking the player!

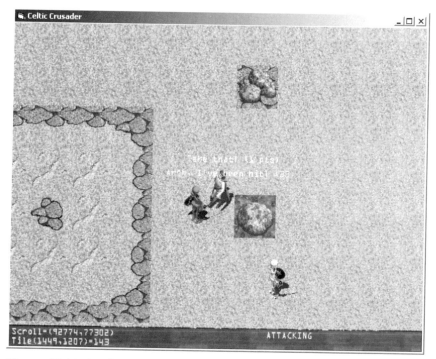

Figure 18.12 Another combat in progress, this time with a Skeleton Knight.

```
        'grab a shortcut to these long variable names
        r.Left = charStates(num).curpos.x
        r.Top = charStates(num).curpos.y
        r.Right = r.Left + charWalkSpr(num).width
        r.Bottom = r.Top + charWalkSpr(num).height

        'remember, images are referred to using the NPC's classindex!
        'the sprite and state arrays are for every single unique NPC,
        'but the bitmap image and class data are shared by all NPCs
        classindex = charStates(num).classindex

        'now check to see if the sprite is within the scrolling viewport
        'sprite's position is actually global, so determine if it's visible
        If r.Left > ScrollX - 1 And r.Right < ScrollX + SCREENWIDTH + 1 And _
           r.Top > ScrollY - 1 And r.Bottom < ScrollY + SCREENHEIGHT + 1 Then

            Select Case charStates(num).state
                Case NPC_ATTACKING
                    AnimateSprite charAttackSpr(num)
                    charAttackSpr(num).x = charStates(num).curpos.x - ScrollX
                    charAttackSpr(num).y = charStates(num).curpos.y - ScrollY
                    charAttackSpr(num).AnimSeq = charStates(num).facing
                    DrawSprite charAttack(classindex), charAttackSpr(num), color

                Case Else
                    'update animation frame if walking
                    AnimateSprite charWalkSpr(num)

                    'draw the sprite--remember, it's using the shared image
                    charWalkSpr(num).x = charStates(num).curpos.x - ScrollX
                    charWalkSpr(num).y = charStates(num).curpos.y - ScrollY
                    charWalkSpr(num).AnimSeq = charStates(num).facing
                    DrawSprite charWalk(classindex), charWalkSpr(num), color
            End Select

        End If

End Sub
```

A Note about Making the Game Modular

The Celtic Crusader game is now becoming rather large and complex. When you think about how far we've come and how simply the game started out, it's pretty amazing how big it is now. At this point, it is important to make the game more modular and expandable. Switching the NPCs and PC to a state-driven model rather than procedural was a big help. Otherwise it can be daunting to maintain the complexity of many animation sequences simultaneously in memory along with tracking what the player is doing and so on.

But the state engines are not good enough to make this game a success. Since the code has now grown a little difficult to wade through, consider how to proceed if you continue completing the game (with your own vision and imagination, of course). I have set up the game so that NPCs have two arrays of animations available—one for walking, another for attacking. If you plan to add more types of animations, insert additional state conditions and new sprite arrays for each type of animation. Giving each character a standard, default number of animations helps you easily insert new characters without having to modify any code for bitmap files with a different number of sprite columns, animation frames, and so forth.

Level Up

This chapter filled in the most important aspect of the game thus far. A combat system is essential to a good RPG, but your list of core techniques were not up to the challenge until this point in the book. Now that you have a rudimentary combat system available, there is no limit to what you can do with this game engine. You have come so far since the first few chapters on building the tile-based scroller! It's incredible that things have progressed so much; it feels like ancient history. You are now working with high-level concepts that brought the game to life! I've been running the game in full-screen mode and it looks fantastic. This is entirely due to the high-quality artwork made available by Reiner's Tilesets, and I take no credit for the artwork (although properly *using* it is no simple feat, as you have seen so far). What's next? This concludes Part IV. Part V begins in the next chapter, where you learn how to liven up the game world with inanimate objects such as trees, buildings, and so on.

PART V

FINISHING TOUCHES

T he last three chapters help put some finishing touches on the game that has been under development throughout the book.

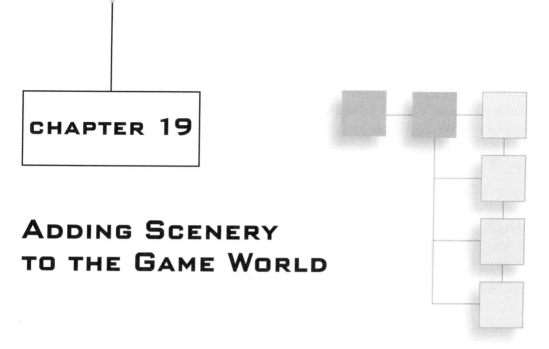

CHAPTER 19

ADDING SCENERY TO THE GAME WORLD

This chapter shows you how to fill the world with scenery. This scenery is added to the game world in such a way that does not require you to edit the map file. Instead, objects such as trees can be added to the game (using sprites) to make it a more lively place in which to host the overall storyline and game play. You learn how to add inanimate objects such as trees, bushes, buildings, and other objects to fill the mostly empty terrain in the game. These inanimate objects are solid so that the player's character (PC) cannot walk through them (similar to solid tiles that are impassable).

Here is a breakdown of the major topics in this chapter:

- Scenery artwork
- The scenery arrays
- Loading the scenery graphics
- Modifying the game loop
- Keeping the player out of the scenery
- Drawing the scenery sprites
- New Warrior Hero animations
- New Black Knight animations

The World Is a Desert

The current game world is a big, empty, barren, desolate, boring place considering that it's supposed to be the home for the characters in the game—not to mention that the game is supposed to be fun! In order to liven up the world, you need to add some scenery. I show you how to add some random trees to the world—with collision detection—and you can adapt this code to just about any cosmetic graphic image that you want to add to the game world. There are a lot of sprites in the graphic collection of Reiner's Tilesets that liven up the world, including 3D renderings of houses, buildings, castles, towers, windmills, and many different types of trees! You can access these renderings at http://www.reinerstileset.de.

There are some great pieces of artwork available that you can use to beautify this game world. I focus on planting a few dozen random trees on the landscape near where the player's character starts off in the game, to show you how such objects are added to the game. You can add any other type of graphic to the game, and it is included in the collision detection routine (so the player can't walk through these solid objects).

The artwork for the scenery in this chapter includes four very highly detailed trees that have been modeled and rendered (like most of Reiner's artwork). You can see the four trees used to spruce up the game world in Figure 19.1. The effect of the trees is even greater when you notice that there are many small transparent regions among the tree leaves, which increases the realism.

Inserting Random Scenery

What I want to do is use these four tree sprites to add a couple hundred trees to the game world. The trees are represented using TSPRITE and randomly placed in the game world. I am purposely placing the trees around the player's starting position so you can easily walk around and run into several trees without having to travel very far to find one. Remember how huge this game world is? Well, even a few hundred trees is rather spartan for this large world, so placing them all near the player's starting point makes it a little more interesting.

When you turn this into a complete game, you can easily change the code that places the trees and have it scatter the trees throughout the entire countryside. Just remember that you can adapt this code to include inanimate objects other than trees; you can randomly place huts, shacks, houses, windmills, rocks, and even small mountains (all of which are available in the Reiner's Tilesets collection). Figure 19.2 shows the new version of Celtic Crusader with scenery added.

Figure 19.1 These four trees help improve the appearance of the game world.

Figure 19.2 The new version of the game now features solid trees (via collision detection).

The Scenery Arrays

Get started working on the new code for the scenery. For starters, I'm just using four pieces of artwork to represent the scenery of the game. These four sprites are randomly placed at 100 different locations in the game world. You can modify these values if you want to add scenery or increase the total number of scenery items that are placed on the map.

```
Public Const SCENERY_IMAGES As Long = 4
Public sceneImage As Direct3DTexture8

Public Const SCENERY_SPRITES As Long = 100
Public sceneSprites(SCENERY_SPRITES) As TSPRITE
```

Loading the Scenery Graphics

A subroutine called LoadScenery is called shortly after Direct3D is initialized and is responsible for loading the scenery images and setting their positions randomly.

```
Public Sub LoadScenery()
    Dim n As Long
    Dim w As Long
    Dim h As Long

    'load scenery image (containing all the trees)
    Set sceneImage = LoadTexture(d3ddev, App.Path & "\trees.bmp")

    'initialize scenery sprites (trees)
    'assumes all are 128x128...change as needed
    For n = 0 To SCENERY_SPRITES - 1
        InitSprite d3ddev, sceneSprites(n)
        sceneSprites(n).width = 128
        sceneSprites(n).height = 128
        sceneSprites(n).FramesPerRow = 4
        sceneSprites(n).CurrentFrame = Random(4)
    Next n

    'randomly place the scenery sprites
    For n = 0 To SCENERY_SPRITES - 1
        'normally you will spread scenery items all over the map
        'but i'm focusing in on just around the starting position
        w = PLAYERSTARTX * TILEWIDTH
        h = PLAYERSTARTY * TILEHEIGHT
        sceneSprites(n).x = w + Random(4000) - 2000
        sceneSprites(n).y = h + Random(4000) - 2000
    Next n
End Sub
```

Modifying the Game Loop

Now I'd like to show the complete game loop so you can see how everything is being handled by the game. The various update and drawing routines are called from here inside the game loop and generally must be in the order that you see here. For instance, the tile and scenery collision code must come before the tile scroller is updated because the collision routines modify ScrollX and ScrollY. You know ScrollX and ScrollY are directly responsible for the current view of the game world on the screen. Within a timed code block section in the game loop are the drawing routines that display everything on the screen.

```
'main loop
Do While (True)
    'erase the bottom toolbar
    DrawSurface wood, 0, 0, 639, 30, backbuffer, 0, 449
```

```
        'poll DirectInput for keyboard input
        Check_Keyboard

        'call various update routines
        UpdateScrollPosition
        CheckTileCollisions
        CheckSceneryCollisions
        DrawTiles
        DrawScrollWindow
        Scroll 0, 0
        MoveNPCs
        CheckNPCCollisions

        'set the screen refresh to about 50 fps
        If GetTickCount - start > 20 Then

            'start rendering
            d3ddev.BeginScene

            'call various drawing routines
            DrawScenery
            DrawNPCs
            UpdateHero
            ShowPlayerInfo

            'stop rendering
            d3ddev.EndScene

            d3ddev.Present ByVal 0, ByVal 0, 0, ByVal 0
            start = GetTickCount
            DoEvents
        End If

    Loop
```

Keeping the Player Out of the Scenery

Scenery is one thing, but realistic scenery is quite another. In my opinion, everything in the game should react to the solid tiles and scenery, but unfortunately it is only the player who does so in this current version of the game. When *non-player characters (NPCs)* are visible on the screen, it is a good idea to force the NPCs to obey collision laws and make the game feel more realistic. When NPCs are not visible in the current view, there's no need to call the collision routines on them.

The CheckSceneryCollisions subroutine first checks to see if a scenery sprite is visible in the current viewport. If so, then the routine checks for a collision with the player's sprite and adjusts ScrollX and ScrollY if necessary. Since this occurs before the tile scroller is updated, it appears as if the player simply cannot pass through (when in fact, the player's sprite is being moved back a few pixels after a collision).

```
Public Sub CheckSceneryCollisions()
    Dim n As Long
    Dim p As point
    Static spr As TSPRITE

    'copy hero sprite location and size into a temp variable
    spr.x = ScrollX + SCREENWIDTH / 2 - heroSprWalk.width / 2
    spr.y = ScrollY + SCREENHEIGHT / 2 - heroSprWalk.height / 2
    spr.width = heroSprWalk.width
    spr.height = heroSprWalk.height

    'look at all the scenery
    For n = 0 To SCENERY_SPRITES - 1

        'let's deal with just one at a time
        With sceneSprites(n)

            'is the global sprite within the scrolling viewport?
            If .x > ScrollX - 1 _
                And .x + .width < ScrollX + SCREENWIDTH + 1 _
                And .y > ScrollY - 1 _
                And .y + .height < ScrollY + SCREENHEIGHT + 1 Then

                'next test: collision with the player?
                If Collision(spr, sceneSprites(n)) Then
                    StopHero
                    Exit For
                End If

            End If
        End With
    Next n
End Sub
```

Drawing the Scenery Sprites

Assuming that a scenery sprite is visible in the current viewport (which represents the visible portion of the game world, centered upon the player's sprite), then the scenery sprites are drawn in the viewport at an adjusted position that corresponds to the player's position: at the center of the screen. One good enhancement to this routine is drawing the scenery sprites when they are outside the bounds of the screen so the objects scroll into view. Currently, the sprites just pop into view at the edge of the screen. This is the best option at this point, but you may want to consider working on the enhanced version to improve the realism of the game.

```
Public Sub DrawScenery()
    Dim n As Long
    Dim p As point

    For n = 0 To SCENERY_SPRITES - 1

        With sceneSprites(n)

            'is the global sprite is within the scrolling viewport?
            If .x > ScrollX - 1 _
                And .x + .width < ScrollX + SCREENWIDTH + 1 _
                And .y > ScrollY - 1 _
                And .y + .height < ScrollY + SCREENHEIGHT + 1 Then

                'save global x,y position
                p.x = .x
                p.y = .y

                'set sprite to viewport position
                .x = .x - ScrollX
                .y = .y - ScrollY

                'draw the sprite
                DrawSprite sceneImage, sceneSprites(n), C_WHITE

                'restore the global position
                .x = p.x
                .y = p.y
            End If
        End With
    Next n
End Sub
```

New Character Animations

I have converted the animation strips for the Warrior Hero's axe attacking and walking animations for the version of Celtic Crusader presented in this chapter. I like the variety provided by having multiple classes of the character, although the game lacks a character creation screen—something that you may want to work on?

---

tip

When you browse the sprites available for download from Reiner's Tilesets at http://www.reiners tileset.de, both English and German versions of the site are available. Reiner Prokein makes this wonderful artwork available for free—even for commercial games. All that he asks is that you give him credit when you use his artwork and that you do not redistribute the artwork outside of a game.

New Warrior Hero Animations

Figure 19.3 shows the Warrior Hero's walking animation sequences, while Figure 19.4 shows the Warrior Hero's attacking animation frames.

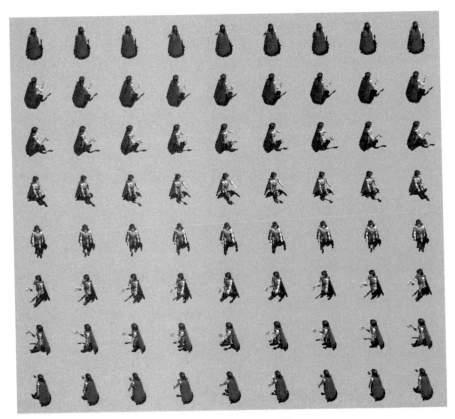

Figure 19.3 The Warrior Hero's walking animation frames.

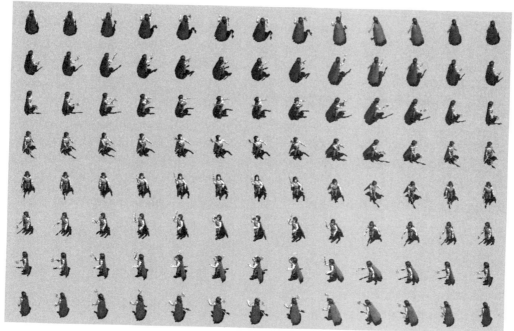

Figure 19.4 The Warrior Hero's attacking animation frames.

New Black Knight Animations

I want to add a new character to the demonstration version of Celtic Crusader shown in this chapter just to add some variety to it. The Black Knight is a truly awesome character to behold, clad in dark, full-plate mail armor with helmet, broadsword, and tower shield. This awesome character is even more impressive than the Warrior Viking that I have been using up until now. In addition to the Black Knight, the Skeleton Knight is still part of the experience. Figure 19.5 shows the Black Knight's walking animation sequences, while Figure 19.6 shows the attack animations.

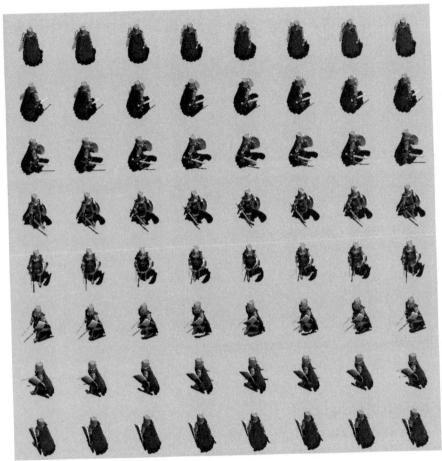

Figure 19.5 The Black Knight's walking animation frames.

Level Up

This chapter provided the ability to add cosmetic improvements to the game in the form of solid scenery. These items of scenery currently include four trees, which are tested for collision with the player to give them a realistic feel in the game. You can add your own scenery objects to the game world using the same basic code provided in this chapter.

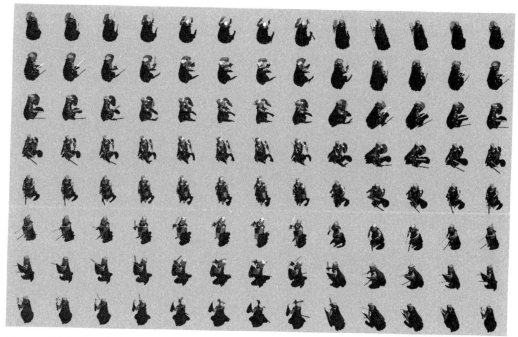

Figure 19.6 The Black Knight's attacking animation frames.

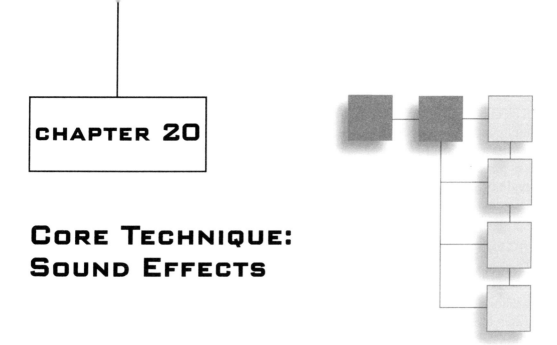

CHAPTER 20

CORE TECHNIQUE: SOUND EFFECTS

In years past, programming sound and music for games was an enormous task. Custom sound code was usually too difficult to write due to the conflicting standards among the various sound cards in the industry. Today, that is no longer a problem. Now a single, dominant hardware maker sets the PC audio standard and a single, dominant sound library sets the software standard. While some may argue the point, I believe that Creative Labs has the sound card market wrapped up with the Sound Blaster products. At the same time, the complicated audio driver industry has been eclipsed by the incredibly versatile and powerful DirectX Audio library. This chapter is a quick jaunt through the DirectSound part of DirectX Audio, with a small program to demonstrate how to use DirectSound to play .WAV files in Visual Basic.

Here are the major topics in this chapter:

- Introduction to DirectX Audio
- Programming DirectSound
- Creating the DirectSound object
- Mixing .WAVs with DirectSound

Introduction to DirectX Audio

Welcome to the sound effects chapter! Audio is always a fun subject to explore because sound effects and music have such an impact on impression and influence our opinions of games so strongly. What is a game without sound? It is nothing more than a technology demo. Sound is absolutely essential for the success of any game, no matter how large or small.

I remember the sound card war of the early 1990s, when several competing companies took on Creative Labs to produce a dominant sound card. This was about the time when multimedia was the next big thing and buzzwords like *edutainment* started to be overused in marketing and by the press. Although CD-ROMs were technically available as far back as 1988, I searched through the entire Las Vegas Comdex convention in 1992 and couldn't find one. It just goes to show how young the multimedia industry is in the overall computer industry!

Accessing the DirectSound Library

DirectX Audio is made up of the DirectSound, DirectSound3D, and DirectMusic components (each of which is comprised of several more components). To gain access to DirectX Audio, you simply reference the "DirectX 8 for Visual Basic Type Library" in the Project References for your VB project. The DirectX type library is huge, providing access to absolutely everything in DirectX with a single reference, including the sound system.

Using DirectSound

DirectX Audio is an enormously complex library for playing, recording, and manipulating sounds of numerous types, from simple mono .WAV files to multisample audio segments to MIDI files. DirectX Audio can be used to write more than just games! This library is capable of handling just about any audio programming need.

DirectSound

DirectSound is the main component of DirectX Audio and the one used most often in games. This component is capable of mixing .WAV sound buffers in real time.

DirectSound3D

DirectSound3D is a support component that works with DirectSound to provide real-time 3D positional audio processing. DirectX 8.0 fully supports accelerated sound hardware, and DirectSound3D is the component that takes advantage of that.

DirectMusic

DirectMusic is now a much more powerful component than in past versions of DirectX because it its performance and audio path objects are the main focus of the DirectX Audio system, which may eclipse DirectSound in the same way that DirectX Graphics eclipsed DirectDraw.

Programming DirectSound

Now, if you are going into this chapter with a desire to grab some code and use it in the Celtic Crusader game right away, you may be pleased with the sample program in this chapter. Rather than theorize about sound hardware and .WAV forms, how about if I just jump right in and show you how to play some cool sounds to spruce up the game? That's exactly what I show you in this section—how to get started programming DirectSound right away.

Understanding Ambient Sound

Ambient sound is a term that I borrowed from ambient light, which you might already understand. Just look at a light bulb in a light fixture on the ceiling. The light emitted by the bulb pretty much fills the room (unless you are in a very large, poorly lit room). When light permeates a room, it is said to be *ambient*; that is, the light does not seem to have a source.

Contrast this idea with directional light and you get the idea behind ambient sound. *Ambient sound* refers to sound that appears to have no direction or source. Ambient sound is emitted by speakers uniformly, without any positional effects. This is the most common type of sound generated by most games (at least in most older games, while the tendency with modern games is to use positional sound).

The DirectX Audio component that handles ambient sound is called DirectSound8. DirectSound is the primary sound mixer for DirectX. While this component is technically called DirectX Audio, it really boils down to using the individual components. Direct-Sound8 is one such component, capable of mixing and playing multichannel .WAV sound buffers (a portion of memory set aside to contain the binary sound data).

Creating the DirectSound Object

In order to use DirectSound, you must first create a standard `DirectX8` object, which is then used to create DirectSound. You can declare the objects like this:

```
Dim dx As DirectX8
Dim ds As DirectSound8
```

Once the objects have been declared, you can then instantiate the objects like this:

```
Set dx = New DirectX8
Set ds = objDX.DirectSoundCreate("")
```

As you can see, the DirectSound object is returned by the `DirectSoundCreate` function. Like all of the major components, DirectSound is initialized and returned by the main `DirectX8` object.

Loading a Wave File

The next step to playing sound with DirectSound involves creating a buffer to hold a waveform that is loaded from a .WAV file. The object that holds the wave is called `Direct-SoundSecondaryBuffer8`. I know this is a large name to learn, but it will be second nature to you in no time. To create a DirectSound buffer object, you must first declare it in the variable declarations section of the program:

```
Dim Sound1 As DirectSoundSecondaryBuffer8
```

There is no need to "New" the object because it is returned by the .WAV loader function, which is called `CreateSoundBufferFromFile`. This function returns an object of type—yep, you guessed it—`DirectSoundSecondaryBuffer8`. (I promise I won't make you endure that object name much longer.) `CreateSoundBufferFromFile` is a member of the main `DirectSound8` object and can be called like this:

```
Set Sound1 = ds.CreateSoundBufferFromFile("filename.wav", dsBuf)
```

Mixing .WAVs with DirectSound

Strangely enough, the `DirectSoundSecondaryBuffer8` object itself is responsible for playing the .WAV buffer. This is something that you must get used to, after working with mainly procedural (non-object oriented) code through this book. A library like DirectSound typically has support objects rather than numerous support functions to do all of the work.

To play back a wave sound that has been loaded into a buffer, you simply use the Play procedure:

```
Sound1.Play DSBPLAY_DEFAULT
```

There is another option that you can use when calling the `Play` procedure. The `DSBPLAY_DEFAULT` constant tells the object to just play the wave once and then stop. Another constant called `DSBPLAY_LOOPING` tells the object to loop the sound, playing it over and over until stopped.

The SoundTest Program

The SoundTest program demonstrates how to create and initialize the `DirectSound8` object, load a .WAV file into memory, and then play the wave with automatic mixing support. Since there is not much to this program other than the simple form, I haven't bothered with a figure.

To create this program, simply start a new Standard EXE project and enter the following lines of code into the code window for `Form1`. The source code does the rest. This program is a simple demonstration of how to use `DirectSound`.

```
'----------------------------------------------------------
' Visual Basic Game Programming for Teens
' SoundTest Program
'----------------------------------------------------------
Option Explicit
Option Base 0

'program variables
Dim dx As DirectX8
Dim ds As DirectSound8
Dim Sound1 As DirectSoundSecondaryBuffer8
```

The Form_Load event initializes the DirectX and DirectSound objects and then loads the .WAV file before playing it automatically (at the end of Form_Load):

```
Private Sub Form_Load()
    'create the DirectX8 object
    Set dx = New DirectX8

    'create the DirectSound8 object
    Set ds = dx.DirectSoundCreate("")
    If Err.Number <> 0 Then
        MsgBox "Error creating DirectSound object"
        Shutdown
    End If

    'set the priority level for DirectSound
    ds.SetCooperativeLevel Me.hWnd, DSSCL_PRIORITY

    'load the wave files
    Set Sound1 = LoadSound(App.Path & "\halleluja.wav")

    'play the halleluja sound
    PlaySound Sound1, False, False
End Sub

Private Sub Form_KeyDown(KeyCode As Integer, Shift As Integer)
    If KeyCode = 27 Then Shutdown
End Sub

Private Sub Form_QueryUnload(Cancel As Integer, UnloadMode As Integer)
    Shutdown
End Sub
```

Now for the `LoadSound` function. You were probably expecting this to be a two-pager, but it is quite simple to load a wave file with DirectSound. First, set up a `DSBUFFERDESC` structure and tell it that the sound buffer is a simple static buffer (in other words, no special effects are applied to the sound). Next, the `CreateSoundBufferFromFile` function (a member of `DirectSound8`) loads and returns the wave file into a `DirectSoundSecondaryBuffer8` variable. Once this is done, the wave file is ready to be played.

```
Public Function LoadSound(ByVal sFilename As String) _
    As DirectSoundSecondaryBuffer8
    Dim dsBuf As DSBUFFERDESC

    'set up sound buffer for normal playback
    dsBuf.lFlags = DSBCAPS_STATIC

    'load wave file into DirectSound buffer
    Set LoadSound = ds.CreateSoundBufferFromFile(sFilename, dsBuf)
    If Err.Number <> 0 Then
        MsgBox "Error loading sound file: " & sFilename
        Shutdown
    End If
End Function
```

Now for the `PlaySound` procedure. This is also surprisingly short and easy to understand, because the `DirectSound` buffer object does all the work. This version of `PlaySound` (yes, there are others in the chapter) first checks to see if the `bCloseFirst` parameter wants it to first terminate any sound currently playing in that buffer. Then it checks to see if the `bLoopSound` parameter determines if the sound will be played back continuously in a loop (in which case the only way to stop it is to call `PlaySound` again with the `bCloseFirst` parameter set to True):

```
Public Sub PlaySound(ByRef Sound As DirectSoundSecondaryBuffer8, _
    ByVal bCloseFirst As Boolean, ByVal bLoopSound As Boolean)

    'stop currently playing waves?
    If bCloseFirst Then
        Sound.Stop
        Sound.SetCurrentPosition 0
    End If

    'loop the sound?
    If bLoopSound Then
        Sound.Play DSBPLAY_LOOPING
```

```
    Else
        Sound.Play DSBPLAY_DEFAULT
    End If
End Sub
```

Finally, the Shutdown procedure stops sound playback, deletes objects from memory, and then ends the program:

```
Private Sub Shutdown()
    'stop sound playback
    Sound1.Stop

    'delete DirectX Audio objects
    Set dx = Nothing
    Set ds = Nothing
    Set Sound1 = Nothing

    End
End Sub
```

Level Up

This chapter was a quick overview of DirectSound, giving you just enough information to add sound effects to your own Visual Basic games. By loading multiple sound files into memory and playing them at certain points in your game, you greatly enhance the game-play experience. DirectSound handles all of the details for you, including loading the .WAV file and playing it through the sound system. All you have to do is instruct it what to do. In that sense, you are the conductor of this orchestra.

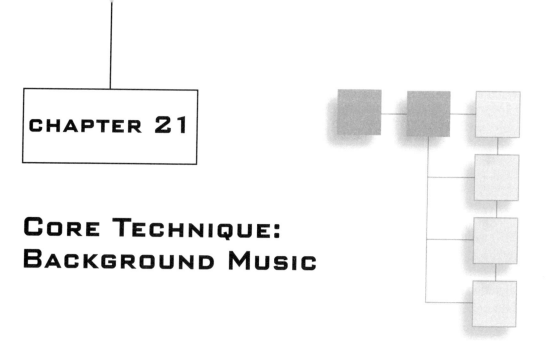

CHAPTER 21

CORE TECHNIQUE: BACKGROUND MUSIC

D irectMusic and DirectSound were once separate components of DirectX. Now these components are integrated into DirectX Audio. What does this mean for DirectX programmers? Basically, these components are still around, and DirectX Audio is just a name that describes the main components that have been a part of DirectX now for many years.

DirectMusic seems to be overly complicated when you consider that all it really needs to do is play a MIDI sound sequence. DirectMusic seems to suffer from feature glut in an attempt to provide a multitude of audio features into DirectX Audio. You could literally run a professional music studio with DirectX Audio, because it includes some incredibly advanced options. However, by avoiding most of the unnecessary features of DirectX Audio and focusing on what is needed for a game, the code is much easier to manage.

Here are the major topics in this chapter:

- Understanding DirectMusic audio paths
- MIDI versus .WAV music
- Playing background music
- The MusicTest program

Understanding DirectMusic Audio Paths

One important factor that you should remember is that DirectMusic does not have an *audio gain* feature, meaning that volume is maxed out by default. The only option for modifying volume is to reduce the volume of a music sequence. Volume is expressed in hundredths of a decibel and is always a negative value. If you want to restore volume to maximum, set the volume to 0. This might seem like a strange way to control volume, but DirectMusic cannot amplify sound.

A DirectMusic *audio path* is an object that controls the output of a single channel. Any changes made to that channel affect all sound operations routed through the channel, such as .WAV, MIDI, or segment playback.

MIDI Versus .WAV Music

Why would anyone consider using MIDI today, when it is far more exciting to go with digital background music such as MP3? The reason is primarily that of performance and size. A very long MIDI sequence might take up only a few hundred kilobytes, while a lengthy digital sample requires multiple megabytes per minute. While digital music provides the best quality and is the most impressive way to handle background music, there are advantages to using MIDI.

One of the main advantages is the sheer number of public domain MIDI files available on the Internet. There are literally thousands of songs that may be freely used in a game, as long as those songs are not copyrighted. In contrast, digital music must be composed and recorded (or licensed by the original composer or musician).

Playing Background Music

Even the simplest game needs some form of background music or it is difficult for the player to remain interested. Remember the golden rule of gaming: Any game without sound and music is just a technology demo. It is absolutely essential that you spend some of your development time on a game working on the music and sound effects. In fact, it is probably a good idea to do so during development. As the game takes shape, so should the sounds and music.

Background music should reflect what is going on in the game, and can even be used to invoke the emotions of the player. Consider a scene where a beloved game character dies. Upbeat music would spoil the mood, while dark and menacing background music engenders the player with feelings of remorse and sorrow (and perhaps even anger).

Keep this in mind when working on sections of a game and try to have a different background sequence for different circumstances. Victory should be rewarded with upbeat music, while menacing or dangerous situations should be accompanied by low-beat, low-tempo songs that reinforce the natural emotions that arise in such a circumstance.

The MusicTest Program

The DirectMusic program (not a very creative name, I know) is very simple so that nothing takes away from the code to load and play a music sequence. Basically, this program creates the various objects needed to get a MIDI file loaded and playing without any bells or whistles.

The key objects in this program include DirectMusicLoader8, DirectMusicPerformance8, DirectMusicSegment8, DirectMusicSegmentState8, and DirectMusicAudioPath8. (See, I warned you that DirectMusic was needlessly complicated.) To make things easier, I have created a couple of classes that take care of these objects internally and provide a means to load and play a MIDI file. In the meantime, I show you how to do it with regular code.

You might be surprised at how easy it is to actually load a MIDI file, considering the long list of objects. Here is all you need to do to load a MIDI file into a DirectMusic segment:

```
Set dmSeg = dmLoader.LoadSegment(sFile)
dmSeg.SetStandardMidiFile
dmSeg.Download dmPath
```

Surprised? I sure was the first time I came across this code. It is similarly easy to play the MIDI sequence, which is loaded into the segment object:

```
Set dmSegState = dmPerf.PlaySegmentEx(dmSeg, 0, 0, Nothing, dmPath)
```

This function, PlaySegmentEx, is all that is required to play a MIDI file once it has been loaded into a segment.

Now, I'm a firm believer in the concept that practice makes perfect. So, without further ado, here is the listing for the DirectMusic program. Like the AmbientSound program earlier, this program is a simple Standard EXE project, and you can type the code into the code window for Form1.

```
'-------------------------------------------------------
' Visual Basic Game Programming For Teens
' MusicTest Program
'-------------------------------------------------------

Option Explicit
Option Base 0

'main DirectX object
Dim dx As DirectX8

'DirectMusic loader object
Private dmLoader As DirectMusicLoader8
```

```
'DirectMusic performance object
Private dmPerf As DirectMusicPerformance8

'DirectMusic segment object
Private dmSeg As DirectMusicSegment8

'DirectMusic segment state object
Private dmSegState As DirectMusicSegmentState8

'DirectMusic audio path object
Private dmPath As DirectMusicAudioPath8

'DirectMusic audio parameters
Dim dmA As DMUS_AUDIOPARAMS
```

The Form_Load procedure initializes DirectX8 and the DirectMusic objects used in this program. Note how the DirectX object creates all of the other objects. Next, the audio path is created, the MIDI file is loaded into memory, and PlayMusic is called:

```
Private Sub Form_Load()
    'set up line-by-line error checking
    On Local Error Resume Next

    'create the DirectX object
    Set dx = New DirectX8

    'create the DirectMusic loader object
    Set dmLoader = dx.DirectMusicLoaderCreate
    If Err.Number <> 0 Then
        MsgBox "Error creating DirectMusic loader object"
        Shutdown
    End If

    'create the DirectMusic performance object
    Set dmPerf = dx.DirectMusicPerformanceCreate
    If Err.Number <> 0 Then
        MsgBox "Error creating DirectMusic performance object"
        Shutdown
    End If

    'initialize DirectMusic
    dmPerf.InitAudio Me.hWnd, DMUS_AUDIOF_ALL, dmA
```

```
    If Err.Number <> 0 Then
        MsgBox "Error initializing DirectMusic audio system"
        Shutdown
    End If

    'create the DirectMusic audio path object
    Set dmPath = dmPerf.CreateStandardAudioPath( _
        DMUS_APATH_DYNAMIC_3D, 64, True)

    If Err.Number <> 0 Then
        MsgBox "Error creating DirectMusic audio path object"
        Shutdown
    End If

    'load the MIDI file
    If Not LoadMusic(App.Path & "\symphony.rmi") Then
        MsgBox "Error loading music file symphony.rmi"
        Shutdown
    End If

    'print some music information to the immediate window
    Debug.Print "Length: " & dmSeg.GetLength
    Debug.Print "Name: " & dmSeg.GetName
    Debug.Print "Repeats: " & CBool(dmSeg.GetRepeats)
    Debug.Print "Clock time: " & dmPerf.GetClockTime
    Debug.Print "Music time: " & dmPerf.GetMusicTime
    Debug.Print "Latency time: " & dmPerf.GetLatencyTime

    PlayMusic
End Sub
```

There is only one user-interface support routine in this program. That's because this is sort of a dumb program. Don't get me wrong—this program does a lot as far as the music playback goes, but it sort of ignores the user, and that's not usually the best way to go in a VB program. But this is just a demo and the code is simple this way.

```
Private Sub Form_QueryUnload(Cancel As Integer, UnloadMode As Integer)
    Shutdown
End Sub
```

Now for the LoadMusic function! Okay, maybe it's not really all that exciting. But this function does a lot more work than the LoadSound function in the AmbientSound program. First, the function determines if a MIDI sequence is already playing by checking to see if dmSeg has been initialized. If a sequence has already been loaded, it is removed from memory. Then the MIDI file is loaded by the `LoadSegment` function (which is a member of `DirectMusicLoader8`). Okay, now the song is ready to be played, right?

Wrong! For some reason, `DirectMusic` forces you to download the segment into an audio path for playback. I think that should have just been included in the `LoadSegment` function, but for some reason the authors of `DirectMusic` chose to put the file loader into a separate object (and for the life of me, I do not know why).

```
Public Function LoadMusic(sFile As String) As Boolean
    On Local Error Resume Next
    LoadMusic = False
    If Len(sFile) = 0 Then Exit Function

    'remove any existing segment
    If Not (dmSeg Is Nothing) Then
        dmSeg.Unload dmPath
        Set dmSeg = Nothing
    End If

    'load the MIDI file
    Set dmSeg = dmLoader.LoadSegment(sFile)
    If Err.Number <> 0 Then Exit Function
    dmSeg.SetStandardMidiFile

    'download the music segment
    dmSeg.Download dmPath
    If Err.Number <> 0 Then Exit Function

    'success
    LoadMusic = True
End Function
```

`PlayMusic` and `StopMusic` include the functionality to play and stop playback of a MIDI file (or any other type of sound loaded). It seems confusing with so many objects until you see which object is actually calling the `PlaySegmentEx` function to start playback; it is called by the performance object, with the segment and audio path objects included as parameters. This sort of makes sense if you think of the audio path as the destination for the music playback, while the segment is the source of the music.

```
Private Sub PlayMusic()
    If dmSeg Is Nothing Then Exit Sub
    Set dmSegState = dmPerf.PlaySegmentEx(dmSeg, 0, 0, Nothing, dmPath)
End Sub
```

```
Private Sub StopMusic()
    If dmSeg Is Nothing Then Exit Sub
    dmPerf.StopEx dmSeg, 0, 0
End Sub
```

As usual, the Shutdown procedure cleans up the program by deleting objects, freeing up memory, and then ending the program:

```
Private Sub Shutdown()
    'stop music playback
    If Not (dmPerf Is Nothing) Then
        dmPerf.StopEx dmSeg, 0, 0
        dmPerf.CloseDown
    End If

    'delete DirectMusic objects
    Set dmLoader = Nothing
    Set dmSeg = Nothing
    Set dmPath = Nothing
    Set dmPerf = Nothing
    Set dx = Nothing

    End
End Sub
```

Level Up

This chapter provided an overview of the DirectMusic component of DirectX, which is used to play background music in the MIDI format. Although many games today use digital music that is just mixed in with the other foreground sound effects, the use of MIDI music for background music is still a viable option. This is especially true if you do not want to cut down on your game's frame rate while DirectX Audio is mixing all of your sound effects along with the music (which is a processor-intensive task). By using the code in this chapter, you can easily add music to any of your Visual Basic games.

APPENDIX

USING THE CD-ROM

The CD-ROM that accompanies this book contains all of the source code in the book, as well as projects not listed in the book. (As explained in the text, some projects were left out of print to conserve space.) In addition, you will find a folder on the CD-ROM containing the DirectX 8 for Visual Basic Type Library that makes it possible to write DirectX programs with Visual Basic 6.0. Although it is not necessary, the DirectX 8 SDK has also been provided, but you should be able to make do with just the Type Library.

Here is the directory structure on the CD-ROM:

\bitmaps

\DirectX8

\mappy

\maps

\sources

I recommend you copy the entire \sources folder off the CD-ROM and onto your hard drive. After doing so, right-click the \sources folder (on your hard drive), select Properties, and then turn off the Read-Only property for all files and subfolders. That way you will be able to open the projects and make changes to the code without Visual Basic complaining about the files being read-only.

The \bitmaps folder contains all of the artwork and graphics used in the book (including sprite animations). I have *not* included the complete Reiner's Tilesets collection, because that is available from http://www.reinerstileset.de.

The \mappy folder contains the free edition of Mappy that is described in this book and is used to create game worlds.

The \maps folder contains the game world maps used in the book in one easy-to-find location.

The \sources folder contains all of the source code projects described in the book (including the various versions of Celtic Crusader that were not printed).

INDEX

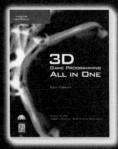

License Agreement/Notice of Limited Warranty

By opening the sealed disc container in this book, you agree to the following terms and conditions. If, upon reading the following license agreement and notice of limited warranty, you cannot agree to the terms and conditions set forth, return the unused book with unopened disc to the place where you purchased it for a refund.

License:

The enclosed software is copyrighted by the copyright holder(s) indicated on the software disc. You are licensed to copy the software onto a single computer for use by a single user and to a backup disc. You may not reproduce, make copies, or distribute copies or rent or lease the software in whole or in part, except with written permission of the copyright holder(s). You may transfer the enclosed disc only together with this license, and only if you destroy all other copies of the software and the transferee agrees to the terms of the license. You may not decompile, reverse assemble, or reverse engineer the software.

Notice of Limited Warranty:

The enclosed disc is warranted by Thomson Course Technology PTR to be free of physical defects in materials and workmanship for a period of sixty (60) days from end user's purchase of the book/disc combination. During the sixty-day term of the limited warranty, Course PTR will provide a replacement disc upon the return of a defective disc.

Limited Liability:

THE SOLE REMEDY FOR BREACH OF THIS LIMITED WARRANTY SHALL CONSIST ENTIRELY OF REPLACEMENT OF THE DEFECTIVE DISC. IN NO EVENT SHALL COURSE PTR OR THE AUTHOR BE LIABLE FOR ANY OTHER DAMAGES, INCLUDING LOSS OR CORRUPTION OF DATA, CHANGES IN THE FUNCTIONAL CHARACTERIS-TICS OF THE HARDWARE OR OPERATING SYSTEM, DELETERIOUS INTERACTION WITH OTHER SOFTWARE, OR ANY OTHER SPECIAL, INCIDENTAL, OR CONSEQUEN-TIAL DAMAGES THAT MAY ARISE, EVEN IF THOMSON COURSE TECHNOLOGY PTR AND/OR THE AUTHOR HAS PREVIOUSLY BEEN NOTIFIED THAT THE POSSIBILITY OF SUCH DAMAGES EXISTS.

Disclaimer of Warranties:

THOMSON COURSE TECHNOLOGY PTR AND THE AUTHOR SPECIFICALLY DISCLAIM ANY AND ALL OTHER WARRANTIES, EITHER EXPRESS OR IMPLIED, INCLUDING WARRANTIES OF MERCHANTABILITY, SUITABILITY TO A PARTICULAR TASK OR PUR-POSE, OR FREEDOM FROM ERRORS. SOME STATES DO NOT ALLOW FOR EXCLU-SION OF IMPLIED WARRANTIES OR LIMITATION OF INCIDENTAL OR CONSEQUEN-TIAL DAMAGES, SO THESE LIMITATIONS MIGHT NOT APPLY TO YOU.

Other:

This Agreement is governed by the laws of the State of Massachusetts without regard to choice of law principles. The United Convention of Contracts for the International Sale of Goods is specifically disclaimed. This Agreement constitutes the entire agreement between you and Thomson Course Technology PTR regarding use of the software.